*Pride In Our Hometowns.*

# P·O·R·T·R·A·I·T·S
## OF
## *Iowa*
### VOLUME II

*Enjoy their magic for a day – or for a lifetime.*

Copyright ©2005 Nonpareil Publishing
All rights reserved
First Edition
ISBN 0-9773067-0-4

*Pride In Our Hometowns.*

# P·O·R·T·R·A·I·T·S OF *Iowa*
## VOLUME II

## ACKNOWLEDGEMENTS

## PUBLISHED BY NONPAREIL PUBLISHING

### Tom Schmitt

*Project Creator-Editor*

### John Bridge

*Creative Design Editor*

### Project Contributors

Pride In Our Hometowns: Portraits of Iowa, Volume II is a cooperative effort of 17 Iowa newspapers serving the communities featured within the pages of this book. Our thanks to the following newspapers:

**Albia** – *The Albia Newspapers*
**Atlantic** – *The Atlantic News Telegraph*
**Carrol** – *Daily Times Herald*
**Centerville** – *Daily Iowegian*
**Chariton** – *Chariton Herald-Patriot*
**Creston** – *Creston News Advisor*
**DeWitt** – *The Observer*
**Fairfield** – *Fairfield Daily Ledger*

**Fort Madison** – *Fort Madison Daily Democrat*
**Jefferson** – *The Jefferson Herald*
**Keokuk** – *Daily Gate City*
**Newton** – *Newton Daily News*
**Osceola** – *Osceola Sentinel Tribune*
**Red Oak** – *The Red Oak Express*
**Sheldon** – *Iowa Information, Inc.*
**Washington** – *Washington Evening Journal*

**Avoca-Oakland-Treynor** – *The Daily Nonpareil*

Nonpareil Publishing appreciates all the efforts and contributions from everyone involved in this publication. Special effort was made to ensure the accuracy of the information for each story and picture. However, historic reviews were, many times, based upon limited available sources.

## Portraits of IOWA

## TABLE OF CONTENTS

ALBIA – *Town With The Beautiful Square* .................................................. **5**

ATLANTIC – *Coca-Cola Capital Of Iowa* .................................................. **17**

AVOCA – *The Spirit Of Small Town Iowa* .................................................. **185**

CARROLL – *We Can Do It* .................................................. **29**

CENTERVILLE – *In The "Center" Of It All* .................................................. **41**

CHARITON – *City Of Lakes* .................................................. **53**

CRESTON – *On Top Of Things* .................................................. **65**

DEWITT – *The Crossroads To Opportunity* .................................................. **77**

FAIRFIELD – *The First...* .................................................. **89**

FORT MADISON – *Cherishing the Past, Embracing the Future* .................................................. **101**

JEFFERSON – *City On The Rise* .................................................. **113**

KEOKUK – *The Gate City* .................................................. **125**

NEWTON – *Red Pride* .................................................. **137**

OAKLAND – *The Spirit Of Small Town Iowa* .................................................. **185**

OSCEOLA – *A City On The Move* .................................................. **149**

RED OAK – *A Shade Better* .................................................. **161**

SHELDON – *Born Of The Railroad* .................................................. **173**

TREYNOR – *The Spirit Of Small Town Iowa* .................................................. **185**

WASHINGTON – *The Cleanest City In Iowa* .................................................. **197**

*Pride In Our Hometowns.*

# P·O·R·T·R·A·I·T·S
## OF
# *Iowa*
### VOLUME II

## FOREWORD

Iowa has many outstanding characteristics, but at its heart are its people and the communities they built. From people who turned the prairie into rich farmland, to those whose pioneer spirit launched businesses that became international successes, Iowans have, since the state's conception, continuously worked to make the world a better place.

Like its people, the communities Iowans forged have seen both good times and bad, but in the end, the communities have become some of America's most favored places to live and raise a family. Places people are proud to call - "My hometown!"

Each community has its own colorful history. Some communities' stories date back long before Iowa even became a state in December of 1846. The histories of other cities are shorter but are equally rich in success. **_Portraits of Iowa, Pride In Our Hometowns, Volume II_**, tells the stories of 19 of the states unique communities.

Communities like Carroll, where a fire in 1879 burned 55 businesses, 10 homes and one of the community's leading churches. Yet, Carroll rebuilt and did so with new regulations on building materials.

Or a quaint little community known across the country for its beautiful town square. New York Times Pulitzer Prize winning architecture critic Ada Louise Huxtable praised the Albia, Iowa town square in 1971. Huxtable told her readers across America that "In southern Iowa there is a town...which has discovered a truth: all change is not progress." She was describing the preservation and restoration of Albia's town square, a project that took over five years to complete phase one (entirely with private dollars) and continues almost 35 years later.

Or, Fairfield, a community situated in the southeastern part of the state, where area residents brought many firsts to the state: the first Iowa State Fair; the first Carnegie Library, the first golf club and the first malleable iron foundry west of the Mississippi River.

Some family names have a long history in these communities, histories that date back for generations. The heritage of some families even date back as far as when the community's roots were first planted in Iowa's rich soil. Other residents are likely relatively new and may just be establishing their roots in their newly found home. Yet others, who may have moved on, remember with pride and love the place they once called home. Regardless of the length of time a family has been associated with a community, if they remain there today or not, an endless number of people lovingly call these communities "My hometown!"

As readers turn the pages of **_Portraits of Iowa, Pride In Our Hometowns, Volume II_**, I believe each will discover this book to be an enjoyable read as they learn dozens of little-known stories about the people of Iowa, some famous, some not so famous; and these 19 outstanding communities they created.

Tom Schmitt
*Nonpareil Publishing*

*Pride In Our Hometowns.*

# P·O·R·T·R·A·I·T·S
## OF
## *Albia*

### TOWN WITH THE BEAUTIFUL SQUARE

*In October of 1971 New York Times Pulitzer Prize winning architecture critic Ada Louise Huxtable wrote in her column, "In southern Iowa there is a town called Albia...which has discovered a truth: all change is not progress."*

*She was describing to her readers across the United States the preservation and restoration of Albia's town square, a project that took over five years to complete (entirely with private dollars) and continues almost 35 years later.*

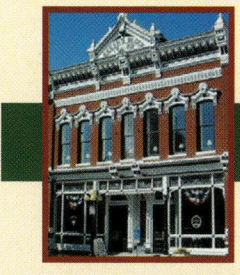  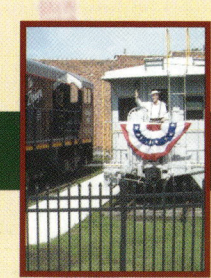 

ALBIA

*Pride In Our Hometowns.*

# P·O·R·T·R·A·I·T·S
## OF
## *Albia*

## TOWN WITH THE BEAUTIFUL SQUARE

*This panoramic photo of downtown Albia was taken circa 1910.*

Albia has been called the "town with the beautiful square," and it is, but it is much more than that. The name "Albia" comes from a Welsh word that means "high plain" and the community sits in the middle of Monroe County nestled in the timbered hills of South Central Iowa.

Monroe County boasts of being the most Irish of any county in Iowa with the tiny Irish community of Melrose and the "Cathedral in the Wilderness," historic St. Patrick's Church located in Georgetown, both a few miles west of Albia.

It is a community steeped in Iowa's rich history of coal mining which brought immigrants from throughout the world as well as African Americans from the South to make better lives for their families. It is why Albia and Monroe County take pride in the rich mixture of Welsh, Irish, Italian and Slavic ethnic influences and why the word "Buxton" brings about the ideas of racial harmony.

### A SNAPSHOT

Albia has become a community built on grit and determination, a community that fought through terrible economic trials with the loss of the coal mining industry beginning in the 1930's and a farm crisis that hit hard in the mid 1980's, to become a beacon of industrial and economic revival in

*There's plenty of fun to be had during the Cruizin' Albia celebration, held the last weekend of June. The event has been held every year for the last 20 years.*

*Albia has a rich tradition in the railroad industry. The town was once a major center for shipping coal from the productive mines in the area. Major railroads that intersected in Albia included the Burlington Northern, the Iowa Central, and the Chicago and Northwestern Railway, as well as the Albia Interurban Railway. The interurban was a passenger line that served the coal mining towns in the area. Today, the BNSF railroad is always busy, and the Appanoose County Railroad provides railroad access to industries in the area.*

ready to pick a site for the county seat. The site was initially called Princeton, then a petition was circulated to change that name to Clark's Point and finally, in the election of 1846 both the county name and the county seat had their names

Iowa in the 1980's and 1990's. It is a community that has not forgotten its past and continues to preserve and restore the Victorian influence that created its downtown and at the same time has built new educational facilities, has completely revitalized its city parks, sports and recreation facilities, has just completed a new aquatic center, has built new most of its churches in the past three decades and continues to work at building a solid industrial and business base to provide good jobs for its citizens.

<u>History</u>

The first white settlers who came into Kish-Ke-Kosh County crossed the Des Moines River near Eddyville in 1844. John B. Gray's trading post and ferry helped push settlers into the area. By August of 1845 settlers were

*Albians are proud of their parks. This playground equipment was recently donated and installed at Albia City Park by the local Rotary Club. Another beautiful park in Albia was also completely updated by the Cruizin' Albia Committee.*

changed. The county became Monroe County and the county seat Albia.

Farmers, including a large number of Irish immigrant farmers entered Monroe County. The Irish settled in the western part of the county, creating the communities of Melrose and Georgetown. Life in

*This photo shows part of the Buxton mine, which was once the location of a bustling community north of Albia. Buxton is still well known today as a place where thousands of African Americans and European Americans all lived together harmoniously in the late 19th and early 20th centuries. Buxton disappeared not long after the coal mines closed*

**7**

# Albia IOWA

> Each year during the last weekend in June, classic muscle cars and rock & roll are celebrated during the Cruizin' Albia celebration. The event features a full schedule of fun events for the whole family.

Monroe County took a huge turn when coal was discovered on Avery Creek in 1860. By 1895 Monroe County was the third largest coal producing county in the state and by 1911 it was number one with 2.5 million tons mined that year.

Dozens of coal mining communities sprang up including Lovilia, Buxton, Hiteman, Avery, Hocking, Foster, Hynes, Ward, Haydock, Lockman, Hilton, White City, Maple, and Coalfield.

Thousands of miners, mostly European immigrants flooded into the area, growing the population from 386 in 1844 to 25,500 in 1910. During the height of mining, Albia became the center of commerce and families turned parts of their fortunes into elegant Victorian era commercial buildings around Albia's square.

But between 1910 and 1920 a new energy source was discovered—oil—and fuel oil and diesel oil began to heat homes and power the nation's locomotives, taking the place of coal. The mines began to close and by the 1930's the mining industry was but a shadow of itself at the turn of the century. By the 1960's many other businesses and industries built on the back of the mining industry had also closed and the once elegant store fronts around the square had been boarded up or covered with false fronts. High unemployment and loss of population plagued Albia and in the early 1960's a state official passing through Albia remarked that it was the "ugliest town in Iowa."

Embarrassed community leaders vowed to make him eat his words. The Albia Area

Left: Albia resident George "Red" Frye was a member of the University of Iowa's fabulous Iron Men football team, which won the Big Ten championship in 1939. Frye played center and linebacker on the team. He continues to live in Albia today, and is one of the last living members of the legendary team.

Right: This is a view of the intersection of Washington and Main on the Albia square. The Peoples State Bank building was recently remodeled and restored to its historic appearance.

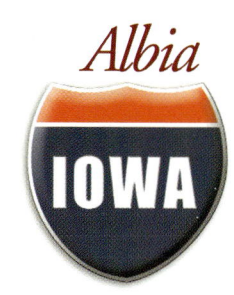

*Christmas time in Albia is a magical experience. The historic downtown square comes alive with the traditional spirit of the holidays. The Albia Victorian Stroll, held each year on the first weekend in December, features living Christmas cards in the storefronts of the historic buildings on the square.*

Improvement Association was formed to plan and work together to turn the community around. In the early 1950's, Robert T. Bates, the son of a prominent turn-of-the-century lawyer and banker who helped build the original square, returned home after establishing himself as a top Hollywood decorator. Joining his family's bank, Bates moved into the second floor apartment in the Bates Building on the northwest corner of the square with a window that overlooked the entire square. From there he helped envision the restoration project. The Albia Area Improvement Association incorporated in 1966 and came up with a name for their project—"Operation Facelift." Over the next five years, entirely financed with private dollars, the square was sandblasted, bricks and mortar repaired, windows and cornices replaced or repaired, buildings were painted and walls, covered with years of coal smoke, cleaned and repaired.

The restoration of the square was celebrated throughout the state and nation, but Albians didn't rest. In 1983, the entire 92 building business district was named to the National Register of Historic Places in time for the city's Quasquicentennial. A year later a three-day community celebration called "Restoration Days" was established to keep the fires of restoration burning brightly. Soon after that, the Albia Historical Preservation Board was established, received important funding from private sources and began a street lighting project that placed modern replica street lights and linden trees around the square.

And while many communities were struggling just to

*Coal miners in a Hiteman area mine are pictured taking a break in this photo taken in 1916. Many of today's Albia area residents are descendants of the coal miners who once toiled deep in the earth of Monroe County.*

*This is the bell that was originally located in the clock tower of the Monroe County Courthouse. It was removed from the tower in 1970 and is now on display on the courthouse lawn.*

# Albia IOWA

maintain their main level store fronts, individuals and businesses in Albia were embarking on a project to restore the second stories of downtown buildings. Robert T. Bates was the original "cliffdweller," moving into his family's spacious second story residence in the Bates Building in the early 1950's. Almost as much museum as a home, Bates' apartment was filled with antiques from around the world, original paintings and other art work. He was well-known for his lavish parties following community theater productions or other community events. In the late 1980's First Iowa State Bank President Robert Kaldenberg and his wife, Betty, Albia Newspapers Publisher Robert W. Larson and his wife, Dorothy, and David and Sandy Johnson, all rebuilt the upstairs of their businesses into beautiful apartments. Others followed and today there are newly remodeled apartments above almost every building around the square.

One of the most difficult projects on the square was taken up by Albia educators Dan and Diana Walker when they restored the old King Theater to its original turn-of-the-century splendor, reopening the business in 1983 after a year of work. Eventually they would add a cliffdweller's apartment above the theater. Today the theater continues to show movies as well as host live entertainment events on its original vaudeville stage, complete with the original orchestra pit. In 1990 the people of Monroe County passed a million dollar bond issue to restore the exterior of the Monroe County Courthouse. In 2000 an interior restoration was started and in 2002 the north steps and the clocktower were restored.

And the work continues. When Mr. Bates died in the mid 1990's he left $2 million to be placed in a foundation so that the work might

*Albia Community High School was built new in 1993, and is part of a state-of-the-art system of educational facilities in Albia. The Mick Technology Center is also nearby, and provides high-tech educational opportunities to local students, thanks to generous donations by the Mick, Hardinger and King families.*

*The magic of Christmas comes alive each year during the Albia Victorian Stroll. The historic downtown Albia storefronts become living Christmas cards during the event, like this one featuring little Becca Mason.*

*The Pabst Law Firm is now located in this historic Victorian house located on Benton Avenue in Albia. The house was originally built by Theodore Bolivar Perry.*

be continued. That legacy allowed the Skean Block Building to be remodeled into a restaurant. It rebuilt from the ground up a key building on the southeast corner of the square that collapsed from Highway 5 roadwork. The Bates Foundation has pumped thousands of dollars into dozens of buildings to help keep them in good shape.

Because of lack of funding, the historic Carnegie-Evans Public Library had fallen on hard times. In the late 1990's, after a failed bond issue, the library board began a major private fund-raising effort to repair and restore the building. Generous gifts from the Denny and Helen Homerin family, Loren and Rowena Hardinger, Jim and Pat King, Robert T. Bates, the Joe and Maxine Cohn Trust and others raised over $225,000 to nearly complete a interior renovation along with window replacement and a new HVAC system.

### Building things new

Even though Albia is known nationally for its downtown restoration efforts, it isn't a one dimensional community and it has worked hard to blend modernization efforts with historic preservation efforts.

The community passed a bond issue in 1993 and constructed a new high school. At about the same time, when the age of two

*The Bates Building is located on the northwest corner of the Albia square. Robert T. Bates was the driving force behind the effort to restore the historic downtown buildings in Albia to their original Victorian charm.*

*Two Albia Lady Dee softball players go after a ball at Lizzie Alexander Field.*

outlying elementary schools and student population made it necessary to bring all of the students into buildings in Albia, there was concern about educational space. That was solved by the generous gifts of Harold and Gloria Mick, the Hardingers and Kings to build the Mick Technology Center, which not only made it possible to reorganize the attendance centers but gave children in Albia (3rd through 12th) accessibility to state-of-the-art computer technology.

Having overwhelmingly approved a SILO tax, the school district is now considering the construction of a new track facility and possibily an auditorium.

## Parks and Recreation

Until 1984, the only quality sports facility in Albia was the Little League baseball park. With the addition of new Musco lighting and other improvements, it is still a top notch facility.

But since 1984 the Albia and Monroe County community has worked tirelessly building and rebuilding its parks and recreation facilities. In 1984, as the farm depression was building, a group of men led by Sonny Williams, Mike Lawrence and Norm Braun set out to build a new baseball and softball facility for Little League, Babe Ruth, high school and adult players. Again, using almost all private financing, over $250,000 was raised to build the Monroe County Sports Complex. The facility includes competition baseball and softball fields, a slow-pitch field, tennis courts, basketball court and concession stand. It has

*Albia Community High School baseball pitcher Justin Stoffa delivers a pitch at the Monroe County Sports Complex.*

*Albia's high school soccer team is one of the best in southern Iowa.*

*Albia*
**IOWA**

The Nathan E. Kendall library in the Monroe County Historical Museum contains thousands of personal items and books. Kendall was Iowa's governor from 1921-1925. Emmalee Kerber is pictured browsing through the library.

become the home of the community's outstanding summer baseball and softball program and annually hosts many tournament events at all levels.

In 2004, under the leadership of Jim Keller, Deb Zaputil and Terri Schofield, a state-of-the-art indoor hitting and pitching facility was completed, allowing youngsters to practice their hitting and pitching skills all year round. In addition, the Sports Complex had new lights installed at the softball and baseball diamonds. An old school building was torn down and a temporary high school softball field built on what became known as Washington Park. When the new Sports Complex was opened, the diamond was abandoned and the area left unattended. Several groups, led by the Cruizin' Albia Committee, took the park on as a project and turned it into a beautiful, multi-purpose city park. The field has been completely restored by the Little League Softball Association, the Cruizin' Albia Committee built a playground, added a shelter house and a restroom/concession building and the Cruizin' Albia/Washington Park has become a jewel in the Albia park system.

Even in worse repair was the 100-year-old Albia City Park. The huge park area included a dilapidated softball field, an aging swimming pool, broken playground equipment and a worn out shelter house. The Albia Soccer Club led an effort to convert the old softball field into a regulation soccer field. The Albia Rotary Club took on the job of rebuilding the shelter house and raised $35,000 to install a modern playground and the citizens of Albia and Monroe County together passed a $2.5 million bond issue to build a new family aquatic center.

Privately, the Albia Country Club is one of the finest

The Monroe County Hospital was recently transformed into one of the most modern hospitals of its kind after a $4.5 million renovation project was completed two years ago.

13

# Albia IOWA

nine-hole golf courses in the state with watered fareways, a remodeled club house, swimming pool and lake. The club is home to the longest running pro-am golf tournament in the state. A group of racquetball enthusiasts even built a 24-hour racquetball/weight-lifting facility on the square using a building gutted by fire.

### Arts and Entertainment

Part of the fun of having an historic square is planning festivals and Albia does festivals about as well as any community in the state. Three major community festivals are held yearly beginning on the third weekend of June with Cruizin' Albia. Cruizin' Albia is an old car/rock and roll reunion where people enjoy looking at antique and custom cars and listening to classic rock and roll music. There's even a night for classic country music.

Restoration Days happens the third weekend of August and it is a direct result of the community's effort to restore the square. An enormous parade, first class quilt show, threshing bee, an art show that draws top artists from four states and the Restoration Days Follies (an all local, all live variety show honoring the days of Vaudeville) highlight the festival.

The Victorian Stroll also shows off the historic square on the first Saturday of December. Living Christmas cards are created in every store window around the square as visitors get a taste of Christmas 100 years ago.

Albia has a large

*The Albia Restoration Days Follies provide tons of laughs and great music each year during the Restoration Days celebration the last weekend in August. The show is held each year in the historic Albia Theatre.*

*Left: During the Restoration Days celebration each year in Albia, a big parade is held featuring dozens of interesting antique tractors. Later in the day, the tractors are paraded out of town to a big threshing display on the Bob Reed farm. Reed is pictured leading the Southern Iowa Vintage Tractor Club in the parade.*

*Right: This photo shows part of the west side of Albia's historic town square. Albia has the distinction of having the entire downtown district named to the National Register of Historic Places.*

# Albia IOWA

*The Monroe County Historical Museum features hundreds of interesting displays of Monroe County's past. This is part of the museum's coal mining display, featuring equipment used long ago in local coal mines*

Welsh community and the tradition of music runs deep. Albia has its own Big Band, a 50's and 60's rock and roll band and a Municipal Band. The Monroe County Arts Council is active and dozens of local artists contribute to the culture and beauty of the community.

### Industry

Once a community with the highest chronic unemployment in the state, Albia Industrial Development Corp. leaders have, in the past 20 years, transformed Albia and the greater Monroe County community into a model of industrial development and recruitment. Beginning with the recruitment of the Cargill Corn Milling plant in the northeast corner of the county in the mid-1980's, the AIDC has helped attract companies like A.Y.M. Inc., DeLong Sportswear, Superior Machine, Quiktron and RELCO while helping to maintain other small industries like Kness Mfg. (makers of the world's best mousetrap), L&S Tools, Iowa Aluminum, Hawkeye Molding and Trophy Glove. The Iowa Biotechnology Center around Cargill includes Ajinomoto, Wacker-Chemi and Heartland Lysine.

*Albia and Monroe County have experienced incredible growth in industry over the last 20 years. The newest industry to open its doors in Albia is the Relco Locomotives facility south of Albia. The company is a leader in refurbishing locomotives for railroad services across North America.*

Two major contractors make their home in Albia—DDVI and Reed Construction.

### Health Care

Monroe County boasts one of the finest rural hospitals in the state, built in 1982 and doubled in size and completely remodeled in 2004, the Monroe County Hospital is consistently near the top in patient and employee satisfaction in national hospital surveys.

Albia also has two excellent nursing homes, three dental practices, two optometric practices, two chiropracters and a well-staffed family medical clinic connected to the hospital.

### Churches

Faith is important in Albia and the importance of church life can

15

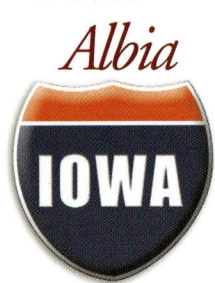

# Albia IOWA

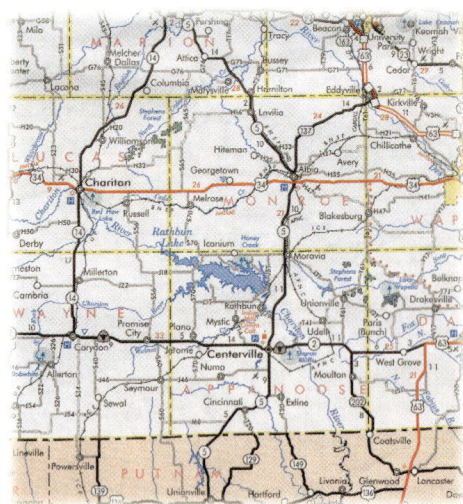

## Learn More

Albia is located in Monroe County

For information, contact the
**Albia Chamber of Commerce:**
641-932-5108

**The Albia Industrial Development Corporation:**
641-932-7233

**The Albia Newspaper:**
641-932-7121

## Story Contributors

*This story compiled from the writings of Dave Paxton, Dien Judge, Janet Jenkins and Sarah Hindman*

---

be measured somewhat by the number of new church facilities built within the last 25 years. St. Mary's Catholic Church, First Christian Church, Trinity United Methodist, St. Paul's Lutheran, First Baptist Church, Cornerstone Community Church, Albia Baptist Temple and River Life Family Worship Center all have new facilities.

### Famous Albians

You can talk about restored buildings, new swimming pools and new churches all you want, but the real strength of the Albia community is her people. And Albia does have some famous people.

George "Red" Frye was a member of the legendary University of Iowa "Ironman" football team of 1939 and retired in Albia after a successful career as a Veteran's Hospital administrator.

*This is the bandstand on the courtyard of the Monroe County Courthouse. The bandstand was constructed in the 1990s, and is designed to appear similar to the original Albia bandstand from the early 20th Century.*

Another favorite son is professional rodeo cowboy, Bill Huber, who has been ranked in the top 15 in the world in calf roping. Rino Della Vedova, a career building contractor, helped establish M.A.S.H. units for the first time in WWII. Ben Grayson was the first African American to serve as state Lions Club President. Ruth Hollingshead was the first female postmaster in Iowa. Patty Judge is currently Iowa Secretary of Agriculture. Nathan B. Kendall was governor of Iowa (1921-1925). Ed St. Clair Gantz worked on the Manhattan Project, developing the atomic bomb during WWII and later worked as a NASA scientist. These and many others are either included in the Albia Community High School Wall of Fame, the Albia Hall of Fame or the Monroe County Ag Hall of Fame.

*Pride In Our Hometowns.*

# P·O·R·T·R·A·I·T·S
## OF
## *Atlantic*

### COCA-COLA CAPITOL OF IOWA

*"The history of the progress of a town is a history of effort, ceaseless effort, and the metamorphosis from a cross roads is a story replete with incidents of tireless energy, boundless ambition and persistency of purpose."*
*From Atlantic News Telegraph, Industrial Edition, 1917*

*Located strategically between Omaha and Des Moines, six miles from Interstate 80, and at the intersection of two major US highways, the city of Atlantic has long served as the crossroads of southwestern Iowa. A dynamic place where people and ideas come together, and more often than not prosper.*

 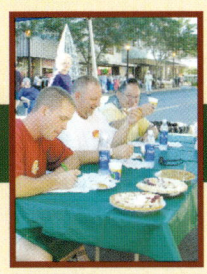  

ATLANTIC

*Pride In Our Hometowns.*

# P·O·R·T·R·A·I·T·S
## OF
## *Atlantic*

### COCA-COLA CAPITOL OF IOWA

*A view looking down Chestnut Street in Atlantic.*

Established in 1868, the communities growth and transportation capabilites soon led to it being named the county seat just a year later. Soon the community would be served by four Rock Island rail lines, and was part of the main line from Chicago to Colorado. Spurs also reached out and connected the surrounding communities of Audubon, Griswold, Kimballton and Villesca.

At one time the depot in Atlantic, was one of the busiest in Iowa. After years of being abandoned the depot became the home of Atlantic's Chamber of Commerce in 2004 after a major renovation.

The community is located along what would become the first paved road from Des Moines to Omaha, Neb. Called White Pole Road it later became part of US Highway 6, the longest continuous US highway connecting Bishop, California with Provincetown, Massachusetts on Cape Cod.

### A SNAPSHOT

It's in Atlantic that the east-west Highway 6 meet the north-south US Highway 71, a road that extends from the Canadian border to near Port Allen, Louisiana.

Like most rural communities its early life was rooted in agriculture and in 1877 boasted the largest corn canning plant in the world. The factory was built in 1877 and soon, supported by hundreds of acres of sweet corn, the plant shipped its product to such far off locales as

*The communities annual Coca-Cola Days parade include a costume class.*

18

# Atlantic IOWA

the Philippines, Alaska and all over the United States.

Throughout the years the community other businesses would be recognized, nationally and internationally for their contributions. Among those is the community's oldest business, the Atlantic News Telegraph, for which former Publisher E. P. Chase won a Pulitzer Prize in 1934 for an editorial entitled, "Where is Our Money ?" Chase was the first and one of only six Iowa journalists to win the award.
The paper continues to serve the community after over 130 years and has won a number of awards from state and national organizations.

But the business most identified with the community didn't even begin in Atlantic. In 1907 Frank P. "Perk" Tyler opened an ice cream business in Villisca. In 1909 he sold the business to his sons, Royal, Harry, and Henry, who expanded the operation and began producing soda named "Tyler's Flavors."

Sales were so strong that the brothers acquired a creamery in Clarinda. In the creamery's safe they found a franchise contract for Coca-Cola. The Tylers had heard of this product and its success elsewhere, but Iowans weren't familiar with it. The Tylers began making Coca-Cola, adding a few bottles to the cases of Tyler's Flavors. In no time, Iowans were requesting more Coke.

From that seed grew the Atlantic Bottling company which serves most of southwest Iowa and led to the communities title of "Coca-Cola Capitol of Iowa."

*Looking down Chestnut Street at night. The street is lined with lights each winter.*

*Some of the younger residents show off their Coca-Cola days t-shirts*

# Atlantic IOWA

In 1923 Royal sold his interest to Harry and Henry, who continued expanding the business by purchasing four additional bottling companies in Shenandoah, Atlantic, Creston, Iowa and Grand Island, Nebraska. In 1929 they acquired the franchise rights for Atlantic to bottle and distribute Coca-Cola.

By 1930 the Tyler Brothers had sold their ice cream business and concentrated fully on soft drinks. In 1949, Harry and Henry divided their business by drawing straws. Harry got Atlantic and Creston; Henry got Shenandoah and Grand Island.

Harry's son Jim was managing the company by 1958, when served customers in a 60-mile radius of Atlantic with Coca-Cola, 7-Up and Tyler's Flavors products. The company had 16 employees then; ten years later there were 40 employees and the company had added Squirt, Dr. Pepper, Frostie Root Beer, Tab and Like to its lineup.

On April 1, 1975, Atlantic Bottling purchased the Des Moines area Coca-Cola franchise, and burgeoned the brand's presence and popularity. This was accomplished in large part due to Jim's son, Kirk Tyler, who was placed in charge of sales for the company in 1981.

In 1991 Kirk Tyler was named President of Atlantic Bottling Company, and Jim became Chairman of the Board of Directors.

Three generations of the Tyler family have built and continue to expand on "delivering the refreshment" of Coca-Cola and related products to customers

*The city's war memorial, located just off Chestnut Street. The monument was recently cleaned and refurbished.*

*The old Rock Island Depot, now home to the Atlantic Area Chamber of Commerce.*

# Atlantic

*A volunteer tends to one of the many flower beds planted along city streets.*

throughout the Atlantic Bottling Company's franchise territories.

The community celebrates it's unique role by holding an annual Coca-Cola days celebration each September that includes Coke-themed activities and attracts collectors from all over the country.

Many of the activities are held in the city's beautiful park that features a monument to area soldiers who have fought and died in war. The monument features brass statues depicting soldiers in uniform while atop stands a statue of Victory. The monument is just the latest example of the communities contribution to the nations defense.

The Grant Memorial Fountain, formerly located in the park was erected in 1886, is said to have been the first memorial in the United States erected to Ulysses S. Grant after his death.

The first U.S. troops sent to fight in World War II came from Iowa, and Iowa's 34th "Red Bull" Division served the longest uninterrupted duty in U.S. military history-about 600 days.

Some of those soldiers were stationed at the city's historic armory that is now in the process of being restored and remodeled. When completed it will not only provide a home to local veterans groups, but a Coca-Cola museum as well.

A total of four "phases" are planned, with a first phase intended to fix the roof and seal up the building so that further deterioration doesn't occur. A second phase includs work on the exterior of the building, with some tuck pointing, door, window and demolition work estimated to come to about $100,000.

*Recently students helped to add improvements to some of the city's walking trails.*

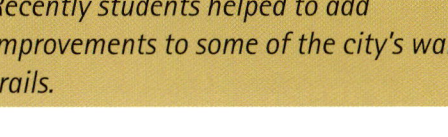

21

# Atlantic IOWA

The third phase would include general work on the inside of the building, including painting walls, refinishing floors, etc. at an estimated cost of $55,000 and the final fourth phase would include mechanical work.

In 2004 a group of dedicated community volunteers completed another important renovation of a historical building. The old Rock Island Depot, the "anchor" of the community downtown shopping district, was completely restored and is now the home to the Atlantic Area Chamber of Commerce. Over 100 years old, the depot was part of a rail system that by 1872 included 317 miles of track in Illinois and 718 in Iowa and 139 in Missouri. It included the line of the Keokuk & Des Moines which was the first railroad to reach Des Moines, when it operated an excursion train into that city from Keokuk on August 29, 1866.

The system got its start in Iowa and was always densest there, with a large number of lines serving most cities in the state.

The Rock Island stretched across Colorado, Illinois, Iowa, Kansas, Missouri, Nebraska, New Mexico, Oklahoma and Texas. The easternmost reach of the system was Chicago, and the system also reached Memphis, Tennessee; west, it reached Denver, Colorado, and Santa

*Each year hundreds of Coca-Cola venders and collectors visit the community to swap collectibles.*

*The old armory is in the process of being restored and is expected to include a Coca-Cola museum.*

# Atlantic IOWA

Rosa, New Mexico. Southernmost reaches were to Galveston, Texas, and Eunice, Louisiana while in a northerly direction the Rock Island got as far as Minneapolis, Minnesota.

Major lines included Minneapolis to Kansas City, Missouri, via Des Moines, Iowa; St. Louis, Missouri, to Santa Rosa via Kansas City; Herington, Kansas, to Galveston, Texas, via Fort Worth, Texas, and Dallas, Texas; and Santa Rosa to Memphis.

The railroad operated a number of trains known as Rockets serving the Midwest, including the Rocky Mountain Rocket (Chicago-Omaha-Lincoln-Denver-Colorado Springs) and the Corn Belt Rocket (Chicago-Des Moines-Omaha).

After sitting vacant for several years a group of local volunteers took on the job of renovating the historic building. While progress was slow initially, the project received a big boost after longtime Atlantic resident, Blanch Rowe, left the group $300,000 to finish the project.

The gift to the depot, given in the name of her father, Wilson Rowe, who worked for the Rock Island and Pacific Railroad until his retirement.

The project also received money from

*Officials look over plans for the renovation of the Armory.*

## CASS COUNTY COURTHOUSE

23

# Atlantic IOWA

the state and other local contributions. In May 2004 the work was officially completed while the building first tenant, the Atlantic Chamber of Commerce moved in. Aside from being home to the Chamber is also provides meetings and is the site of the community's Farmer's Market.

While keeping in touch with its historical past, the community hasn't neglected it's future. In 2004 the doors opened on a new $6 million community recreation center.

Operated by the Nishna Valley YMCA, the building boasts an indoor pool, two gymnasiums, two racquetball courts, an indoor walking track, weight room and day care facilities.

Within months of opening membership at the facility nearly doubled and continues to grow.

The success of the Rec center followed on the heels of another successful project, the construction of the nearly $1 million Cass County Community Building. Built with a combination of state and local funds, the project began in 1998 because of a need to accommodate large groups with up-to-date communication services.

The 173 foot x 80 foot building includes office space a 7,700

*The Atlantic municipal pool recently underwent and extensive refurbishing.*

*Area organizations recently received a number of donations from officials at the newly opened Wal-Mart.*

24

air-conditioned auditorium with the ability to seat 544 people at tables, and/or divide the area into one of three smaller rooms with high quality acoustical folding walls, a large lobby, the local extension service office, restrooms and a storage area. In the south end is a kitchen, a restricted bar, restrooms and an area for more storage. Separate entries are available so deliveries could be directly made to the kitchen or for access to different parts of the auditorium if there is more than one meeting going on.

It has become the site of numerous meetings, conventions, wedding receptions and each year plays host to the Cass County Fair.

The city also recently completed a $500,000 update of the its city pool, increasing the size by approximately 400 square feet larger and including a zero-depth entry, six 25 meter racing lanes, a slide and diving board. The project was funded with state and local money and came in on time and under budget.

The most recent project is the $6 million expansion of the community airport. The project, funded primarily through Federal Aviation Administration funds, includes the construction of a 5,000 foot runway along with other improvements. City officials say the extended runway will allow for larger airplanes to land and provide another benefit to local businesses. While the project has run into

## BIG PROJECTS

*Each year area youth participate in the Cass County Fair held in Atlantic every August.*

# Atlantic

*Work began recently on a new park that will include three lakes, camping and hiking trails.*

lost culture. Artifacts from the site have been removed and continue to be studied.

Education has always played an important role in the community.

a number of road blocks, the city is in the process of acquiring the final piece of property need for the project and work has already begun rerouting nearby roads and improving hangers and taxiways.

In 2004 state archeologists were busy studying ancient Indian artifacts found at the site. While little is known about the archaic culture, archeologists are hoping the Cass County site can help piece together information found from a several similar sites stretching from Cherokee County in northwest Iowa to the Missouri border. It's unlikely the site will yield the ancient Indian equivalent of the holy grail, but the information gained here, coupled with what has been learned at other sites will add to the overall knowledge of the

*With two eighteen-hole golf courses a birdie putt is never far away.*

# Atlantic IOWA

*The Nishna Valley YMCA opened last year and is already setting membership records.*

With modern buildings and a dedicated staff, the Atlantic Public School system is one of the best in the state. Along with top notch academics, the district also featuring award winning extracurricular activities including an award winning marching band, and state championships in football, and a state record seven girls state track championships.

As a sign of the communities commitment to education the district along with the booster club have committed to building a 60 x 90 foot multi-purpose building, that will include a multi-purpose area, a concession area for athletic and community event, additional physical education space and additional storage space. Officials hope to have the nearly $329,000 addition completed by the end of year.

Throughout the year the community holds a number of celebrations including Harvest Days, AtlanticFest and others. It is also the home to the states Tournament of Champions, golf tournament.

Held in August, AtlanticFest is a celebration of ...well Atlantic. Each year residents pack the streets for the event that includes games, contests, entertainment and specialty shows.

In October the community celebrates it's rural roots with a HarvestFest. Residents and visitors enjoy a Harvest Market and Flea Market, with vendors selling pumpkins, gourds, homemade crafts, antiques and other collectibles. In addition, there is a Quilt Show, Children's Pumpkin Decorating, Homemade Apple Pie Contest, Entertainment, and more.

*Pumpkin decorating was just one activity held at the annual HarvestFest.*

27

# Atlantic IOWA

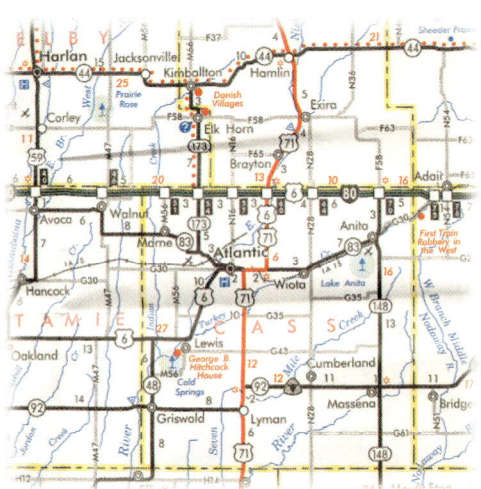

## Learn More

Atlantic is located between Omaha and Des Moines just south of Interstate 80 in southwestern Iowa.

For more information Contact the Atlantic Area Chamber of Commerce at 712-243-3017 or visit its website at www.atlanticiowa.com.

## Story Contributor

Jeff Lundquist
Atlantic News Telegraph

## Recreation

With two 18 hole golf courses, the community also hosts the annual Tournament of Champions, in which club champions from across the state gather for an annual event.

The community continues to evolve, and recently embarked on a new project that city officials hope will improve not only the quality of life for residents but provide a boost to the economy and an incentive for attracting new residents.

With studies showing that areas with the most recreational opportunities experience the most growth, plans are currently underway for the development of a 177 acre park that will feature three lakes, RV campsites, hiking and biking trails and native prairie.

At least $250,000 has been set aside for the project which will get underway in the fall of 2005 and will be completed in stages. Located at the site of an old rock quarry, the new park will be a first step in redeveloping the north west side of the community and provide residents with a place to enjoy the solitude of nature or take a quick walk around the a lake.

Atlantic, a town born at the crossroads, has continued to be a place where ideas and people come together. It's a place where the vision of those early settlers, along with the promise of a thriving, committed, community has not gone unrealized.

*Officials with the Nishna Valley YMCA celebrate the facilities one year anniversary.*

*Pride In Our Hometowns.*

# P·O·R·T·R·A·I·T·S
## OF
## *Carroll*

### WE CAN DO IT!

*The "Can do" attitude of the citizens of Carroll is exemplified in many varied projects and amenities in Carroll. Economic development activities, revitalization projects in the central business district, and a strong medical community anchored by St. Anthony Regional Hospital makes Carroll a vibrant community.*

*The schools and churches, recreational facilities, historic restoration, beautiful residential areas, and community events and celebrations lead the way in addressing quality of life issues.*

  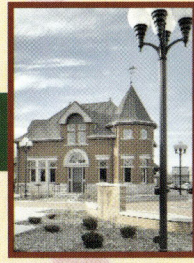 

CARROLL

*Pride In Our Hometowns.*

# P·O·R·T·R·A·I·T·S
## OF *Carroll*

## WE CAN DO IT!

*Through the Corridor of Commerce Program, downtown Carroll has a new look that invites shopping and relaxing.*

For years Carroll, Iowa was known as the "Hub of Western Iowa" reflecting the junction of the two major highways of 30 and 71 just west of Carroll.

### A SNAPSHOT

Transportation has always been a factor in the development of Carroll. The Indian Trail that ran north and south through the county came through Carroll just east of where the court house stands today, according to legend. The Chicago and North Western Railroad was a major influence first in the development of the county and then in platting the town of Carroll.

Highway 30, originally known as the "Lincoln Highway" is routed through the middle of town. This highway, a creation of Carl Fisher, originated in Times Square in New York City and ended 3,389 miles later in San Francisco. Highway 71 carries traffic north and south on the west side of Carroll. The three major cities of Des Moines, Sioux City and Omaha can be easily reached with a hundred mile drive.

*Similar markers were placed along each mile of the Lincoln Highway Sept. 1, 1928 by the Boy Scouts to designate the route of the first Transcontinental Highway.*

*Many airplanes fly in for the flight breakfast, an annual event at the Arthur Neu Airport.*

The Municipal Airport was rededicated in 1963 in honor of Arthur N. Neu who was mayor of Carroll from 1934 to 1960. The airport that has served the community since the mid 40's has a 5500 foot concrete runway to accommodate the air traffic from those who call Carroll "home" and business people coming to Carroll.

## THE HISTORY

The County and City of Carroll were named for Charles Carroll of Carrollton who was the only Catholic and last surviving signer of the Declaration of Independence.

Carrollton was the first county seat when the county was formed in 1856 which was logical since the settlers were clustered around the North and Middle Raccoon Rivers in the eastern part of the county at the time.

But a more central location seemed a better idea as the county grew. So by a vote of the settlers, Carroll City became the second county seat of Carroll County in 1867. The first courthouse was a railroad warehouse which was used until a new court house was built sixteen months later. Carroll City was renamed Carroll in 1875.

Carroll has a unique layout in that the businesses are not clustered around the courthouse square, but are to the west of the square. This was typical of a railroad plan with the tracks and depot at one end of

*Harvest time in Carroll County means long days in the field.*

31

# Carroll IOWA

*Carroll Community Theater performers present delightful plays for everyone to enjoy.*

town and the Main Street of the business district at a right angle to the tracks. The residential area was on both sides of the track surrounding the business district.

On September 24, 1879, when a train engineer saw a fire burning in one of the businesses of Carroll, he blew his whistle to sound the alarm. There was little to do since there was no fire equipment and little water to protect the buildings made of wood. When the fire was out, all of the businesses between Fourth and Sixth Streets and Adams and Main Streets were burned. Fifty-five businesses and ten residences were burned including the Burke Hotel and the Presbyterian Church. Carroll did rebuild, but with new regulations about building materials used.

The Chicago & North Western built through Carroll in 1867 and the Chicago Great Western built in 1902 created an avenue for getting

*The unique building that houses the Des Moines Area Community College offices was once the site of the bathhouse for the American Legion Pool.*

supplies in and shipping farm produce out of Carroll. The railroads also provided passenger service, which allowed people to travel to other communities in the county with relative ease.

Before the county was settled, a major event occurred near Swan Lake. An Indian battle that was so fierce only a few survived of the many hundreds who fought the battle. There are differing accounts of what tribes were involved with the Sioux on one side of the battle and the Meskwaki, Potawatomie, or Sac and Fox on the other. It is reported that remnants of the battle were found years later as farmers plowed the soil near the lake.

A man who had a profound influence on the development of Carroll County was Father Joseph Kuemper. Through his

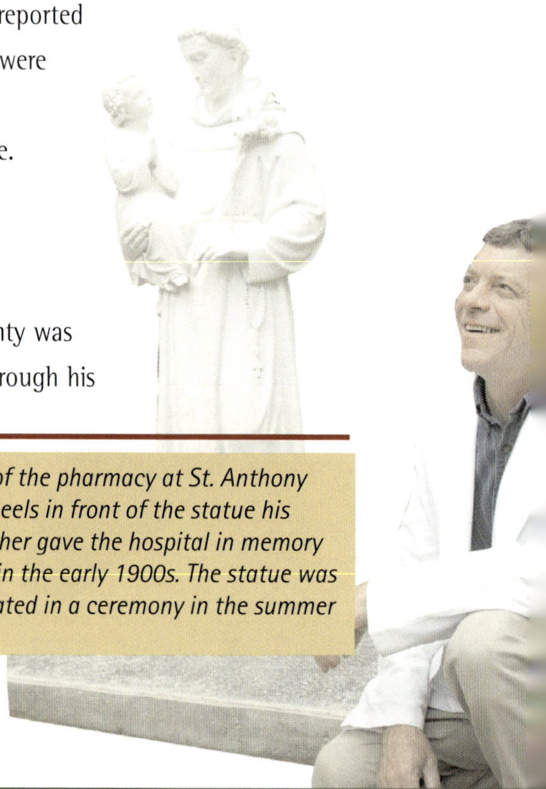

*Paul Dieter, director of the pharmacy at St. Anthony Regional Hospital, kneels in front of the statue his great, great grandfather gave the hospital in memory of his wife who died in the early 1900s. The statue was restored and rededicated in a ceremony in the summer of 2005.*

32

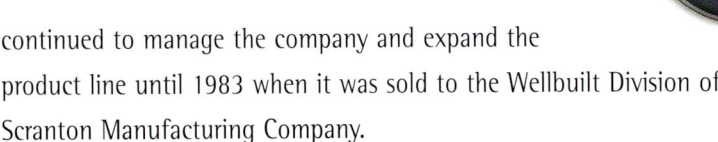

## Father Joseph Kuemper

efforts St. Anthony Hospital and St. Angela School of Domestic Science were started in Carroll along with three parishes in the county. Kuemper Catholic High School was named for him.

A well known company in Carroll was the result of the unique partnership that was formed in 1903 when Henry and John C. Heider began building four-horse eveners. Little did they know that their business would grow into a major manufacturing enterprise that would include tractors, wagons and ladders. Henry, who was the inventor, was granted twenty-three patents during his lifetime while John C. was in charge of the business details. After the brothers died within months of each other in 1946, family members continued to manage the company and expand the product line until 1983 when it was sold to the Wellbuilt Division of Scranton Manufacturing Company.

### Education

Two major school systems serve the community of Carroll. Carroll Community School District and Kuemper Catholic School System. Both are pre-Kindergarten through the twelfth grade. An array of academic opportunities is offered by each school system both individually and collaboratively. In addition to academic programs, the two school systems share some sports facilities and transportation.

DMACC has been an educational force that has given many students in Carroll and the surrounding area an opportunity otherwise not available to them. Since its inception in 1979 it

*Tim Fitzpatrick welcomes students on the first day of classes outside Kuemper Catholic Grade School. The parochial school system recently celebrated their 50th anniversary.*

*Farner-Bocken, a company that was founded in Carroll in 1939, is headquartered in a spacious facility on the east edge of the city.*

33

# Carroll IOWA

has continued to grow, expanding its campus and adding many courses including 2 + 2, a four year program offered through the University of Northern Iowa in elementary education and technology management. The latest is a four year nursing program in collaboration with the University of Iowa.

When DMACC was given the property in 1979, the Spanish Mission bathhouse of the American Legion Swimming Pool that was originally on the site was converted to offices for the college. It is a very interesting entrance to the college.

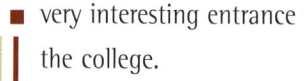

*Saints and angels grace the alter of Holy Guardian Angels Church.*

### Religion

That religion is very important in the lives of the people of Carroll is apparent in the many lovely churches throughout the town. The oldest church building, Trinity Episcopal Church, is a white frame structure that was built in 1886. There is a strong Catholic presence in Carroll and Carroll County that is evident in the many Catholic churches that dominate the communities throughout the county. But there is a diverse choice of worship options as evidenced by newly formed evangelical churches and the presence of vibrant mainline Protestant churches.

### Business Community

Varied would describe the business climate in Carroll with a diverse base of industries in manufacturing, technology, whole distribution, telemarketing and value added agriculture. Local companies both large and small have made Carroll their home base. Many companies have chosen Carroll as a place to expand with its

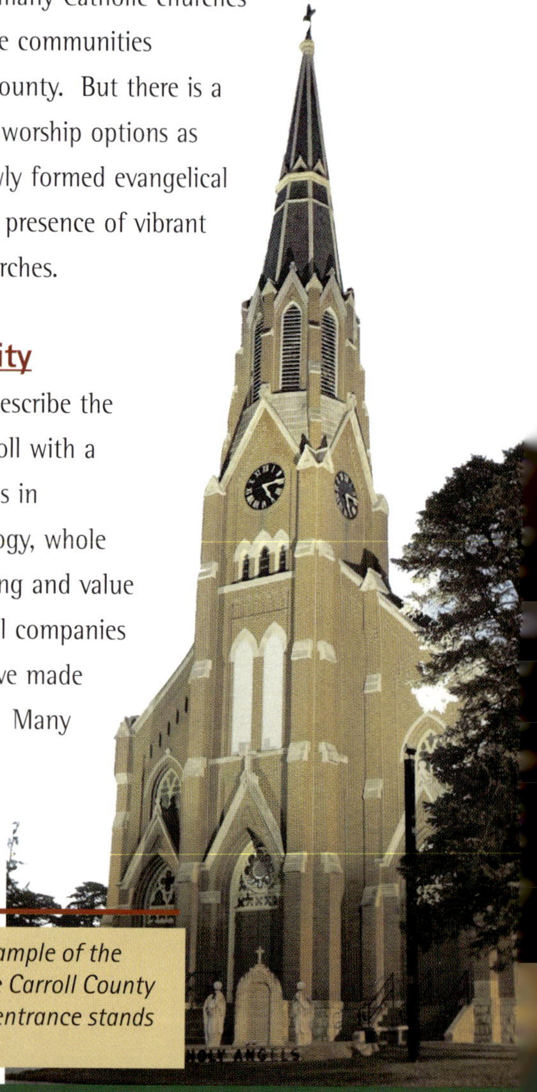

*Children practice their football skills for the future at the area's recreation youth camp.*

*Holy Guardian Angels Church is an example of the exquisite Gothic churches that dot the Carroll County countryside. The flood lit west facing entrance stands against the day's first light.*

**34**

transportation system and large employment pool.

Downtown Carroll has a new look with the complete redesign of Adams, Main and Fifth Streets through the Corridor of Commerce project. The new street scapes of many varied retail shops are anchored by kiosks with maps and information about the Lincoln Highway on the edge of the retail district.

## People

Carroll has been the starting point for many young people including the leaders of major corporations. Ken Macke, CEO of then Dayton Corporation began his career in retail in Carroll. Walt Neppl started as a stockman at (JCPenney) in Carroll and went on to become Chairman of the Board before he retired in 1982. Both men are graduates of Carroll High School. Dan Neary, presently President of Mutual of Omaha, is a graduate of Kuemper Catholic High School. Marian Rees graduated from Carroll High School as valedictorian and went on to produced award-winning films including ten for the Hallmark Hall of Fame. Among the awards she has won are eleven Emmy Awards, two Golden Globe and one Peabody.

*The Chicago and Northwestern Railroad Depot is in the final stages of a restoration project.*

*Pella Corporation, Carroll Operations is a supplier of premier window components and is one of the large employers in the county.*

35

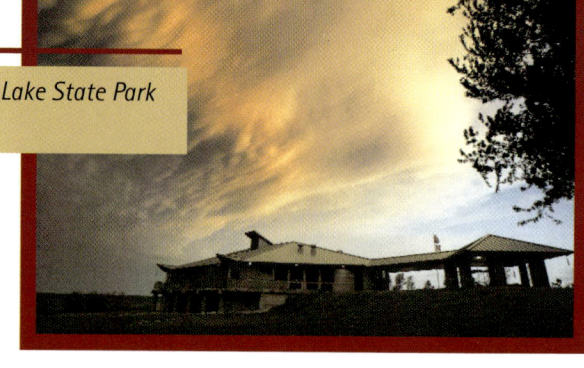

# Carroll IOWA

*The Carroll Education Center at Swan Lake State Park was completed in spring 2005.*

## Medicine and other support services

The impressive complex of St. Anthony Regional Hospital that dominates a hill-top south of Carroll began as a modest 30 bed hospital created by Father Kuemper. He offered the administration of the hospital to The Franciscan Sisters of Perpetual Adoration from La Crosse, Wisconsin who still own and operate it today. The hospital celebrated 100 years of service to the Carroll area in 2005 with a yearlong celebration and a new addition. The state-of-the-art complex serves as a regional medical center with comprehensive patient care and many specialists. Besides the main hospital facility, a doctor's clinic, nursing home with separate Alzheimer's unit, specialty clinic building and an assisted living apartment complex are included. Independent of the hospital are additional clinics and other health services.

New Hope Village is a success story of which Carroll is very proud. Since it was established in 1977, it has provided a lifestyle for adults with special needs in a home like setting. Through training at the handicap and disabled adult facility, the residents learn skills that make them a vital part of our work force.

## Recreation and Leisure

Throughout the city of Carroll are many neighborhood parks with Graham Park a favorite for family gatherings in the summer.

The 500-acre Swan Lake State Park, a mile southeast of Carroll, has an array of

*A DNR biologist shares information about one of the swans at the park.*

*The Civil War Memorial obelisk in the Carroll Cemetary was built by the WPA in the 1930s and today it is surrounded by markers honoring those who have served in recent conflicts.*

36

# Carroll IOWA

*Games of chance from the early 1950s helped raise money for the Carroll Stadium, home of the Carroll Merchants semi-pro baseball team and a facility that is considered by some to be one of the best fields in the Midwest. Today, high school and collegiate teams play at the facility.*

activities that makes it a destination for many people. Paddling a canoe around the 100 acre lake or camping at one of the campsites can be a great way to relax. Taking in the exhibits at the newly opened Education Center or participating in one of the many activities planned by the staff can be very rewarding. A stroll around the section of the Sauk Rail Trail that circles the lake invites enjoyment of all the beauty the park has to offer.

For the more active, the Sauk Rail Trail takes hikers, bikers and cross country skiers on a 33 mile journey to Lake View passing through small towns, fields, and lush country sides on the way.

Two golf courses offer 18 holes of enjoyment on a summer day. The municipal course, which is open to the public, has watered greens and fairways. The country club, which is private, has a golf pro and shop along with watered greens and fairways. Both courses host many local and regional tournaments as well as high school competition.

For year around activities, the Carroll Recreation Center offers a wide choice of activities including the swimming pool with slide, basketball court, exercise facilities, theater and meeting rooms, making it a gathering place with something for everyone.

*Students explore one of the interactive exhibits at the Swan Lake Education Center.*

*A family enjoys a baseball game at the Carroll Stadium.*

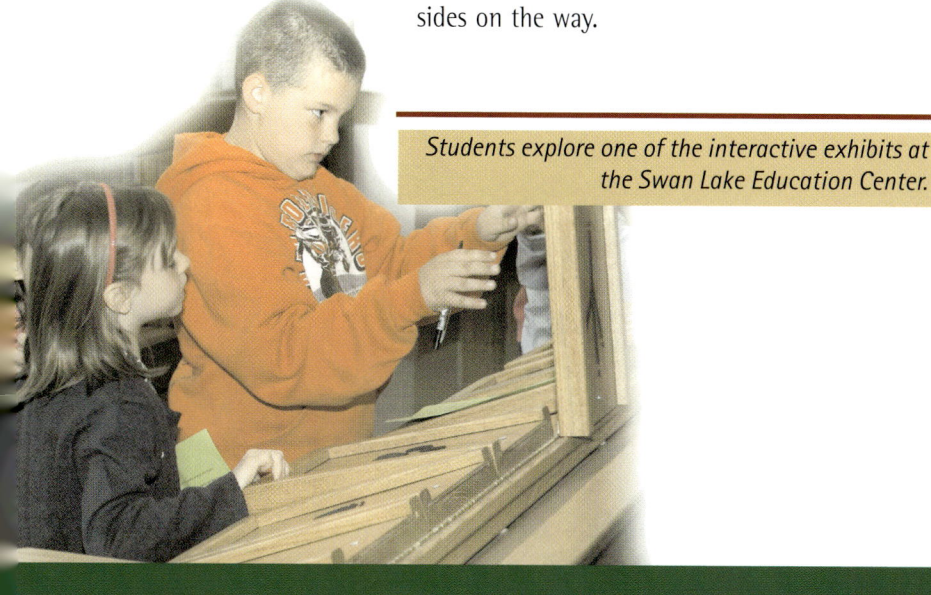

# Carroll IOWA

*The Festival of Trees is an annual celebration held between Thanksgiving and Christmas featuring more than 85 trees decorated by individuals, business, churches and civic groups. It is a delightful way to get in the holiday spirit.*

The theater at the Recreation Center is the setting for many delightful plays put on by the Community Theater.

What better way to spend a summer evening than watching a baseball game and what better place than the Carroll Baseball Stadium that was built in 1949 for the Carroll Merchants, a semi-professional team. Today, the facility hosts various high school, college and amateur team play.

## Points of Interest and Events

The recently renovated Chicago & North Western Depot designed by Charles Summer Frost the son-in-law of the Chicago & North Western President, Marvin Hughett, is a reminder of how important the railroad was to both Carroll the city and the county. The original depot and American Express baggage building along with a replica of a passenger platform create a pleasant setting to relax or watch the Union Pacific trains travel through Carroll, a reported sixty a day.

The Carroll County Historical Museum housed in the hundred year

*A bicyclist enjoys a pleasant ride on the Sauk Rail Trail.*

*Students at Fairview Elementary School perform a skit about Abraham Lincoln.*

38

# Carroll IOWA

*Luminaries have been lit for the evening ceremony of Relay for Life.*

*The Carroll County Historical Museum housed in the Carnegie Library Building is a treasure trove of historic artifacts*

old Carnegie Library Building near downtown Carroll, has an array of artifacts relating to the history of the county from the time of it's beginning in the 1850's to the mid twentieth century.

The rock walls and buildings in Carroll are reminders of WPA projects from the 1930's. In Graham Park and Swan Lake State Park are entrance pillars, shelter houses, and other buildings. The wall around the city cemetery and the Civil War Veterans Monument are more examples of work done by the WPA.

The Civil War Memorial monument in the City Cemetery has been enlarged to include veterans of all wars up through the Persian Gulf. The markers along with a small circular stage form a circle around the Civil War Memorial. Every Memorial Day a ceremony is held at this site.

*Luminaries have been lit for the evening ceremony of Relay for Life.*

39

# Carroll IOWA

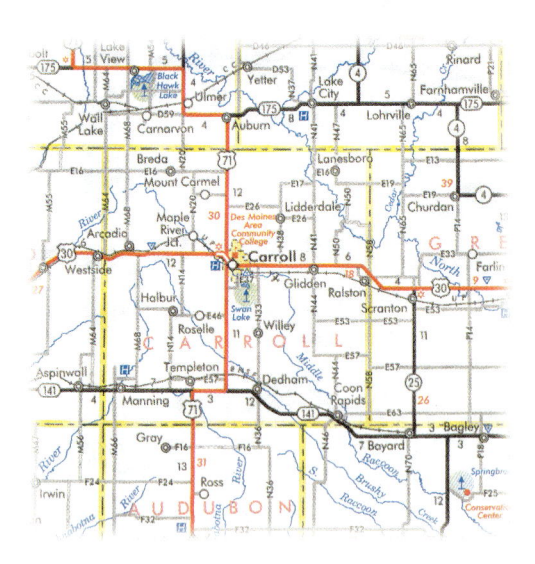

## LEARN MORE

To learn more contact the Carroll Chamber of Commerce at: 712-792-4383 or find us online at:

www.carrollspaper.com
www.chamberatcarrolliowa.com

## STORY CONTRIBUTORS

Marilyn Setzler is the author of two books on the history of Carroll County and she is the curator of the Carroll County Historical Museum.

A lifelong resident of Iowa, Jeff Storjohann is a staff photographer for the Carroll Daily Times Herald.

Christmas is a time to celebrate in Carroll with the Festival of Trees, a collection of trees decorated by organizations and individuals of Carroll, the Festival of Lights, a drive through lighting display at Swan Lake and Christmas Carroll tours, a daylong tour of community events.

The American Cancer Society Relay For Life of Carroll County is a year-long campaign that involves thousands of volunteers from all over the county working to make a difference in the fight against cancer. As a result, Carroll County has been number one per capita for funds raised in the United States in its population category for several years running.

When driving through Carroll County, there is a stunning architectural element in many of the small towns – a church steeple rising high above the town. These gothic churches built by the early settlers in the county are still in use today. They are striking in their beauty and worth the trip.

*A tranquil evening at Swan Lake State Park belies the bloody battle that took place over 150 years ago between waring tribes of Native Americans.*

*Pride In Our Hometowns.*

# P·O·R·T·R·A·I·T·S
## OF
## *Centerville*

### IN THE "CENTER" OF IT ALL

The Southern Iowa community of Centerville is situated in the midst of an outdoor recreation paradise. Deer and wild turkey hunters travel from all over the U.S. to walk the wooded hills of Appanoose County. For fishing and boating enthusiasts, the second largest lake in Iowa, Rathbun Lake, is located only minutes away.

Founded in 1846 by Jonathon Stratton under the name Chaldea, the town was planned around a unique two-block wide city square - which residents of Centerville claim is the biggest county seat square in the world.

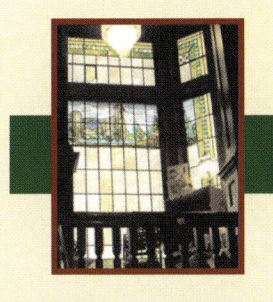

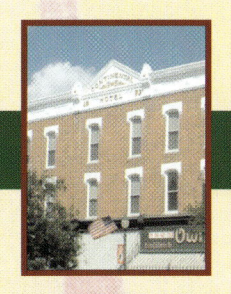

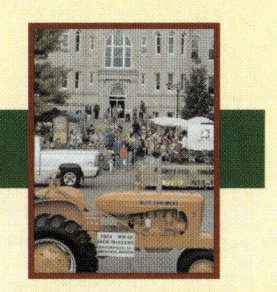

CENTERVILLE

*Pride In Our Hometowns.*

# P·O·R·T·R·A·I·T·S
## OF
## *Centerville*

## IN THE "CENTER" OF IT ALL

*Cherishing its heritage while looking toward the future. Every September Centerville's population more than triples for the Pancake Day festivities.*

Centerville came by its current name through a fluke. Town leaders planned to change their community's name to Senterville in honor of a Tennessee politician. Upon the paperwork's arrival in in Des Moines, a state government bureaucrat decided the locals couldn't spell and filed it as Centerville.

### A SNAPSHOT

The town experienced its peak population in the early 1900s with a boom in coal production. After that point, as coal usage dwindled and the harder coal of western states became more popular, the mining industry that had been the town's life blood collapsed. Through the 1950s, 1960s and 1970s, community efforts to promote new industries began. This push also culminated in the building

*Centerville is the county seat of Appanoose County, known for its scenic wild areas.*

42

# Centerville IOWA

of Iowa's ssecond largest recreational lake, Rathbun Lake, in 1971.

From the 1990's to present day, the town has focused on quality-of-life issues, in an attempt to attract and keep young families in the area.

A new volunteer effort is promoting the arts, culture and local history - much which centers on the Centerville Square area. Projects under way or completed include renovation of the Square's band shell, renovation of a 1930s' "California style" movie theater - the Ritz, renovation of the city's 100-year-old Drake Public Library and face lifts for many of the store fronts in Centerville's historic square area.

*Nearby Rathbun Lake has the longest shoreline in Iowa and is known as "Iowa's Ocean."*

## THE ARTS

The Appanoose County Coalition for the Arts was formed in 2000 to take ownership of the Ritz Theatre. Its board is made up of representatives from a number of local arts groups.

Upon the completion of the theater's renovation, plans call for the hiring of a professional theater manager who will schedule live

*The Appanoose County Railroad is "The Little Engine That Could" -created by the community when regular train service was dropped to Centerville.*

43

# Centerville IOWA

performances, business meetings and other functions to be held at the theater. The manager's duties will also include seeking outside performance groups.

The Ritz is to include a stage, orchestra pit, lighting, sound and support facilities for live performances for an audience up to 235 people. Performances would be by the local theater group, Curtain Up, as well as equity theater groups.

The Ritz will also be used for summer theater workshops, dinner theaters, performances by the Centerville Concert Association, musical and dance recitals and blue grass and Branson shows. "State-of-the-art" multi-media-equipment would allow for live feeds from Broadway and movies transmitted digitally by satellite.

Volunteers are currently raising funds to purchase an additional 20 acres to be used as an extended hiking and biking trail around the Centerville Reservoir. The extension will be part of a long-range goal that will someday include a trail to Rathbun Lake, a trail from

*A flag procession during the Courthouse's centennial celebration marks the numerous nationalities of Appanoose County residents listed in the 1904 census.*

*The Drake Public library was built by Gov. Francis Drake in 1903. The Des Moines college is also named after Centerville's former resident.*

44

# Centerville IOWA

Centerville to Sharon Bluffs State Park and a network of trailsd within the city.

This community spirit is also reflected in its railroad - the Appanoose County Community Railroad. The tiny railroad of two diesel engines and 36 miles of track is possible only because area leaders refused to let their community be cut off from rail service. When the Burlington Northern rail connection ended to Centerville in 1982, the community and business leaders stepped forward to create the nonprofit rail company.

*An familiar evening scene on the historic Centerville Square where soldiers have been seen off to battle since the Civil War.*

Residents contributed $50,000, local businesses contributed $120,000, two banks loaned $250,000 and the city and county pledged a total of $85,000 to see that Centerville and its industries would not lose the badly needed transportation system.

Then came the difficult task of receiving

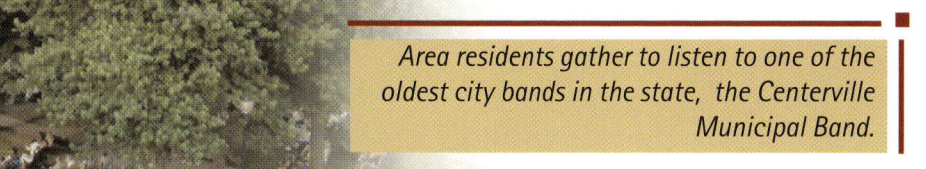

*Area residents gather to listen to one of the oldest city bands in the state, the Centerville Municipal Band.*

# Centerville Iowa

grants, which resulted in more than $1.7 million from state and federal sources.

The original track purchase was 10 miles of rail to Moulton where it could connect with the Norfolk Southern. In a repeat of history, that railroad company abandoned its track from Albia to Moulton and once again local leaders stepped forward to see that the additional 26 miles of track was purchased, which today such Centerville industrial plants as Rubbermaid and Curwood depend upon - retaining employment for 1,000 residents.

Other major employers include Alliant Energy Operating Center, the Barker Company that manufacturers refrigeration display cases, Iowa Steel and Wire and Modern Muzzle Loading - known in the industry as Knight Rifle. The creation of the state's first destination park and resort at Rathbun Lake is no accident. When Department of Natural Resources officials were holding interest meetings across the state in 2001, more than 600 area residents packed the meeting in Centerville to

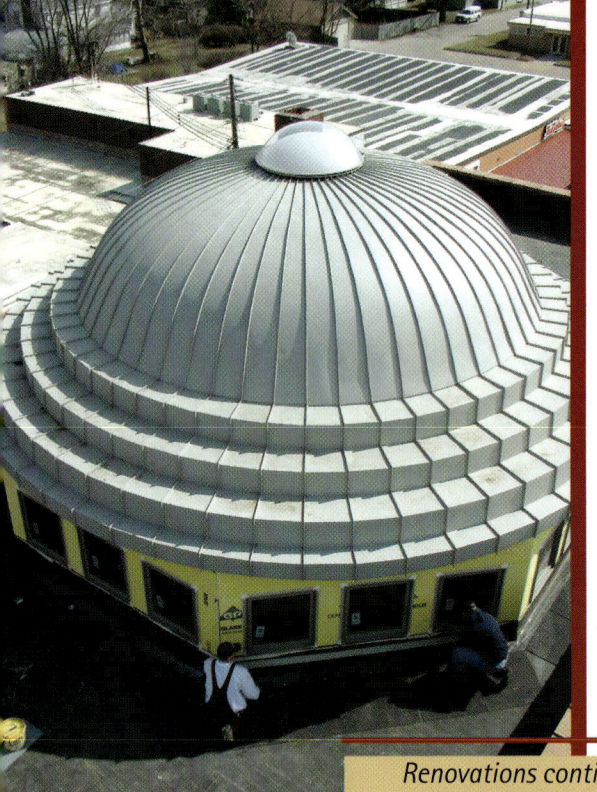

## INDUSTRY

*Renovations continue at the historic Drake Public Library, including a facelift for the dome.*

*An ugly metal exterior siding has be removed to reveal the "California style" Ritz Theatre, which is undergoing restoration.*

46

# Centerville IOWA

show their support for the project.

The effort culminated after the 2005 Iowa Legislative Session with Gov. Tom Vilsack signing a bill for the park's initial $28 million financing. He noted that it took 30 years and the perseverance of Southern Iowans to make a resort complex on Rathbun Lake a reality.

The official signing ceremony took place at the park site and was viewed by a crowd of approximately 250, many who have worked for years to see the resort an actuality.

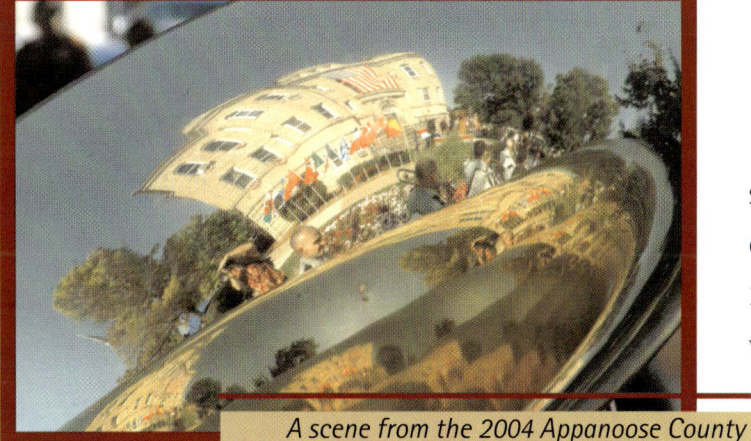

*A scene from the 2004 Appanoose County Courthouse Centennial as seen in the reflection of a 34th Army Band tuba.*

At Centerville is a satellite campus for Indian Hills Community College. The campus is located on the western edge of the city. Students can take arts and sciences courses, as well as enroll in the technical programs of administrative assistant, building trades and drafting/virtual reality, and the health occupations program of practical nursing.

A new program deals with sustainable agriculture, alternative crops and land use management.

Approximately 400 students attend this campus. This is the home campus of the Indian Hills Falcons

*If hunting or fishing is your thing, take a trail ride on the rolling hills to the east of Centerville.*

# Centerville IOWA

*Centerville business leaders take a tour through a former factory donated to Centerville and now under repair as part of an economic development effort.*

baseball team and the beautiful Pat Daugherty Field, named for a former coach of the Falcons. Centerville residents treasure their historical roots and observe it with a Hometown Heritage Day every summer, as well as a Croatian Fest in July to celebrate the community's Croatian legacy.

The Historical and Coal Mining Museum is located at 100 West Maple and opened from 1 to 4 p.m. on Sundays from Memorial Day through Homecoming week in October. It is also opened during Croatian Fest, Labor Day, Pancake Day and by appointment. The museum is located in a 1903 post office building and houses a collection beginning with the settlement period of 1843. Many exhibits depict a pioneer farm and village as well as a historic post office display. Artifacts from the Mormon Trail of 1846 are on display, and maps and detailed information about the trail are available. The research library contains all available histories, plat books and directories of

*The renovated Second Baptist Church is one of the few early Black American churches left in Iowa.*

48

Appanoose County. Coal mine replica on the lower level shows mining tools and equipment.

Another historic site is the Chicago, Burlington and Quincy Railroad Depot located on Highway 5 in the south part of the city. This picturesque brick building is a monument to the old railroad days, Built in 1910 by B.S. Staley Construction, it is still a beautiful structure and brings back memories of a busy railroad serving passengers and providing freight and baggage service to the surrounding area. The building also housed the telegraph office. The Depot was used until March 1982 when it was abandoned. At the present time it has been renovated and is home to the VFW.

## HISTORIC LIBRARY

The Drake Public Library has its roots beginning in 1896 with a group of ladies opening a library reading room. The ladies struggled with expenses for six years to keep the reading room open.

In 1901, a delegation of community leaders went to Centerville resident Gov. Francis Drake for his help in a request to the Carnegie Foundation to build a library. He listened to their request, but

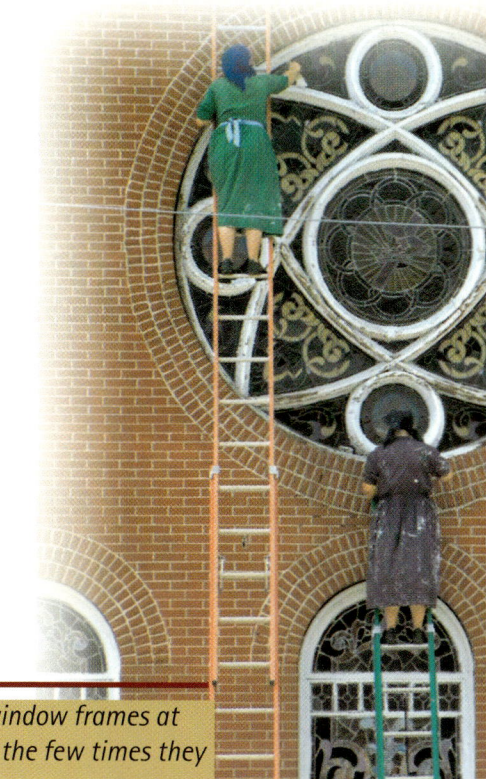

*Every year the wind and water is celebrated at Rathbun Lake with a sailboat regatta.*

*Local Amish women paint the window frames at the Presbyterian Church, one of the few times they are seen in colorful garb.*

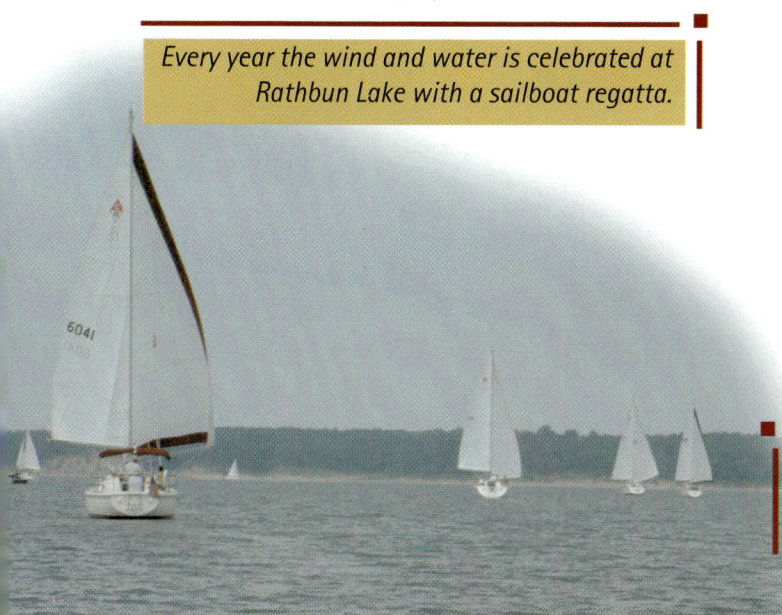

49

# Centerville IOWA

*Centerville's Drake Avenue is lined with beautiful old homes like the Beck Mansion.*

The Drake Public Library is located on Drake Avenue.

Centerville is the home to many stately mansions - a number which have been recently renovated. Leading the effort is Morgan Cline, a former Appanoose county resident who has returned to purchase and renovate a number of historic structures. His most visible project has been the beautiful brick Continental Hotel on the Square - now independent living apartments for area senior citizens.

Among the mansions Cline has restored is the D.C. Bradley Home. The architectural design of this interesting house, built in 1900, is so delightfully unconventional that it defies description. It definitely has Japanese influence but also a hint to Dutch Colonial and the effect is harmonious.

refused. If Centerville wanted a library, he would build it. The ladies turned over 2,630 books and other property valued at $3,000 to the new board of directors. The cornerstone was laid Nov. 16, 1901, and the library was dedicated to the city in 1903 by Gov. Drake to show his love for the city in which he had lived so long.

*A driver sizes up her competition during the Centerville Annual Soapbox Derby.*

50

# Centerville IOWA

The formal interior is characterized by the stately elegance of the great entrance hall, heavy beamed ceilings, paneled walls and a railed stairway to the upper floors. French doors with leaded panes and high mahogany wainscoting blend gracefully into the design. Located on Drake Avenue, this home has served many purposes over the years and is now the home of The Shoppes at Bradley Hall.

Other fun activities and places to go include:

- **The Centerville Concert Association's concert series.** The series of four or five concerts feature a variety of instrumental and vocal performances.
- During June and July the Municipal Band performs at the band shell on the historic courthouse square on Thursday evenings. Bring a lawn chair and enjoy homemade ice cream and a slice of pie provided by

*Volunteers remove the steeple roof from the Second Baptist Church as renovation efforts by a handful of volunteers begins.*

*Appanoose County native son Morgan Cline came home to renovated the Continental Hotel and a number of old mansions and other stores on the Square.*

51

# Centerville, IOWA

## Learn More

*For more information contact the Centerville Area Chamber of Commerce at: 641-437-4102.*

## Story Contributor

*Photos by Dan Ehl
Story written by a number of Centerville sources.*

---

local churches and organizations.

- **The Appanoose Country Club** has a 9-hole golf course and a lovely club house with large dining room, bar and enclosed porch. A new 9-hole course, the Manhattan Golf Club, is now located on the south side of Centerville on Highway 5.

- **Centerville City Park** has a large public pool as well as excellent facilities for picnicking and playing tennis. Just southwest of Centerville, the Lelah Bradley Park and Reservoir is a wonderful place to spend the day picnicking, fishing or camping. There is also a hiking and biking trail beginning at S. 11th St. in Centerville.

- **Pancake Day** - you don't want to miss this one when the city's population of 6,000 more than quadruples on the last Saturday of each September. A huge parade, free pancakes, Pancake Day Queen pageant and many family activities attract people from around the country.

- **Appanoose County Fair** - Livestock judging and exhibiting, rodeos, music, Bill Riley Talent Show and demolition derbies are just some of the activities that go on every year at the Appanoose County Fair.

## Activities

*Pride In Our Hometowns.*

# P·O·R·T·R·A·I·T·S
## OF
## *Chariton*

### CITY OF LAKES

*Named for a French trader and founded in 1851, when most people hear the word "Chariton" they immediately connect the south central Iowa community with Iowa grocery store giant, Hy-Vee.*

*People living in Chariton and Lucas County are exceedingly proud to be the home of the Hy-Vee Food Store, but there are reasons why companies like Hy-Vee, Johnson Machine Works and others decided to make Chariton their home — great people, beautiful country and wonderful traditions.*

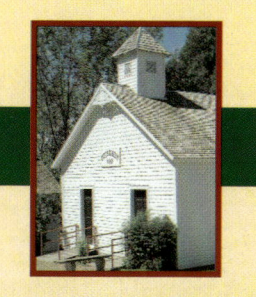

CHARITON

*Pride In Our Hometowns.*

# P·O·R·T·R·A·I·T·S
## OF *Chariton*

### CITY OF LAKES

## A SNAPSHOT

Chariton was originally called Polk after U.S. President Polk, was declared the county seat of Lucas County in 1849 and a log courthouse was built in 1850. The name of the town was changed to Chariton (Polk was already taken by a county and city to the north) in honor of a French trader. The city was officially established in October of 1851.

A temporary Mormon settlement was established just south of the present city in the spring of 1848 and evidence of the Mormon Trail still exists in Lucas County. Irish immigrants were among the first people to enter Lucas County and establish farms.

Jonas Wescoat and his brother were the first settlers in Chariton, building two log buildings on the current square. One was their home, the other their store.

Like most communities in south central Iowa, Chariton, coal mining played an important role in its development. In fact, United Mine Workers president, John L. Lewis, was born in Lucas, a small mining community nine miles west of Chariton and began his career as a union organizer in

*Miss Merry Christmas crowned during the annual Holiday Open House.*

54

# Chariton
## IOWA

*White tailed deer will make frequent appearances at Red Haw State Park.*

Lucas County. Railroads also played a pivotal role in the development of Chariton with the construction of a rail hub including a roundhouse.

Histories of Chariton and Lucas County will tell you the community was by the turn of the century a prosperous southern Iowa town of just under 5,000 with a wide variety of business and industry serving a large agricultural and coal mining community.

In January of 1930 a business partnership between Charles L. Hyde and David Vredenburg would eventually change the face of Chariton, turning it into the home of one of the nation's leading grocery wholesalers and retailers.

Hyde and Vredenburg came from pioneer farm families who left the farm to open their own small grocery stores in small communities in southern Iowa. The two met in 1921 and eventually established The General Supply Company to serve members of the Reorganized Church of Latter Day Saints headquartered in Lamoni. In 1930 the two created a new partnership and opened a grocery store in tiny Beaconsfield, Iowa. Throughout the years of the Great Depression the two men expanded their grocery businesses into other southern Iowa and northern Missouri communities. In

*Dual Gables House — restored by the Lucas County Arts Council.*

# Chariton IOWA

1938, 16 stockholders incorporated under the name of Hyde & Vredenburg and in 1945 the company relocated its headquarters from Lamoni to Chariton where the first warehouse was built.

Dwight Vredenburg, David's son, joined the company as a young man and became company president in 1949. His imagination, drive and philosophy of doing business not only shaped Hy-Vee for the next 40 years, but in large measure helped shape the attitudes and vision of Chariton itself.

A lot of people think of Iowa as miles and miles of flat farmland and rows and rows of corn fields. Lucas County has its share of fine Iowa farmland, but the Iowa stereotype stops there when you consider Chariton.

Chariton is surrounded by lakes on three sides, a state park borders the city to its south and the city maintains 11 parks. Red Haw State Park with Lake Red Haw is literally a minute's drive from the south edge of town. To the east sits Lake Ellis and Lake Morris twin lakes used as the city's reservoir and to the west is Crystal Lake at the Lakeview Country Club.

*The restored Carnegie Public Library night view.*

## CITY OF LAKES

Abundant wildlife and great fishing is within arm's length of Chariton residents. Within a few minutes' drive are huge tracts of largely undisturbed timber called Stephens State Forest. Portions of Stephens State Forests border Lucas County to the east and portions run almost parallel with Highway 34 throughout the county to the south of Chariton.

The Lucas County Conservation Board operates Pin Oak Lodge, an education center and

*Chariton Municipal Band performs on Chariton's new bandstand.*

wildlife exhibit at Pin Oak Marsh, an Iowa Department of Natural Resources marshland just south of Chariton on Highway 14.

Parks and recreation are important to the community. A brand new girls softball complex which includes Championship Field sits next to a new soccer complex in Northwest Park are just the latest of many park projects. Northwest Park also includes a disc golf course built by the Rotary Club. Brooke, Franklin and Railroad Parks are located in different neighborhoods providing easy access to families. Constitution Park, across from the restored Carnegie Library is ablaze in beautiful flowers and red bud trees. North Park is home to little girls softball, Little League baseball is played at Eikenberry Park and Yocom Park offers a fabulous children's playground and picnic facilities.

Several years ago, an abandoned rail line was used to build the Cinder Path, a 13.5-mile bicycle trail that begins at the south edge of Chariton and travels beyond Derby to the south.

With so many opportunities for outdoor park recreation, the community has not left other forms of recreation wanting. The Chariton Community Center and Johnson Auditorium are connected to the high school and provides first class sports facilities for youth and adults and also provides a wonderful theater for school plays and an active Chariton community theater.

The facility was built in 1984 with generous corporate contributions from the Johnson Machine Works and Hy-Vee foundations, along with citizen donations.

The Chariton Booster Club went to

*Playing Disc Golf at Northwest Park.*

*A beautiful summer day and great fun can be had at Vredenburg Family Aquatic Center.*

**Chariton IOWA**

57

# Chariton IOWA

the other side of the high school and built a state-of-the-art weight lifting facility for Charger athletes.

Dwight and Ruth Vredenburg presented the community with a $1 million gift to match a one-cent local option sales tax passed by the communities of Derby, Lucas, Russell, Williamson and Chariton to build the Vredenburg Family Aquatic Center, a magnificent outdoor swimming pool and aquatic facility built in Bingham Park (named after Dennis Bingham, who was killed in Vietnam). The aquatic center opened in 2000.

The Vredenburgs, before Dwight's death, also made possible the construction of a brand new movie theater, Vision II.

One of the finest private golf and country clubs in Iowa, Lakeview Country Club, sits on Chariton's western edge. The nine-hole competitive course wraps itself around beautiful Crystal Lake. The club house acts as a hub for dining and social activities in Chariton.

*A spectacular aerial view of the Lucas County Courthouse and Chariton Square.*

### Social And Cultural

In 1992 the Chariton Public Library, an historic Carnegie Library with a magnificent red tile roof, underwent a $750,000 remodeling and building project. An addition nearly doubled the size of the library and the exterior addition matched perfectly the building's original design. A complete interior remodeling created an extremely usable, modern library.

*Brand new Vision II theater built with a gift from the community.*

*Ice fishing at Red Haw State Park.*

## Chariton IOWA

### RED HAW LAKE

In 1996 the city council created the Chariton Historical Preservation Commission and it has been busy ever since. The preservation commission continues to support the library, it has helped the Lucas County Arts Council restore the Dual Gables House and the Freight House and is currently working on downtown building restoration. Dual Gables House was built in 1889 and has a unique architectural design with a Y-shape at a 45-degree orientation to the street. The two gables each has its own outside door. The house was gifted to the Lucas County Arts Council which uses it for classes and other occasions.

The CB&Q Freight House was part of a thriving railroad industry in Chariton. The 100-year-old structure was built in 1904 and served as the center of city commerce in Chariton for many years. Everything shipped in and out of Chariton went through the Freight House. In the fall of 2000 a massive restoration project was started after the Lucas County Arts Council obtained ownership of the building. Restoration has been ongoing since then.

The Lucas County Historical Museum is operated by the Lucas County Historical Society and includes the Stephens home, the "Puckerbrush" country school house, the Otterbein Church, the John L. Lewis building, an old red barn and an original log cabin. The museum contains an incredible array of Lucas County and Chariton artifacts.

People traveling through Chariton's downtown will immediately notice its bandstand. In the late 1800's an ornate gazebo stood on the southwest corner of the

59

# Chariton IOWA

*A night view of Lucas County Courthouse adds beauty to the area.*

courthouse square. Eventually it was replaced by a bandstand on the northeast corner of the square and it was used until the early 1940's when it was moved to Russell.

In 1999 the Retail Division of the Chariton Chamber of Commerce, Chariton Rotary Club and the Historical Preservation Commission raised $35,000 to build a new (historical replica) bandstand. The new bandstand was dedicated in June of 2000.

There are dozens of other clubs and organizations in Chariton, including the Chariton Rotary Club. The Chariton Rotary Club is well-known throughout the state for its sponsorship of student exchanges as well as other adult exchange programs.

Another organization that draws attention to Chariton is its 35-member volunteer fire department. In addition to protecting Chariton and much of Lucas County from the threat of fire, department members compete annually in state fire department competition and generally bring home the top awards. The department also takes care of "Old Betsy," a fire fighting apparatus that was first put into service Dec. 12, 1877 and still works today.

The people of Chariton don't create museums, parks and recreation facilities to let them sit around. The community sponsors all sorts of fun events throughout the year.

## CELEBRATIONS

One of the biggest events is the annual Fourth of July celebration, a three-day festival with parade, games, live entertainment and fireworks.

Halloween is really big in Lucas County with the Haunted Forest and Lavitsef (festival spelled backwards) and the Pierce's Pumpkin Patch

*Children have a blast as they sled down a wooded hill at Red Haw State Park.*

60

# Chariton IOWA

*Football Friday nights at Reynolds Field is always a hot spot to be.*

Festival held in October. Another delightful celebration is the All-Iowa Corvette weekend that occurs over Memorial Day weekend. During the Christmas season, Chariton goes all out to make the holiday season special. There are also wonderful festivals in outlying towns including the John L. Lewis festival at Lucas on Labor Day, the Old Time Music Festival at Williamson and the Russell Homecoming.

## Business and Industry

What makes Chariton different than many communities its size is the solid industrial base that has developed over decades of hard work. People move to Chariton and stay in Chariton because of excellent job opportunities.

Hy-Vee is the largest private employer in the state and even though its corporate headquarters have been relocated to West Des Moines, it still boasts a work force in Chariton of over 1,500 people at the distribution center. The Hy-Vee grocery store is also one of the main employers in town.

Johnson Machine Works was established

*Girls enjoy the rides during a 4th of July event that takes place in Chariton.*

# Chariton Iowa

*Biking down the Cinder Path Bike Trail provides exercise and leisure activity.*

in 1907 by David F. Johnson and remains a family owned business, operated by fourth generation Johnson family member, Jeffrey Johnson. David F. Johnson, a machinist for the Northwestern Railroad took over management of Chariton Foundry shortly after the turn of the century. Beginning with iron and steel repairs for the railroad, local farmers and builders, the company began building fabricated steel bridges during the Great Depression, built buoys and depth charge release racks for the U.S. Navy in WWII and following the war began fabricating steel for commercial buildings, built products and machines for the sewage treatment industry and eventually began fabricating gates for hydroelectric power plants and transportation waterways.

A wonderful corporate neighbor, Johnson Machine Works helped the community build Johnson Auditorium and gave a prototype fabricated steel pressbox to the high school for its football field.

## Industry

Astoria Industries is a relative newcomer to Chariton industry, relocating from Minnesota in 1995. The company builds fiberglass bodies for the service vehicle industry.

Stratford Homes is another recent addition to the industrial base in Chariton and last summer celebrated building its 400th home in Chariton. A beautiful new factory in Chariton's south industrial park builds customized modular homes.

Wayne Mfg. is a manufacturer of Christmas and holiday decorations.

You can't really call a corner grocery store a major employer, but Piper's Store is one of the most unique and best known businesses in Chariton. Walk in the store today and you'll find it not a whole lot

*Chariton's Volunteer Fire Department provides the area with great pride and service*

# Chariton

*This aerial shot of the Hy-Vee Distribution Center shows its great size.*

different than when Joe L. Piper opened his grocery store on the northeast corner of the square in 1905.

In the early years, Pipers had its own slaughterhouse and a bakery which shipped bread by rail to small towns in the area. The free delivery Joe L. offered then, still exists today. Son, Bob and his wife, Ruth, took over the store in 1946 and they entered the candy-making business in 1947, a portion of the business that is probably most famous today. After Bob's death in 1987, Jim and Anne Kerns bought the store and retained the Piper name. Anne worked with Bob Piper six years to learn the secrets of the candy-making business and handed that knowledge over to her daughter, Jill, who bought the business in 1999. Piper's is one of Chariton's main tourist attractions.

A modern airport that is capable of landing small jet airplanes is one of the many important services provided for businesses and individuals. Lucas County Health Center, is both a major employer in Lucas County, and the center for community health care. In addition to providing a critical care hospital and emergency services LCHS also includes Northridge assisted living center and Kid's Life Discovery Center.

Chariton is also proud of its Iowa Army

**LUCAS COUNTY HISTORICAL MUSEUM'S STEVENS HOUSE**

# Chariton, Iowa

## Learn More

Chariton is located in Lucas County.

For information, contact the Chariton Chamber of Commerce: 641-774-4059 or go online to:

www.charitonchamber.com

## Story Contributor

This narrative was compiled by Chariton Newspaper Publisher Dave Paxton using several sources including the "Lucas County Heritage 2000," "History of Hy-Vee" and the Pictorial History of Lucas County.

Photos were provided by Bill Howes, Christy Hirschy and Jeri Reeve.

---

National Guard, an air maintenance unit that has provided troops for both the Persian Gulf War and the wars in Afghanistan and Iraq.

Chariton takes great pride in its educational system. The community has newer elementary buildings, a recently built middle school and a high school with modern additions, including the Johnson Auditorium and Hy-Vee Recreation Center.

## Schools and Churches

Reynolds Field is a first rate facility for the school's outstanding football and track programs. Excellent sports, music and drama facilities help create excellent programs in athletics, music and drama.

Chariton's faith community is vibrant as well with several older denominations caring for historically significant buildings and a number of new congregations building new facilities.

First United Methodist Church dates back to a log cabin church built in 1851. The current stone church was erected in 1938. Sacred Heart Catholic Church was founded in 1869 and the current church constructed in 1914.

Another beautiful, historically significant church is First Presbyterian, located just across the street from the historic Carnegie Public Library building.

*Pride In Our Hometowns.*

# P·O·R·T·R·A·I·T·S
## OF
## *Creston*

### ON TOP OF THINGS

*Creston has been known for many things throughout its 136-year history. Established at the highest point along the line of the Burlington and Missouri Railroad - thus the name "crest town" - the city once had the largest railroad roundhouse west of Chicago.*

*It was also the home of Frank Phillips, founder of petroleum giant Phillips 66. And, for several years, Creston was known as the bluegrass capital of the world.*

*Today, Creston is surrounded by rolling hills, perfect for cow/calf production, has area lakes, among the best in the state for fishing, and fields and timbers that attract hunters from all over the nation.*

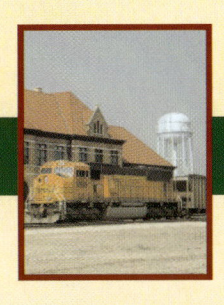

CRESTON

*Pride In Our Hometowns.*

# P·O·R·T·R·A·I·T·S
## OF *Creston*

## ON TOP OF THINGS

*Taylor Street (Highway 34) has become a bustling retail corridor through the city.*

With a population of 7,500, it is the largest town in South Central Iowa. Surrounded by smaller communities, it is the hub for retail, governmental and health services for the area. Creston is on the crest of the divide between the Mississippi and Missouri river basins at an altitude of about 1,310 feet.

Established in 1869, Creston became an overnight boom town populated by hundreds of railroad construction workers and their families. Engineer Dan Scullen piloted the first train into Creston.

In 1855, public land grants were offered for the building of railroads from the Mississippi to Missouri rivers, on a route running west from Burlington. Several surveys were run that year, but no lines were completed in the county until 1868, when Afton became the western end of the Burlington and Missouri Railroad (later Chicago, Burlington and Quincy, now Burlington Northern Santa Fe).

### A SNAPSHOT

A division point was desired for the area, a site upon which a roundhouse, shops and other facilities would be located. After first selecting a site near Cromwell, railroad officials altered their plans and chose a spot on the highest point or 'crest' of the line in Iowa.

*Fans vigorously support their basketball team at the state tournament. The Panthers won the state 3A boys title in 1997, and have gone to state three times since 1996.*

66

# Creston IOWA

*The Blue Grass Palace was a major attraction in Creston in the 1800s. The palace was rebuilt each year from bales of bluegrass and became the site for areas counties to display locally-grown product. It was also the site of entertainment as chautauquas were held there each year.*

The roundhouse gained fame as the largest west of Chicago and reportedly the second largest in the world at that time.

Development of rail facilities in Creston changed the area very quickly from lonely frontier to a populated industrial center. Creston's rapid growth led to the the eventual transfer of the county seat from Afton to Creston in 1890. A major landmark of that era remains today, Creston's former depot. Built in 1899, it now houses Creston City Hall and other offices and is on the National Register of Historic Places. Creston's railroad heritage is another attraction.

Inside the depot there is a large model railroad display, depicting Creston's railroad history.

There is also a presidential doll collection, giving an accurate depiction of the first ladies in their inaugural gowns, along with their presidential husbands.

Today, Burlington Northern Santa Fe Railroad employees get on and off trains at Creston. In addition to the number of coal and freight trains that pass through town, Amtrak passenger trains stop twice daily. Surrounding fields also put Creston on the map in earlier days. Creston was known as the bluegrass capital of the world about the turn of the 19th century.

Blue Grass Palaces fabricated from tons of bluegrass hay became popular tourist attractions at the site of the current high school on Townline Street. Bluegrass was cured and stacked in ricks for threshing and several threshing facilities were set up.

In its prime, the Blue Grass League was organized in Creston to unite bluegrass

*Gibson Memorial Library, the community's public library, was renovated in the mid-1990s.*

# Creston IOWA

*Crestmoor Golf Club along Highway 25 on the west edge of Creston is one of two nine-hole golf courses in the city. The other is Pine Valley Golf Club on Highway 34 West.*

production in 18 surrounding counties. The league had a vision of creating a palace made of baled bluegrass and display their products to other members.

The first Blue Grass Palace was erected in 1889 and attracted thousands of people. Creston's Louis Syberkrop designed the place. Fellow Crestonian J.C. Woodruff was the architect and builder of the palace.

The palace was square, 100-feet on each side. Towers were constructed on each corner and visitors entered the palace through a large horseshoe-arch made of hay and straw bales. The palace had a castle-like appearance.

Inside the palace, walls were made of a variety of grains and grasses. Each county in the league had its own space in the palace to display all their fruits, vegetables, grasses, grains, dairy products, wood, coal and other items produced in the bluegrass region.

In 1890, the palace was built three times larger. A 16-day festival, open to the public, complemented the palace. The last palace built was in 1891.

Bluegrass production returned to Europe by the 1950s, however, primarily because of climate advantages. Idaho, Oregon and California also had bluegrass production.

Actress Marcia Wallace, born in Creston, played Carol Kester (Bondurant) on "The Bob Newhart Show." She reprised that role in a guest spot on "Murphy Brown" for which she received an Emmy Award

*Located in McKinley Park, the Union County Historical Complex is a historical village of replicated buildings.*

68

*Creston supports a five-day a week newspaper, the Creston News Advertiser.*

nomination. She won an Emmy Award for her work as the voice of Mrs. Krabappel on the popular animated series "The Simpsons."

Wallace made numerous appearances on "The Merv Griffin Show" early in her career and guest starred on "The Brady Bunch" in the classic episode Getting Davy Jones. Other guest spots include roles on "Columbo," "The Love Boat," "Taxi," "Murder, She Wrote" and "Magnum, P.I." She has also done numerous films and television movies including "The Castaways on Gilligan's Island" (1979). Currently she appears on the Comedy Central series "That's My Bush."

William Bell, born in Creston on Christmas Day 1902, was known to the musical world as "Big Bill" Bell, the greatest tuba player in the world. He played with various bands and symphonies and taught music.

Drum player and Creston native John Robinson has played with a variety of popular musical acts from Elton John and Madonna to Ray Charles.

Creston native Walter Cunningham was one of the first three-man crews of the Apollo 7 mission - the first manned flight in the Apollo series, which preceded the moon landing.

Frank Phillips, an ambitious barber turned bond salesman from

## CRESTON TO FAME

*Left: A walking/biking trail stretches more than two miles through northern Creston, connecting McKinley Park and the Southwestern Community College campus. It will eventually extend north to Green Valley State Park.*

*Right: Balloon pilots fill the skies with color above Creston on the third weekend of each September for the Southwest Iowa Professional Hot Air Balloon Races.*

Creston, visited Bartlesville, Okla., in 1903 to assess business possibilities in the surrounding oil fields. After a series of failures that nearly caused him to abandon the business, a string of 81 straight successful oil wells insured success. Philips founded petroleum giant Phillps 66.

Creston uses its potential for tourism, especially when it comes to outdoor recreation.

"Hunting and fishing brings a lot of people to Creston," said Ellen Gerharz, Executive director of the Creston Chamber of Commerce. "That's the majority of tourists that come here."

## WATER WORLD

There are five major lakes for fishing, and more than 2,500 acres of publicly-owned woodland and prairie, all located within a 20-mile radius of Creston. Convenient for a tourist whose main interest is hunting and fishing and doesn't want to waste a lot of time driving from place to place.

Three Mile Lake is a 900-acre lake, well stocked for fishing, offers swimming, boating, water skiing and hiking. It was recently named one of the top 10 fishing lakes in Iowa by the Department of Natural Resources. Three Mile also offers year-round, all-weather cabins. Green Valley State Park, the largest park in the Creston area, also has a lot to offer. It's located 2 ½ miles northwest of town. There is a beach for swimming, boat ramps for easy boating access, fishing, water skiing, hiking and camping. Green Valley, like Three Mile, offers rental of all-weather cabins.

Summit Lake is another

*Memorial Day services are offered each year at Graceland and Calvary cemeteries.*

*Creston basketball players raise their state tournament trophy in 2005. The school qualified for state tourney play three times in nine years, beginning in 1996.*

# Creston IOWA

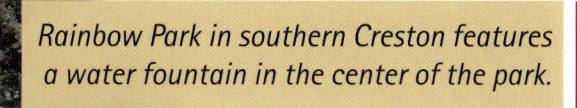

*Rainbow Park in southern Creston features a water fountain in the center of the park.*

lake known to be good for fishing. It's located on the edge of town and is said to be plentiful in crappie, largemouth bass and bluegill.

Twelve Mile Lake is perhaps one of the more popular fishing lakes. Over 650 acres of lake, Twelve Mile draws fishermen from all over the state.

McKinley Park, nestled within the community, is the home of a much smaller lake than the rest, but it, too, offers its share of the fish population for visiting fisherman. A mile-long walking and bike trail is also near McKinely Park.

There isn't just a lot of fishing going on. Creston is a town known for its ample amount of hunting targets. It's been said that Creston has the best pheasant and quail hunting around. There are also turkeys, waterfowl and plenty of deer.

Another attraction is the Union County Historical Complex. Located in McKinley Park, the Historical Complex is a historical village. It can be described as a museum of replicated buildings, arranged as a pioneer settlement during the late 19th century.

"The historical complex is a treasure in this town," said Gerharz. This detailed little village contains a general store, home, church, school, railroad switch and caboose, harness shop, barber shop, blacksmith shop, fire station, machine building, mill house, log cabin and barn. The complex is open 1-5 p.m. daily June through Labor Day weekend. Tours are available year round.

Tourists visiting Creston can stop by the Frank Phillips Tourism Information Center, located on the corner of Taylor (U.S. Highway 34) and Park streets.

The information center is a tourist attraction in itself. The brick

*Greater Community Hospital opened Crest Ridge Estates, a contemporary apartment complex for senior residents, in 2003.*

*Burlington Northern Santa Fe Railroad (BNSF) rolls by the restored railroad depot that now serves as Creston's City Hall. Amtrak also serves the area daily.*

*Fishing is the area's most popular tourist attraction. Green Valley State Park, north of Creston, offers one of five major lakes in the area.*

building is one of the first original Phillips 66 gas stations in Iowa. Creston offers a legion of annual events.

Creston is pure Americana during the Fourth of July. McKinley Park is the heart of the holiday in Creston. A volunteer group, called 10,000 Crestonians, plans the events. Over the Fourth of July weekend there is a carnival, talent show in McKinley Park, parade, fireworks display and flea market.

"Creston has one of Southwest Iowa's best fireworks displays," said Gerharz.

The Union County Historical Complex opens its doors to show Creston's yesteryears. Crowds line Adams Street for a parade. A talent show draws performers of all ages from across Southwest Iowa. The holiday concludes with a dazzling fireworks show. The colors multiply as they reflect off McKinley Lake.

Balloon Days is another big event held in Creston. The balloon festival, held the third weekend in September, is the second largest hot air balloon event in Iowa. There are more than 50 balloons, a parade, craft fair and flea market. Since 1977, Creston has hosted the Southwest Iowa Professional Hot Air Balloon Races. Balloon pilots from across the country come to Creston to compete and qualify for the national race in New Mexico.

The 2004 event, organized by a volunteer committee, was the biggest on record - 58 pilots attended. In addition to the races, which start at Creston Airport, crowds can check out a variety of other entertainment and parade throughout town.

*The tradition built by coach Dick Bergstrom has produced 18 winning seasons in 19 years through 2004.*

# Creston IOWA

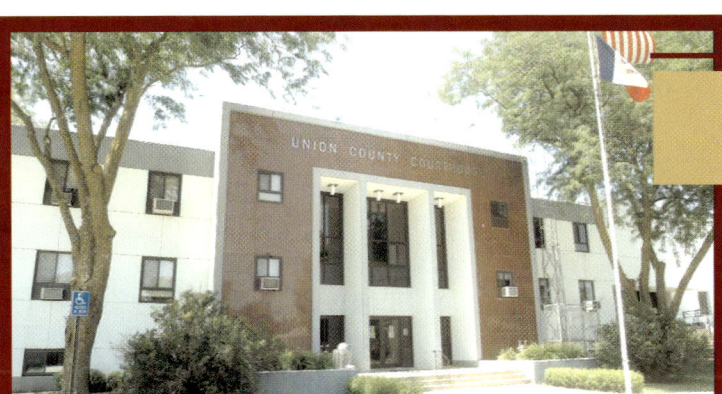

*County offices moved to Creston from Afton in 1890.*

In early December, a lighted Christmas parade shines down Adams Street. Christmas comes to town bringing with it the lighted parade with more than 40 festive entries. The town is decorated and lit up every night with wreaths, lights, bows and other decorations.

Creston's industrial park and atmosphere is diverse.

Originally known as Hills-McCanna, a magnesium foundry, in 1975, the operation changed hands and name to what is known as Fansteel/Wellman Dynamics. The company has been recognized for delivering highest-quality castings and sand-casting technology. The company is best known as a primary supplier of complex components for helicopters, missiles, rocket engines, jet engines, and structural parts for both military and commercial aircraft. It also supplied parts for the 2005 launch of the space shuttle Discovery.

In 1945, Gits Brothers Manufacturing Co., a Chicago maker of lubrication devices, looked for a less congested production area and settled in Creston. In 1944, story has it, Mr. Remi Gits was traveling via train to Chicago after vacationing in Colorado. He was forced to stay overnight in Creston because of a terrible snowstorm and was so overwhelmed by the hospitality toward him and helpfulness of the Creston people, he decided to open an assembly plant in Creston. Today the company produces an assortment of mechanical and electrical devices.

## PRODUCTIVE

*Taylor Park is a new family-oriented recreational area located along the city's walking/biking trail.*

*Creston was once the home of Frank Phillips, founder of Phillips Oil. The city had one of the first Phillips 66 gas stations, now serving as a Visitors Center on Highway 34.*

# Creston IOWA

What ends up in Halloween bags across the country, started in Creston. Since 1986, Gummi Bears candies have been produced in Creston.

Used in homes, hotel rooms and restaurants across the country, Bunn-O-Matic has produced a variety of coffee makers in Creston since 1977.

In addition to the industries, agriculture plays a strong part in the local economy. The agriculture products are diverse and reflect traditional Iowa farms from cattle, hogs, corn, soybeans and hay. Cow-calf operations are popular among area farmers.

## Education

Creston Community School District is enjoying its new surroundings. In January 2005, the school district opened a new elementary and middle school building valued at $13 million.

The building houses second-through eighth-grades and is located on the north side of town near the 15-year-old high school. The new building replaced three buildings, which date back to the 1930s.

Creston High School won the boys 3A state basketball championship in 1997. The football team is coached by Hall of Fame coach Dick Bergstrom. The Panthers wrestling team traditionally finishes in the state's top 10, with 12 state champions and three two-time winners since 1973.

After students graduate from Creston High School, they don't have to go far for a college education. Since 1926, Creston has had a junior college. The first classes were held in Creston High School. In 1960, the college changed its name to Creston Community College and was housed in

*Southern Prairie YMCA has served the community with a variety of recreational offerings since it began in the city's Area Arts and Wellness Center in 1995.*

*Southwestern Community College's main campus is in Creston, with satellite centers in Red Oak and Osceola.*

*Creston*
**IOWA**

> Growth of the Roman Catholic Church in the area in the late 1860s led to development of a parochial school. St. Malachy serves students through the eighth grade.

former Creston Community School District buildings.

In 1966, the college again changed its name, to Southwestern Community College, and became part of the state's community college system.

The college's School for Music Vocations is nationally renowned.

Southwestern's current campus facility, along Townline Street, opened in 1970 and has grown since then.

Southwestern Spartans coaches include veteran Ron "Fox" Clinton for softball and volleyball coach Rita Schroeder has more than 600 victories. Former baseball coach Bill Krejci has coached a USA national junior team.

Hair Tech, a cosmetology school, has been operating in Creston since 1979. Located in downtown Creston in the former Masonic Temple, students learn a variety of skills.

In addition to the public schools, Creston has two different private-education facilities. Because of the growth in the Roman Catholic Church in the late 1860s, a parochial school was opened in 1870. St. Malachy serves students through the eighth grade.

Mayflower Heritage Christian School opened in 2002. The school's initial enrollment was 11 students, but at the beginning of the 2004-2005 school year, enrollment was at 25. Mayflower's classes are through the eighth grade.

Being one of the largest towns in

### A Go-To Place

> Union County is cattle country. The rolling hills are sprawling with pasture land, and the county is also a thriving pork production region.

75

# Creston IOWA

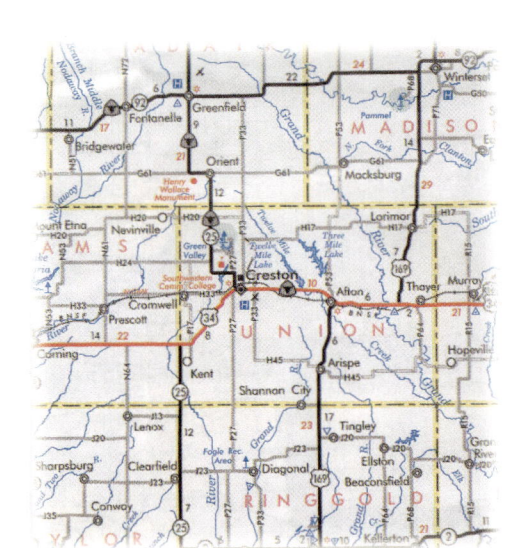

## LEARN MORE

*Creston is located in Southwest Iowa along U.S. Highway 34. Iowa Highway 25 intersects with U.S. Highway 34 in Creston. Creston is 70 miles from metro-Des Moines and 100 miles from Council Bluffs.*

*For more information: Creston Chamber of Commerce, 641-782-7021*
*www.crestoniowachamber.com*

## STORY CONTRIBUTOR

*Story and picture contributors: Creston News Advertiser*

---

Southwest Iowa, Creston is a retail hub of the area, including three new-car dealers, three grocery stores, a variety of fast-food restaurants and specialty shops. Creston supports a five-day a week newspaper, the Creston News Advertiser, and a radio station.

In addition to is business community, Creston's hospital is growing to provide additional services. Since 2002, Greater Community Hospital has added the Medical Arts Plaza, an office building holding many health-care providers who were previously located across town. The hospital also opened Crest Ridge Estates, a contemporary apartment complex for seniors, in 2003. Now known as Southwest Iowa Regional Medical Facility, additional growth including a cancer treatment center is planned.

2005 marks the 10-year anniversary of Creston's Area Arts and Wellness Center located near Southwestern Community College. After extensive community planning, the $3.2 million facility was funded only with donated dollars and grants. Owned by the city of Creston, within the center are Southern Prairie YMCA and Southwestern Community College Performing Arts Center auditorium.

Creston has elevated itself over its 136 years of exisitence, and not just because it rests on a high point along the divide of the Mississippi and Missouri rivers. The largest town along U.S. Highway 34 between Osceola and the Nebraska border, Creston has established itself as the hub of Southwest Iowa in so many ways. At the same time, Creston and its residents have preserved the small-town ways of life. The only direction Creston can go further, is up.

*Creston High School, built in 1990, serves approximately 500 students and is surrounded by various athletic facilities along Townline Street on the north edge of the city.*

*Pride In Our Hometowns.*

# P·O·R·T·R·A·I·T·S
## OF
## *DeWitt*

### "THE CROSSROADS TO OPPORTUNITY"

*DeWitt, population 5,046, is one of Iowa's quintessential communities. Situated at the once busy intersection of U.S. highways 30 and 61 in Clinton County, DeWitt is easy to get to. It offers many of the amenities of a larger city, the friendliness of a small town, and is just a short drive to the beautiful and historic Mississippi River.*

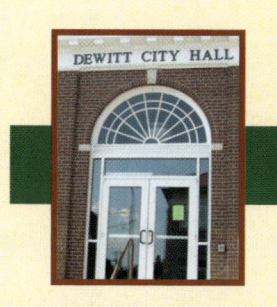

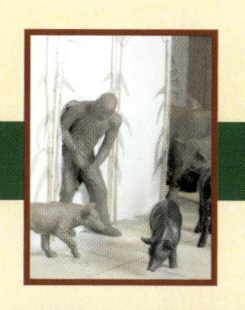

*Pride In Our Hometowns.*

# P·O·R·T·R·A·I·T·S
## OF
### DeWitt

## "THE CROSSROADS TO OPPORTUNITY"

*In 1868, iron rings in the sidewalk marked "parking" places, and gasoline was used only for cleaning soup from vests. Although several of the buildings still are standing, modern day DeWitt is a far cry from this photo showing a horse-drawn buggy and dirt streets.*

You can see DeWitt's distinctive spheroid water tower from miles away, and if you want to know more about the community, its web site address — www.DeWitt.org — is painted prominently on the base of the tower.

### A SNAPSHOT

The water tower marks the original "Crossroads of the World," where two major highways crossed. Although both are now four-lane bypasses around the city, Highway 30 runs coast to coast, and Highway 61 runs border to border.

Long before the highways were built, however, James D. Bourne, became one of the first settlers in Clinton County. He established a ferry across the Wapsipinicon River in 1836 and became one of the first citizens of the settlement that later would be known as DeWitt.

He was known as one of the first "movers and shakers" in the community and is credited with building the first frame house in DeWitt, serving three terms as county sheriff and later as county recorder and county treasurer. He also was the county's first postmaster.

The first county post office opened at Bourne's Ferry and carried mail between Davenport and Dubuque by pony. When the ice on the Wapsi

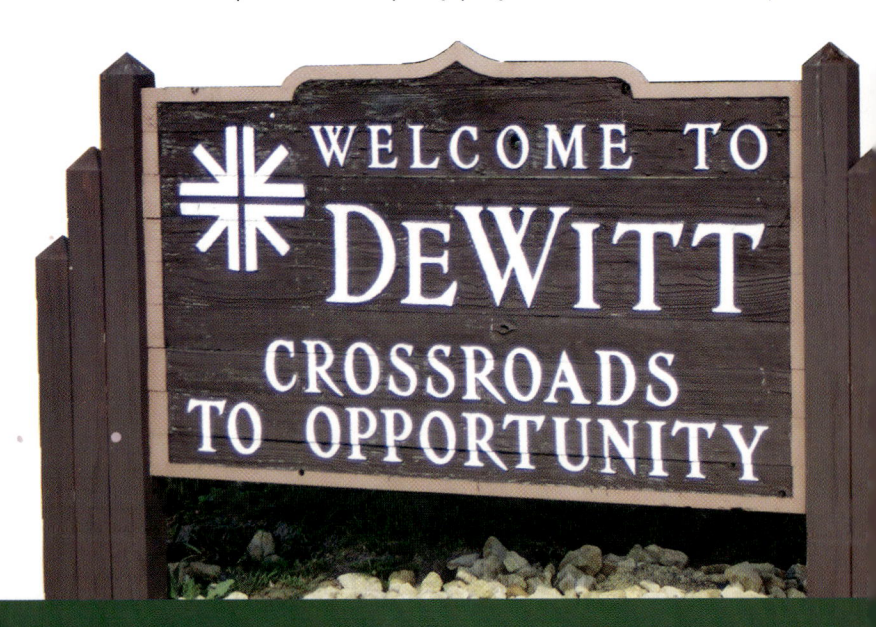

# DeWitt IOWA

*The steeple at St. Joseph Catholic Church has been a local landmark since the church was built in 1880. Attached to the church is St. Joseph School for students in kindergarten through eighth grade. Addition of a parish hall and gathering space were completed in 2004 along with a computer lab and offices at the school.*

River was too thin to support the pony, a large dog carried the mail bag across the river.

The influx of settlers was heavy in the late 1830s as more and more pioneers made their way West.

In 1840, the settlement held its first election for a justice of the peace — J. F. Hamer — and a constable — Jacob Lepper.

The first school was a log house in which Miss Fannie Brown held classes in the summer of 1840. It was located near Silver Creek, about two miles northwest of the present city.

In 1841, the House of Representatives of the Territory of Iowa named a three-man commission to select a new site for the county seat, which had been in Camanche for two years.

The commissioners chose their site, drove a stake and named the new town Vandenburg. Commissioner Miller had hoped to name the village Millersburg, but Col. William A. Warren, also a member of the board, was in love with a girl named Vandenburg, and his choice prevailed.

Meanwhile J.D. Bourne hurried to the land office in Dubuque to purchase the 160-acre parcel for the town for $200.

Even before lots were offered for sale, a log structure — the town's first building — was erected by Robert Bedford. Some say the next building was Loring Wheeler's tavern, but others believe it was the log courthouse.

For some time, Thomas Butterfield was the town's only merchant, selling "a conglomerated stock of a little of everything."

Before long, residents had tired of the name Vandenburg, and they petitioned the legislature for a name change. This time, they chose DeWitt after the first name of the prominent governor of New York. His last name already

*One of DeWitt's landmarks is a clock donated to the city by Mr. and Mrs. A.R. Beard in memory of their parents. It stands outside city hall.*

*The Paul Skeffington Memorial Race has been an annual event in DeWitt for 18 years, attracting about 500 participants each June for 2-mile and 5-mile races plus a fun run. The event honors the late Paul Skeffington, a community activist and grocer. Proceeds from the event have been earmarked for several years for the construction of a trail at Westbrook Park that also bears Skeffington's name.*

# DeWitt IOWA

had been taken by neighboring Clinton, 16 miles away. The change was approved in 1842.

A brick courthouse with stately white columns was built in 1854 at a cost of $6,000.

A short time later, DeWitt's first newspaper was founded by O.C. Bates. The present Observer, however, is a descendant of the paper established by S.H. Shoemaker in 1864 — when Abraham Lincoln was president. Shoemaker was an arch Republican and a Temperance man.

Although DeWitt had become a flourishing community, the population center of the county had shifted to the river towns of Clinton and Lyons. A petition for relocation of the courthouse resulted in an election in the fall of 1869.

The DeWitt folks did everything they could to retain the county seat, but the vote failed. Meanwhile, Clinton had been so confident of victory, a new courthouse already was nearly complete by the time of the vote.

It was bad enough to lose the election, but when the city fathers were told they also had to turn over the bell in the courthouse tower, it was too much to swallow.

After being tipped off a party of Clinton men planned to take the bell by force the following Monday, ten DeWitt men devised the Great Bell Heist scheme during a meeting at Bill O'Brien's Saloon.

At midnight Sunday, two of them climbed the bell tower, loosened the bolts, stuffed rags around the clapper and the bell's movable parts and oiled the bell metal.

They cut a four-foot hole in the courtroom ceiling and lowered the bell to the main floor. With some of the others pushing and some pulling, they carried it to a waiting delivery

*DeWitt enjoyed a brief period as the Clinton County seat. When the population center of the county shifted to Clinton and Lyons, an election called for the relocation of the county offices. While the city lost its courthouse, a band of 10 men rescued the bell from its tower and buried it in an open grave at Elmwood Cemetery.*

*DeWitt's hospital was built in the 1950s in response to a gas station explosion which severely injured several men. The badly burned victims had to be transported to Clinton for treatment. DeWitt Community Hospital was constructed in a cornfield at the edge of town after several fund-raising drives. Today the facility, known as Genesis Medical Center - DeWitt, continues to provide high-tech, high-touch care through an affiliation agreement with the Genesis Health System of the Quad Cities.*

*Like many Iowa communities, DeWitt has had its share of men and women serve in Operation Enduring Freedom. Throughout the years, military personnel have served with pride, even giving their lives for our country's freedoms.*

wagon and drove it to the cemetery.

The men lowered the bell into an open grave where a body recently had been removed for re-burial in another cemetery and covered it with earth, taking a vow of secrecy the old bell would stay there until DeWitt had need of it again.

About a year later, that need was met when the Campbellites built a church. The ten bell rustlers made another midnight trip to the cemetery to retrieve the bell for installation in the new belfry. Today it still calls worshipers to services at Grace Lutheran Church.

In 1878, townspeople saw the need for a place to perform "Uncle Tom's Cabin," and S.H. Shoemaker, publisher of The Observer, who was looking for a place to hold Temperance lectures, led the move to build the Operahouse Theatre. The original theatre was built with $10 shares purchased by 400 townspeople.

In 1929, DeWitt became the first city of its size in the world to offer the newest amusement acquisition, the "talkies," at a local theatre.

After serving the community more than a century, the Operahouse Theatre's renovation once again pulled citizens together in the 1980s. Today, the publicly owned theatre provides a venue for plays and concerts as well as first-run movies at bargain prices.

The Operahouse renovation – at the height of the Farm Crisis – marked the beginning of a move to reinvent DeWitt, which no longer

*The Clinton County 4-H Club Show and County Fair provides family entertainment and an opportunity for youngsters to show off their projects. The 2005 fair marked the 72nd annual event. The fair is held the last week of July, and concludes with the ever-popular demolition derby.*

*Renovation of the Operahouse Theatre in the 1980s was the impetus for many projects that have improved the quality of life for DeWitt area residents in the last two decades. The theatre is a venue for plays, concerts and special events in addition to first-run movies.*

# DeWitt IOWA

enjoyed its strong agricultural business base.

The DeWitt Development Co. (DDC) was formed and set about attracting new industry to the community. Through a partnership of investors known as Crossroads Unlimited, the first of four speculative buildings was erected and a business park developed.

Today the Crossroads Business Park is home to 11 industrial manufacturers and employs more than 1,200 workers.

The success of the DDC has bred more success. Once vacant storefronts again are occupied, and there has been a swell of housing development. More than 40 new houses were constructed in 2004.

Admittedly, much of the community's success is based on its location. The two major highways and the Union Pacific Railroad, whose tracks run along the south side of town and its business park, make DeWitt a prime location for manufacturing and distribution of products.

The highways attract visitors and out-

## THRIVING ECONOMY

of-town factory workers because of the easy access to DeWitt, and they also make it possible for residents to enjoy big-city amenities in the neighboring Quad-Cities and Clinton.

That's not to say DeWitt doesn't have plenty to offer on its own.

While many Iowa communities have been losing population, DeWitt boasted a 10 percent increase in the last census, surpassing the 5,000 mark.

Much of that increase can be attributed to the outstanding quality of life that results from community pride and leadership that sees a need and works to fulfill it.

For example, the city is home to a local hospital that is affiliated with the Genesis Health System in the Quad-Cities. The affiliation agreement offers control by a local hospital board of directors but also provides financial advantages, access to cutting-edge

DeWitt
IOWA

technology and equipment and state-of-the art medical care.

Also associated with the hospital is Westwing Place, a 75-bed long-term care facility.

The community has two medical clinics, five physicians, a nurse practitioner, numerous chiropractors, dentists and optometrists.

It also has Amber Ridge Assisted Living to provide an alternative for those not yet ready for a nursing home, and United Manor and Senior Heights – independent living facilities for senior citizens.

Community Care of Clinton County recently completed four new group homes for exceptional residents who enjoy independent living with supportive services that assure their health and safety.

Recreational offerings abound in DeWitt. The city-owned DeWitt Fitness Center has been a jewel in the city's crown, offering free weights and workout machines, an indoor lap pool, a walking/running track and wallyball/racquetball courts plus a variety of classes to fit the needs of persons of all ages and stages of fitness.

The center was established by Dr. Wallace and Velma Ash as a cardiac rehabilitation center. Later, DeWitt Bank and Trust Co., First Central State Bank and Iowa Mutual Insurance Co. assumed ownership before the city purchased the facility, which is operated on a membership basis.

The city has several neighborhood parks as well as Westbrook Park, an

*Left: Ekstrand Elementary School, which houses the Central district's kindergartners through fifth-graders, has been recognized as a FINE (First in the Nation in Education) school.*

*Right: Central Community Schools' Saber athletic teams have a long tradition of excellence — from the football field and basketball courts to the cross-country courses and many other sports in between.*

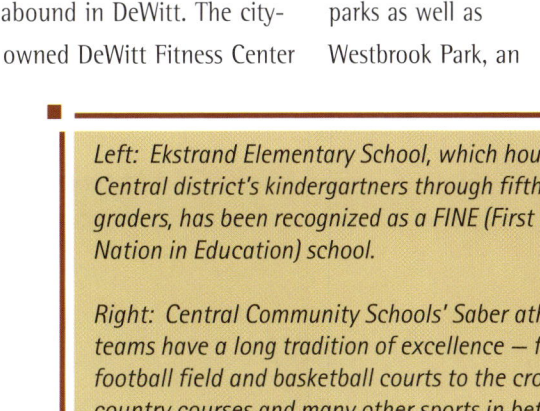

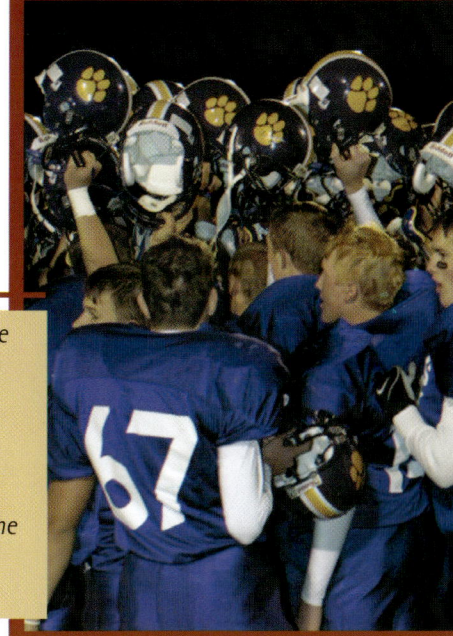

83

# DeWitt IOWA

approximately 100-acre multi-purpose recreation area with facilities that include lighted baseball and softball diamonds, rest rooms and a concession stand, playground equipment, a disc golf course and the soon-to-be-completed Paul Skeffington Memorial Trail, for runners, walkers, bicyclists and cross-country skiers.

A large aquatic park, built in 1999, was one of the first of its kind in eastern Iowa. With its two slides, a lily pad walk and other attractions, it remains a popular destination for children and families on hot Iowa days.

Ashindel Park, adjacent to the aquatic center and fitness center, sports two ball diamonds for younger children as well as an outdoor walking path and a basketball court.

Soon to be added at Ashindel is a skate park, which is being developed through the efforts of young skate boarders who have been raising funds to build a place to practice their skating skills.

Other parks include Paarmann Park in southeast DeWitt, which was developed through the generosity of the Paarmann family, who had a deep desire to make their community a better place.

That feeling was echoed two years ago when Car Freshner Corporation, a community partner which manufactures "Little Tree" air fresheners in the Crossroads Business Park, topped off the fund drive with a generous donation to acquire what is now known as "Little Trees Park" in southwest DeWitt.

> *One of DeWitt's hometown heroes is David Hilmers, an astronaut who flew several space shuttle missions with NASA. Among them was the Discovery mission that signaled America's return to space as the first flight after the Challenger accident. Central Community High school honored its alumnus by naming its Discovery science rooms named after him.*

> *Westwing Place nursing home, adjacent to the DeWitt hospital, operates as an Eden Alternative facility, which encourages resident interaction with children and pets and provides many of the aspects of living at home.*

> *During the WPA (Works Progress Administration) era, John Bloom received a commission for the DeWitt Post Office and installed his mural, "Shucking Corn," in 1937. Bloom was born in DeWitt in 1906.*

*Grace Lutheran Camp, with two retreat centers and other facilities, is situated on the west edge of town and holds camps and other activities in the summer for people of all ages. It is best known, however, for its Christmas luminary, which draws thousands of visitors each year.*

Nearby to the east are Lake Kildeer and Lake Malone, operated by the Clinton County Conservation Board. Both lakes are stocked with pan fish, and Lake Malone also features a swimming beach.

To the west is Crystal Lake, now a private lake, but one which was a popular summer destination before it was developed into a housing addition.

The summer of 2004 marked the expansion of Springbrook Country Club into an 18-hole course. The fairways are lush, rolling and shaded by many mature trees. Water comes into play several times in a round, making "The Brook" as challenging a course as any in the area.

Springbrook is one of the oldest DeWitt recreation areas. While it once featured a number of summer cottages, it now boasts year-round homes, and clustered around the back nine holes are two new housing subdivisions and a condominium neighborhood.

Annual DeWitt events include the Paul Skeffington Memorial Race, the Crossroads Triathlon, several benefit golf tournaments and the Eastern Iowa Threshers Association Steam Show.

Cultural activities and amenities include the Frances Banta Waggoner Community Library, the Central Community Historical Society Museum and annual events, consisting of a fine arts fair and the John Bloom Art Festival during Autumn Fest. The Bloom festival is named for the town's favorite son, who studied under Grant Wood and created a mural which is displayed at city hall.

DeWitt's Fourth of July parade

*The addition of nine holes to Springbrook Country Club a year ago made the golf course one of the most challenging in eastern Iowa. In the background are new condominiums which are a part of the city's housing boom.*

85

# DeWitt, IOWA

traditionally is one of the best in the area, enhanced by a spectacular fireworks show in neighboring Grand Mound.

The Clinton County Fair is held each summer at the fairgrounds in DeWitt, which also features an outdoor living classroom that abounds in beauty and color.

Local service clubs and fraternal organizations provide a significant part of the community leadership, spearheading and/or supporting many of the projects that make the community a better place to live. Among them are two Lions Clubs, Knights of Columbus, a Masonic Lodge, two Federated Women's Clubs, the American Legion Post and its Auxiliary, the hospital auxiliary, a PEO chapter, several sororities and various booster organizations for school interests.

The Central Community Education Foundation and the DeWitt Area Fine Arts Foundation both operate under the umbrella of the DeWitt Area Foundation to address philanthropic educational, cultural, social and quality of life needs in DeWitt and area communities.

St. Joseph Catholic Church, built in 1880, is one of the oldest local landmarks with its tall spire, but religion played an important role in

*Lake Malone, near DeWitt, is stocked with pan fish and has a swimming beach, which provides a great summertime destination.*

*In its inaugural year, 2003, the First Central State Bank Crossroads Triathlon was named the best new triathlon competition by area triathletes. Participants swim in Lake Malone, ride the country roads to the north and run throughout town as part of the triathlon course.*

*One of DeWitt's most popular recreation spots is the aquatic center, built in 1999. The zero-depth facility features two slides, a lily pad walk, a climbing castle with miniature slides for little ones, water features and deep water for lap swimming.*

# DeWitt, IOWA

DeWitt, even in its early days.

The Congregational Church was organized in 1842 and its first church was built in 1852. A Methodist class of six members formed in 1843 and built a church in 1850.

Bishop Loras organized St. Simon's Parish in 1848 and bought a log house to serve as a church whenever a priest could come to town. That church burned to the ground in 1879 and was replaced with St. Joseph's in 1880.

Today, the 12 churches of DeWitt include most denominations.

The Central Community School District of Clinton County provides quality educational opportunities for approximately 1,600 students from DeWitt and the neighboring communities of Grand Mound, Welton and Low Moor. Facilities include a high school, a middle school and an elementary school.

DeWitt also is home to St. Joseph Catholic School, which educates students in kindergarten through eighth grade.

There are two child care centers, both of which offer preschool classes.

Clinton Community College, located in nearby Clinton, also offers college-level classes for high school students, both via the Iowa Communications Network and on campus.

DeWitt has an elected mayor and five city council persons as well as a city administrator, a director of public works, a director of parks and recreation and a police chief, who oversees a department of nine full-time and one part-time officers, plus a K-9 unit that is an active member of the regional drug

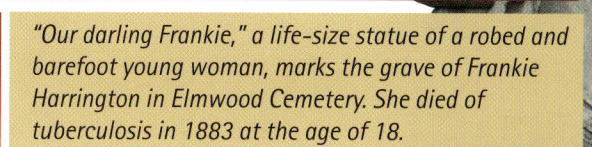

*WMT-Radio's annual Tractorcade concluded in DeWitt in the summer of 2005.*

*"Our darling Frankie," a life-size statue of a robed and barefoot young woman, marks the grave of Frankie Harrington in Elmwood Cemetery. She died of tuberculosis in 1883 at the age of 18.*

# DeWitt IOWA

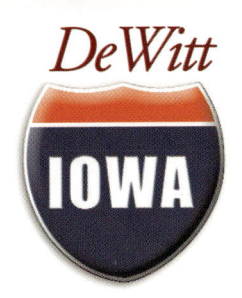

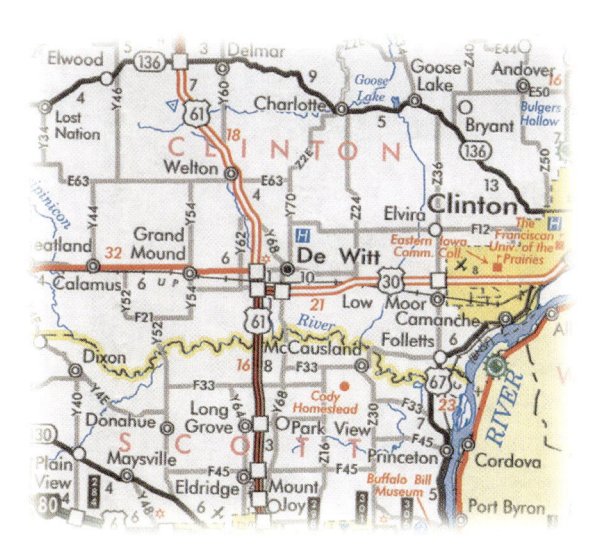

## Learn More

DeWitt is located in Clinton County in eastern Iowa at the Crossroads of the World —the intersection of U.S. highways 30 and 61.

Contact the DeWitt Chamber of Commerce, 563-659-8500; the DeWitt Development Co. at 563-659-8508; or web sites at:
www.DeWitt.org
www.dewittdevelopmentcompany.com
www.dewittobserver.com.

## Story Contributors

**Mary Rueter**, General manager, The Observer, DeWitt

**Ann Soenksen**, President, Central Community Historical Society

Photos by Mary Rueter, Steve Thiltgen, Kate Howes, Jeremy Huss, Kristall Laursen and courtesy of Central Community Historical Society

---

enforcement task force.

The city's volunteer fire department was organized in 1879 and has a fleet of state-of-the-art fire-fighting units plus 30 volunteer firemen.

DeWitt has the distinction of being the site of the first airplane fatality in Iowa in 1911; home to Iowa's first baseball team – the Hawkeyes – in the 1870s; and the boyhood home of an astronaut – David Hilmers – and a noted artist – John Bloom. Still, local folks believe the best is yet to come for this thriving, bustling, forward-looking community.

Sixth Avenue, DeWitt's main street, is slated to undergo renovation and reconstruction in 2006. The $4 million project will feature a streetscape reminiscent of the days of yesteryear with period street lighting, flowering baskets and benches and a specially commissioned sculpture honoring the work of John Bloom.

## The Future

The enhancements all are a part of the welcome feeling the city of DeWitt wants to extend to visitors and potential residents as well as businesses and industry looking for a great place to locate.

"As mayor I am proud of DeWitt, as a father is proud of his child," says mayor Don Thiltgen. "This is a great town, and we are happy to share with others what we are all so proud of."

*Today, just as for many years in the town's past, railroads have played a significant role in the economic health of the community.*

*Pride In Our Hometowns.*

# P·O·R·T·R·A·I·T·S
## OF
## *Fairfield*

### THE FIRST...

*Since its beginning, Fairfield area residents have brought many "firsts" to the state and the nation: the first Iowa State Fair; the first Carnegie Library, the first golf club and the first malleable iron foundry west of the Mississippi River; and the nation's first permanent public power installation.*

*More recently, Fairfield has gained distinction for being home to Transcendental Meditation and the Maharishi University of Management that attracts students from around the world and helps create a community of diverse cultures and opportunities.*

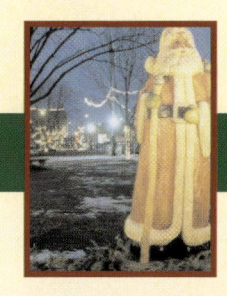

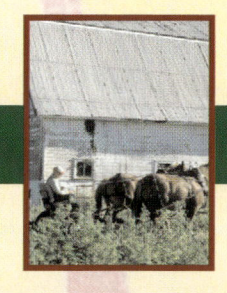

FAIRFIELD

*Pride In Our Hometowns.*

# P·O·R·T·R·A·I·T·S
## OF
## *Fairfield*

### THE FIRST...

*Flags in memory of deceased veterans are flown in Central Park on Memorial Day and Veterans Day by volunteers who arrive by 6 a.m. to put them in place. Volunteers remove the flags at 4 p.m. (Photo by Julie Johnston)*

American Indians and adventurous explorers had lived in and visited Jefferson County for many years before families started moving into the area in 1836.

The first white child born in the area, William Henry Coop, the son of William G. and Nancy Harris Coop, was born July 13, 1836, in a covered wagon where his family was living while busting sod and building a home.

Today, a statue of Coop as an older man telling his history to a young boy of today sits near the bandstand in Central Park signifying a link between the past and the present.

In 1839, the western part of Henry County became Jefferson County, and a group set out to find a site for the county seat. After selecting a bit of prairie near the center of the county, they marked the spot by driving a stake into what is now Fairfield's Central Park.

One of the early area settlers, Nancy Bonnifield, suggested naming the new town Fairfield for the fair field in which it sat.

The Bonnifield cabin, where Fairfield was named, was built in 1838. It was moved eight miles from its original site

### A SNAPSHOT

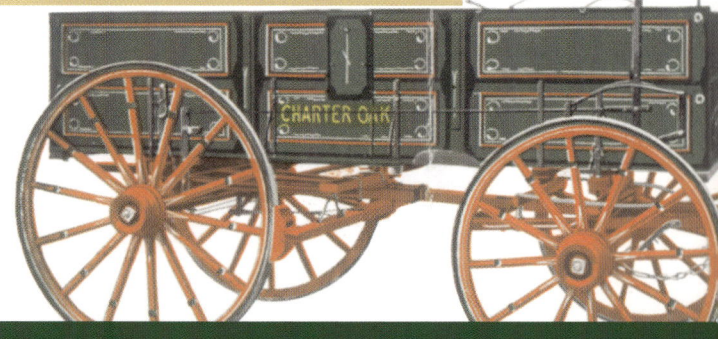

*A line drawing from a Turney Wagon Works brochure early in the 20th century. At its peak, the Turney company produced more than 500 wagons per year. It was said that if you had a Charter Oak farm wagon, you had the best. (Courtesy of Gene Luedtke)*

*The statue of William Henry Coop in Central Park was created by local sculptor Chris Bennett. Born July 13, 1836, Coop was the fifth child of Col. William and Nancy Coop, the first white child born in Jefferson County. (Photo by Julie Johnston)*

# Fairfield IOWA

*A page from the Louden Company general catalog #50 of 1920 shows a Louden planned and equipped barn at Iowa State University as well as one in Ohio. Louden-designed barns are located throughout the United States and also in several foreign countries. (Courtesy of Gene Luedtke)*

into Old Settlers' Park in 1912, and is now the oldest, still-standing dwelling built by a white man in Iowa.

Just a month after surveyors plotted the new city, the first general store opened, and since then, Fairfield has grown into a community influenced by agriculture, industry and education.

## Historic Review

Fairfield has the distinction of being the "first" — the city with the first Carnegie Library west of the Mississippi River, the site of the first golf club west of the Mississippi, the first malleable iron foundry west of the Mississippi, the nation's first permanent public power installation — but the first the city is most proud of is being the site of the inaugural Iowa State Fair.

The idea for a state fair began with an article in the April 11, 1853, Ledger newspaper suggesting a fair and recommending Fairfield as the location because, at the time, it was the center of the state's population.

Later that year, the newly organized statewide agricultural association scheduled the first state fair to begin Oct. 25, 1854, in Fairfield.

The fair was on six acres of land donated by Henn, Williams & Co. between West Grimes and West Lowe avenues and North Second and North Fourth streets.

The entrance to the fairgrounds was on the corner of North Fourth Street and West Grimes Avenue. A 10-foot-tall rail fence surrounded the grounds, which included a long shed protecting a five-foot-wide, 250-foot-long table; 130 stalls; 60 pig pens; an office; a 25-foot-wide, 1,500-foot-round track with a rope guard, a platform in the center for speakers and judges; and space for visitors. It cost $322.20.

Families came by covered wagons and horseback and stayed all three days camping near the grounds. On its busiest day, the fair drew 8,000

*Left: During Fairfield Farmer's Market in October, one Saturday is designated October Morn with knitting, spinning, and cider making demonstrations. Entertainment and an art show as well as farm products for sale offer something for everyone. These children were helping make cider. (Photo by Julie Johnston)*

*Right: The Dexter Double-Tub washer, illustrated in an early company brochure, was once a household word throughout the nation. The Dexter Company built its first washing machine of wood held together by metal bands in 1910 and currently manufactures one-fourth of the commercial laundry machines sold in the United States. (Courtesy of Gene Luedtke)*

91

# Fairfield IOWA

*Left: 2004 reenactment of the 1954 trip with Margaret Carlson, Mike Carlson, Sheryl Carlson Payne(in the wagon) and Butch Downey (holding the horse). (Photo by Vicki Tillis)*

*Right: The Jack and Margaret Carlson family, including children Sheryl and Mike, and Butch Downey with his horse, participated in the 1954 caravan to the Iowa State Fair. (Ledger file photo)*

visitors, who each paid a 25-cent admission fee to see the farm animal, crop and domestic manufacturing contests, events and exhibits.

Receipts totaled about $1,000. After funds for bills and prizes were taken out, there was a balance of $50, and the association decided to hold the second state fair beginning Oct. 10, 1855, in Fairfield.

The second state fair was on 10 acres opposite the southeast corner of the city limits at the time. It drew 12,000 people on its busiest day.

After the second year, other cities hosted the event until it moved to Des Moines in 1879.

In Fairfield, the state fair grounds grew up to grass, the fence was torn down, and the grounds divided into lots and covered up by buildings, walks and roads of a growing city.

Seventy-one years after the first fair, a historical marker, a gift from the Log Cabin Chapter and Iowa Society, Daughters of the American Revolution, was set up at Fourth Street and Grimes Avenue. The large boulder's bronze tablet proclaims it "Marks the Entrance to the Site of the First Iowa State Fair, Held at Fairfield October 25, 26, 27, 1854."

To open the 100th Iowa State Fair in 1954 and to commemorate the first state fair in Fairfield, an Iowa Centennial State Fair Caravan left Fairfield at 8 a.m. Tuesday, Aug. 24. By the time it pulled into the state fairgrounds Friday evening, Aug. 27, it totaled 578 people from 95 towns in Iowa, six states and the District of Columbia; 526 animals; and 30

*Fairfield High School, home of the Trojans, is part of the Fairfield Community School District which also includes four elementary centers and a middle school. Other educational opportunities for area children include Fairfield Christian School and Maharishi School of the Age of Enlightenment. (Photo by Julie Johnston)*

92

# Fairfield IOWA

horse-drawn vehicles.

Saturday, Aug. 28, the two-mile-long caravan opened the Centennial State Fair by parading around the track in front of the grandstand.

A historical marker, set up by the Fairfield Jayceettes in 1955 on the southwest corner of Fairfield's Central Park, designates the park as the starting point of the caravan.

A second plaque added to the marker in 1970, states, "Official records of 1954 Caravan are buried below. Not to be opened until 2054 A.D., the 200th anniversary of the Iowa State Fair."

About 400 people from 17 states, with 45 wagons and around 250 horses made a second caravan trip from Fairfield to Des Moines in August 2004 to commemorate the 150th anniversary of the fair and the 50th anniversary of the 1954 caravan.

The caravan kickoff celebration Saturday, Aug. 7, in Central Park included the showing of a trophy won by Jesse Hinshaw for his 2-year-old colt at the first Iowa State Fair.

The small, less than three-inch tall, engraved silver cup trophy is believed to be the only existing memento from the first Iowa State Fair.

The 2005 caravan set out Sunday morning Aug. 8 on its four-day trip to Des Moines.

*A Dexter Company worker pours hot molten iron into molds in The Dexter Company Foundry, established in 1920, which makes parts for its laundry division as well as for other companies. (Photo by Julie Johnston)*

*One of several Fairfield residences on the National Historic Register, the James A. Beck house, built in 1896, is described as an extremely fine example of Queen Anne residential architecture, at times referred to as "magnificently ostentatious." (Photo by Julie Johnston)*

*The Leapfrog sculpture, sculpted by nationally-known area artisan Chris Bennett, sits in front of the Carnegie Library building. The sculpture represents Ledger newspaper carriers having a moment of fun. (Photo by Julie Johnston)*

# Fairfield IOWA

*Believed to be the only remaining item from the first Iowa State Fair, this silver cup trophy is engraved, "Iowa State Fair; Jesse Hinshaw; First 2 yr. Colt, Fairfield, Iowa 1854." (Photo by Vicki Tillis)*

The procession, including special guest riders from the 1954 caravan, paraded through the state fairgrounds during opening day ceremonies Thursday, Aug. 12.

### First library

The Fairfield Public Library institution, organized in 1853, was thought to be the first public library in Iowa.

When Andrew Carnegie began donating money to build libraries, U.S. Sen. James F. Wilson of Fairfield, persuaded him to give $30,000 to the Fairfield County Library Association to build the first Carnegie Library outside of Carnegie's home state of Pennsylvania.

The square, red brick building built in 1893 housed the Fairfield Public Library until 1996 when it moved into a new building better suited to meet its modern-day needs.

The Carnegie building now houses the Indian Hills Community College's Jefferson Center, the Iowa Workforce Development offices and the Carnegie Museum collection of American Indian artifacts, Parsons College and other local memorabilia.

### First permanent public power

The most famous early landmark was a 185-foot light tower built in 1881 in Central Park when Fairfield became the second city west of the Mississippi River to have electricity.

The tower displayed six 1,800-candle power arc lights that were visible more than 20 miles away in Keosauqua.

According to the American Public Power Association, the tower was the nation's first permanent public power installation and it marked the birth of the electric industry.

Fairfield's public power venture ended in 1899 when the city council sold the tower and equipment to the Fairfield Gas

*Left: Partners For Play, a playground built in 2000 with $161,000 in donated funds and materials, is located in O.B. Nelson Park. In addition to 12 city parks, there are 10 parks located in the county with facilities for picnicing, camping, hiking, birdwatching and a host of other outdoor activities. Partners For Play II was recently constructed in Chautauqua Park for $60,000, all donated. (Photo by Julie Johnston)*

*Right: A boulder marks the site of the entrance to the first Iowa State Fair in 1854. The monument was a gift to Fairfield by the Daughters of the American Revolution in 1925. (Photo by Julie Johnston)*

and Electric Company. The tower remained in service until 1910 when it was declared unsafe and torn down.

### First golf course

Fairfield's Kahgahgee Golf Club organized in May 1892 shortly after Dr. James F. Clarke returned from a medical conference with a wooden driver and three balls. The first game was played in a pasture, with seven empty tomato cans as holes.

In 1900, the club purchased its own land near D Street and Jackson Avenue, and is now the Fairfield Golf & Country Club.

### Top-rated hospital

Jefferson County Hospital, Iowa's second oldest county hospital, opened Oct. 2, 1912. A bond issue of $25,000 was voted to build the three-story, 25-bed hospital. It was only the second time in world history that rural people voted a tax on themselves to build a hospital; Washington County had been the first by a few months.

Various building projects were completed in 1949, 1963, 1970 and 1993. The only remaining portion of the original 1912 structure is the basement.

The hospital is among the top-rated hospitals nationwide for patient satisfaction.

### From kindergarten through college

Beginning with Fairfield's first settlers who taught their children at home, education has always been valued.

Although today's parents have the option of sending their children to one of the private schools in Fairfield or even

*City reservoirs offer local fishing opportunities. (Photo by Julie Johnston)*

*The 224th Engineer Battalion of the Iowa National Guard is headquartered in Fairfield. This photo is of Headquarters and Headquarters Company soldiers waiting in the rain before a departure ceremony in October 2004 before they left to support Iraqi Freedom and the Global War on Terrorism. (Photo by Julie Johnston)*

# Fairfield IOWA

*Bonnifield Log House in Old Settlers' Park, built for the Rodham Bonnifield family in 1836, is believed to be the oldest, still-standing dwelling built by a white man in Iowa. The house is where Fairfield was laid out and named.*
*(Photo by Julie Johnston)*

homeschooling them, most enroll their youngsters in the Fairfield Community School District.

The district encompasses 354 square miles, the fourth largest in Iowa in geographic area. In 2005, the official kindergarten through 12th grade enrollment was 2,068.5 students at the six attendance centers.

Parsons College was founded in 1875 and named for Lewis Baldwin Parsons, a New York Presbyterian who willed his estate to create an institution of higher learning in Iowa. Classes began that fall with 34 students in a brick mansion built by Bernhart Henn.

The college achieved national notoriety in the 1950s and '60s, under the direction of Millard G. Roberts, who instituted what he called the "Parsons Plan" and raised enrollment from 236 to more than 5,000.

Under Roberts' plan, the college began making a profit. He hired more professors and enrolled students who had been academically unsuccessful. Life magazine labeled Roberts "the wizard of Flunk-out U" in 1966.

Parsons lost its accreditation in 1967, and Roberts was dismissed. The college regained its accreditation, but couldn't recover from the financial damage and closed June 2, 1973.

Although Parsons College no longer exists, its alumni still gather in Fairfield to mark the anniversaries of important events in its history.

A year after Parsons closed, the campus was purchased by Maharishi International University, now Maharishi University of Management.

Maharishi Mahesh Yogi, who teaches a Transcendental Meditation technique and has revived the ancient Vedic tradition of India, founded MIU in 1971.

All academic disciplines are taught in the "light of pure consciousness," which promotes success in learning and life by systematically developing the total functioning of a student's brain.

About 700 students from around the world are

*The Carnegie Library building was the first library outside of Pennsylvania to receive funding from Andrew Carnegie. Home of the Jefferson County/Fairfield Public Library from 1892-1996, the building now houses the Carnegie Historical Museum, Iowa Workforce Development and Indian Hills Community College service center. IHCC Ottumwa/Centerville is one of the country's top technical schools offering adult basic education, adult career supplementary and relicensure classes, and is a resource for business and industry, with service centers in each of the counties it encompasses.*
*(Photo by Julie Johnston)*

# Fairfield IOWA

*Jefferson County Courthouse, built in 1893, sits north of the downtown area. In October 1949, the peaked roof on the clock tower was damaged during a violent windstorm, deemed unsafe and removed. Nearly all the $49,000 needed to restore the tower, installed in November 2004, was raised through a fundraising effort. (Photo by Julie Johnston)*

enrolled in on- and off-campus studies.

The most recognized buildings on campus are the golden Patanjali Dome for men and Bagambhrini Dome for women, where TM practitioners meditate twice daily. The domes are sometimes opened for demonstrations of meditation techniques, which include levitating. Spectators often describe the meditators' levitation as "bouncing" or "leaping."

Many of the original Parsons College structures were torn down to make way for new buildings that meet the needs of M.U.M. and are constructed in sthapatya veda style, which places precise attention to orientation of direction, placement of rooms, specific measurements and use of natural materials.

Parts of razed Parsons College-era buildings were saved and were or will be incorporated into other buildings. Some of the Barhydt Chapel stained glass windows were saved and installed at First Presbyterian Church. Other pieces and memorabilia may be included in the city's new civic center.

### First new city of the 21st century

Maharishi followers started Maharishi Vedic City, Iowa's first new city in 25 years in 2001, near the Fairfield Municipal Airport north of the M.U.M. campus and Fairfield.

Vedic City is home to The Raj, a health spa of traditional Ayurveda rejuvenation treatments to help restore balance and re-awaken the body's natural healing mechanisms.

The French county-style facility encompasses 36,000 square feet and is on 100 acres of rolling meadows and woodlands. It is the only facility outside of India specifically built to offer traditional Ayurveda rejuvenation treatments. The premier health spa often draws national celebritries.

Like the new buildings on the M.U.M. campus, Vedic City buildings and homes also are built in the sthapatya veda style. Several new homes in Fairfield also have been built with those guidelines.

### Restoring the courthouse

The three-story brick Jefferson County Courthouse was dedicated in 1893.

After an

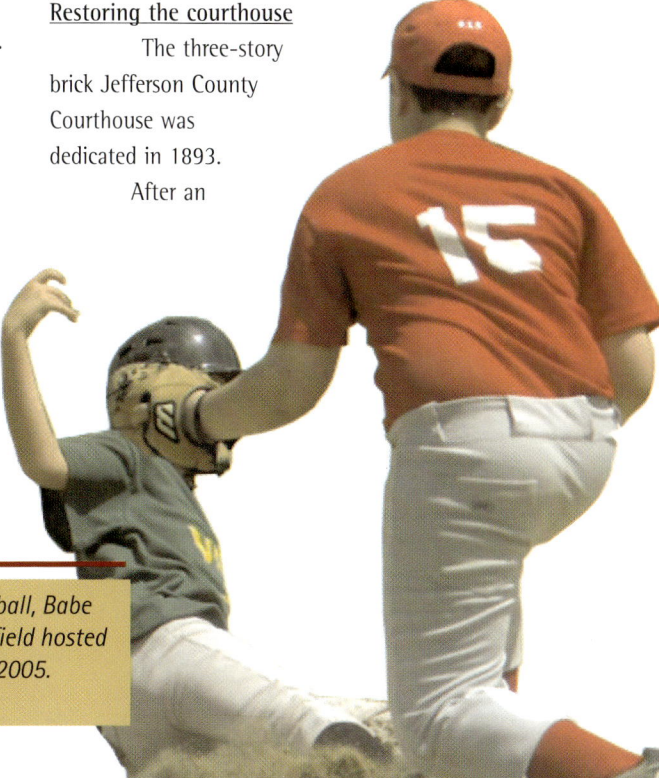

*Home to 58 Little League baseball and softball, Babe Ruth baseball and ASA softball teams, Fairfield hosted the Little League State Tournament in July 2005. (Photo by Julie Johnston)*

97

# Fairfield IOWA

October 1949 windstorm damaged the 36-foot-tall steeple atop the 142-foot-tall clock tower, the spire was removed for safety reasons.

In recent efforts to restore the building to its original splendor, funds were raised to replace the steeple, and a huge crane lifted the 7.5-ton replacement structure into place on a cold November morning in 2004.

The restoration effort is continuing.

### Industrious leaders

One of Fairfield's earliest manufacturers was Turney Wagon Works. It started in 1848 near Trenton, but moved to Fairfield to be closer to a railroad in 1888.

The factory built eight different models of Charter Oak wagons and a line of Fairfield wagons, producing more than 500 wagons each year.

Turney Wagon Works was Fairfield's largest employer for many years, but it ceased operations in 1932.

William Louden started Louden Machinery Co. in Fairfield in 1887 after patenting his hay carrier 20 years earlier.

The hay carrier, which eliminated the task of pitching hay from the ground into a hayloft, was transformed into the nation's first industrial monorail system in 1917 and was used to move scrap metal in munitions production plants during World War I.

Louden also started a barn planning service in 1906 and by 1939 had planned more than 25,000 barns throughout the world. In later years, the barn line was phased out and the company concentrated on overhead conveyer systems.

Louden Machinery Co., known by several different names throughout the years, closed in early 2004.

Harper Brush Works started when A.K. Harper began making brooms in 1900 to pay his way through Parsons College. The company, headquartered on Second Street, expanded several times before opening a second plant in the Fairfield Industrial Park. The company also has a plant in Stockton, Calif. Its line of brooms, brushes and other items can be found in home

*A summertime favorite is the city's outdoor pool and waterslide. The indoor pool at the Roosevelt Aquatic Center, the sand beach at Waterworks Park and the pool on Maharishi University of Management campus offer other locations for swimming.*
*(Photo by Julie Johnston)*

*One of two domes on Maharishi University of Management campus, used by practioners of Transcendental Meditation.*
*(Photo by Julie Johnston)*

98

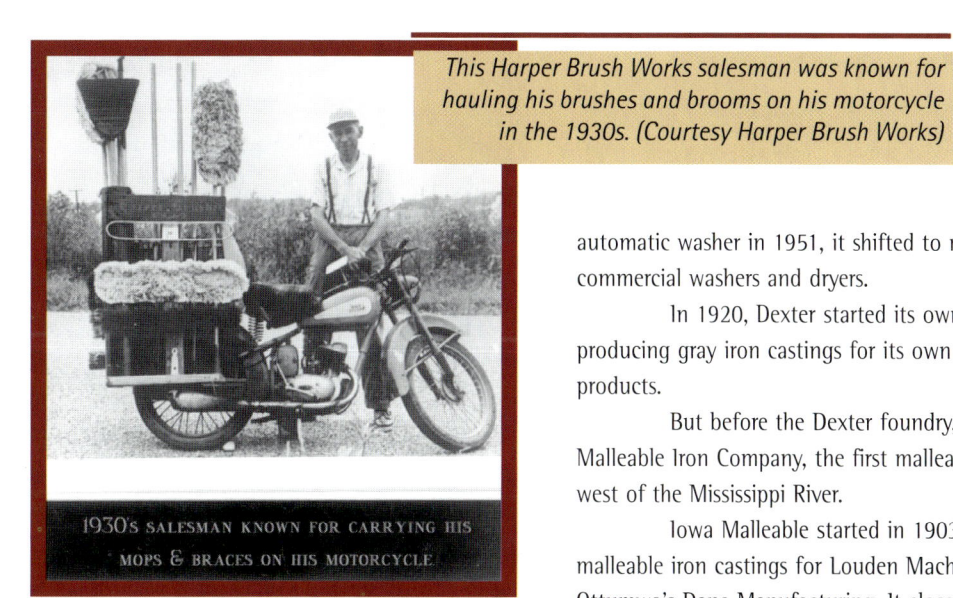

*This Harper Brush Works salesman was known for hauling his brushes and brooms on his motorcycle in the 1930s. (Courtesy Harper Brush Works)*

1930'S SALESMAN KNOWN FOR CARRYING HIS MOPS & BRACES ON HIS MOTORCYCLE

improvement stores across the nation.

Fairfield Line, a manufacturer of athletic and advertising apparel items, was first known as Fairfield Glove and Mitten Company and later Fairfield Glove Company. The company got its start in 1900, and continues today.

The Dexter Company, founded in 1901, moved to Fairfield in 1912. The company made washing machines; the Dexter-Double-Tub became a household word throughout the nation.

A few years after it produced its first automatic washer in 1951, it shifted to manufacturing commercial washers and dryers.

In 1920, Dexter started its own foundry producing gray iron castings for its own and other firms' products.

But before the Dexter foundry, there was Iowa Malleable Iron Company, the first malleable iron foundry west of the Mississippi River.

Iowa Malleable started in 1903 to supply malleable iron castings for Louden Machinery and Ottumwa's Dane Manufacturing. It closed in the 1990s.

Although many of the early industries no longer exist, they laid the groundwork each succeeding generation continues to build on to meet the demands of the community, state, nation and world.

### Recreational pastimes

Fairfield has almost a dozen parks where families can picnic and play. Chautauqua Park boasts new play equipment as of 2005. It also has a disc golf course and a horseshoe pit.

O.B. Nelson Park is home to the city's outdoor pool, baseball fields, a BMX bicycle track and two children's play areas, including an elaborate wooden structure.

Waterworks Park offers a swim-at-your-own-risk beach, as well as a playground and picnic tables.

Howard Park is home of the Fairfield Farmers'

*Jefferson County Hospital, Iowa's second oldest county hospital as it appears today with the Living Care Center to the left and Emergency to the right, provides top-quality health care to area residents. (Photo by Julie Johnston)*

Fairfield IOWA

## Fairfield IOWA

### LEARN MORE

Fairfield is the county seat of Jefferson County in southeast Iowa at the intersection of US Highway 34 and State Highway 1.

To learn more about Fairfield, contact the Fairfield Area Chamber of Commerce at (641) 472-2111 or visit the Web sites www.cityoffairfieldiowa.com, www.fairfieldiowa.com, fairfieldsfuture.org

### STORY CONTRIBUTORS

Vicki Tillis, The Fairfield Ledger news editor

Julie Johnston The Fairfield Ledger photographer

---

Market. Vendors offer locally grown produce, foods and crafts Wednesday evenings and Saturday mornings from May through the end of October. The market has grown to include activities, such as plant exchanges, contests, quilt displays and more.

Jefferson County Park, just outside the city limits, offers picnicking, camping, cabin rentals and trails for hiking and biking, which are tied into the 15-mile Jefferson County Trails system. The park also has a nature center with American Indian artifacts and wildlife displays. Special programs, like moonlight hikes, maple syruping and owl calling, are planned periodically.

The community comes together for a Kids' Day parade and pancakes sponsored by the Fairfield Kiwanis Club each September, an Independence Day Celebration sponsored by the local Jaycees; the Jefferson County Fair each July; a Memorial Day service each May; and a Veterans Day service each November.

Other events include concerts by the well-known 34th Army Band, Fairfield Municipal Band and Live on the Square shows in Central Park, theater productions featuring local talent, an annual gathering of Dodge Power Wagon enthusiasts, and a Central Park holiday lighting display switched on during a dedication ceremony the Friday after each Thanksgiving.

Plus, Fairfield's service, community and social clubs, schools, churches and other organizations plan many events throughout the year.

1st Fridays Art Walk has been a monthly event since October 2002. The free walk is 6:30 to 9:30 p.m. the first Friday of every month on and near the Fairfield square.

About 20 galleries and art venues showcase regional, national and international art exhibits, and the events are splashed with family-friendly entertainment, music and activities.

### Future plans

Fairfield leaders today are laying plans in hopes of drawing more visitors, businesses and residents to continue the community's success.

Fairfield Convention and Visitors Bureau is promoting the city as a tourist destination; the city council is looking into downtown improvements to make the area even more attractive to businesses and visitors; and Fairfield Area Chamber of Commerce is assisting companies interested in moving to or expanding and staying in Fairfield.

Groundbreaking for the $5 million-plus civic center is planned for the fall of 2005. Plans are for the center to be a venue for community activities as well as a draw for larger state or national events.

The Fairfield Community School District is making millions of dollars worth of improvements to its buildings, and the Jefferson County Hospital is planning to expand into a medical mall.

Fairfield businesses and residents, as they have throughout history, will continue to evolve to meet and surpass the needs of the community.

*Pride In Our Hometowns.*

# P·O·R·T·R·A·I·T·S
## OF
# *Fort Madison*

### "Cherishing the Past, Embracing the Future"

*Nestled along the Mississippi River, with the world's longest double decker swing span bridge connecting it to the Illinois riverfront, Fort Madison is a small, yet progressive community boasting a cozy environment of Victorian homes and scenic parks.*

*Fort Madison is also home to the state's only maximum security prison dating back to 1845 and the site of the last federal hanging in 1963; a house once owned by the granddaughter of the famous American seamstress Betsy Ross and said to be haunted; yet another mansion owned by the Ringling family of the Ringling Brothers' Circus fame; the site of the first military post built on the upper Mississippi, and the birthplace of every Sheaffer pen ever made, bought, or sold.*

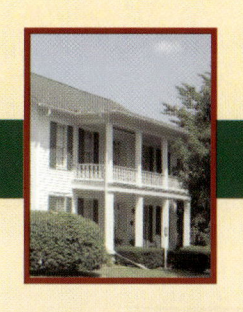

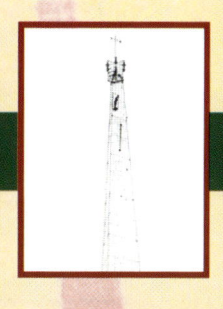

FORT MADISON

*Pride In Our Hometowns.*

# P·O·R·T·R·A·I·T·S
## OF
## *Fort Madison*

### "CHERISHING THE PAST, EMBRACING THE FUTURE"

*Only on a Sunday morning could one car have Avenu of the Riverfront Business District to itself. That's because Sunday mornings are reserved for attending church, however, the theater, specialty shops, and fiv antique shops will open for shoppers, or just casual browsers, later - most at 1 p.m.*

## A SNAPSHOT

Its roots date back to 1808, when Fort Madison became the first military post built on the upper Mississippi in what then was just a "territory," and what would later become the State of Iowa. In part, the fort served to protect the "government factory" or trading post, where area Indians could exchange furs and hides for hunting knives, animal traps, iron tools, and other manufactured goods.

Soldiers of the First U.S. Infantry Regiment, under the command of Lt. Alpha Kingsley, built much of the fort between 1808 and 1809. Kingsley named the fort "Fort Madison" in honor of James Madison, who was then the president of the United States.

The majority of area Indians were friendly toward the fort and its occupants, trading peacefully with the government factory. However, sometimes, bands of Sauk, Fox (Mesquakie), and Winnebago menaced with Fort Madison. These Indians, under partial leadership of the noted Sauk warrior Black Hawk, became known as "Black Hawk's Band" and conducted several sieges on the fort and its soldiers.

Following the outbreak of the War of

*Left: Even those without a boat to enjoy love walking down to the marina just to watch the boaters come and go and to admire the many boats docked there.*

*Right: Younger cowboys and cowgirls love the Tri-State Rodeo, from its kick-off pancake breakfast and Lil' Spurs Rodeo on Labor Day Weekend to its rodeo performances, Miss Rodeo Iowa Queen Contest, and Tri-State Rodeo Parade the following week and weekend.*

102

# Fort Madison IOWA

1812, British agents from Canada incited Black Hawk and his followers further against the Americans. In September, 1812, hostile bands of the Sauk and Fox besieged Fort Madison, killing one soldier caught outside the stockade, slaughtering the garrison cattle, and burning several nearby cabins.

During this siege, the commander ordered the burning of the government factory, located just outside the fort, to prevent the Indians from doing so on another day when the winds might very well carry burning debris to the post buildings. Attacks and hostility continued. In July, 1813, a party of Winnebago and Sauk killed two soldiers cutting timber to build a new blockhouse at the fort, and a week later, hostile Indians killed four U.S. Rangers guarding the unfinished blockhouse.

Faced with constant harassment and frequent attacks, Lt. Thomas Hamilton ordered the abandonment of the fort in September, 1813. During the night, the soldiers slipped away downriver in boats, having set fires and watching the fort be devoured by flames. While the fire left only charred remains of this time period, a replica of old Fort Madison stands in its place along the Mississippi riverfront in what is now Riverview Park. Visitors can tour the Fort, seeing the soldiers' quarters as they were when occupied almost 200 years ago. Authentically dressed historic interpreters take visitors through the day-to-day tasks of the soldiers and their families, and encourage visitors to enjoy hands-on experiences of candle making, military drills, and cooking.

Nearby, also in Riverview Park, tourists need only turn to the east to see the world's longest double decker swing span bridge, built in 1927 with a 525-foot swing span, and to gaze at the Illinois riverfront on the other side.

> The 26-room Albright House was built in 1858 by brothers William and Jacob Albright. The two operated a dry goods store nearby. Originally, the home was two residences with separate addresses. William and his wife occupied one half, or one residence, while Jacob and his wife Rachel, who was Betsy Ross' granddaughter, occupied the other residence.

> Those who love trains, past and present, will find out why Fort Madison is considered by many train buffs to be one of the best viewing sites, with 60 to 70 trains passing by daily.

# Fort Madison, IOWA

While remaining in Riverview Park, more history awaits the inquisitive, as well as the railroad/train enthusiast. The railroad industry is well-rooted in Fort Madison's history. In 1880, the Santa Fe Railroad partnered with the community and opened rail traffic in all directions, prompting a boom in prosperity and population to the small community.

Paying tribute to its roots in the railroad industry, visitors will find the old Santa Fe Depot Historic Center, built in 1909, which is now the North Lee County Historical Museum. Because of its unique architecture, the mission revival-style depot, also in Riverview Park, is listed on the National Register of Historic Places. Inside the museum is a gold mine of artifacts and history related to the railroad, military post, pioneer days, and Fort Madison's landmark business, the Sheaffer Pen Company.

Trains remain at the heart of Fort Madison, as 60 to 70 trains can be observed daily passing by the Historic Center, situated along the mainline of the Burlington Northern Santa Fe Railroad. Engine 2913, proudly displayed in Riverview Park and built in 1943 and capable of speeds up to 120 miles per hour, as well as the A.T.&S.F. Caboose, retired and given to Fort Madison by the Santa Fe Railroad, adds yet another taste of an era gone by.

Separate remains, yet historically connected to the railroad industry, are the numerous Victorian homes in Fort Madison. Since it was first settled in 1833, Fort Madison experienced several "booms" in both prosperity and population, but nothing compares to the one from 1887 to 1893 in reaction to the Santa Fe Railroad setting up its shops here and its river bridge. In anticipation of the arrival of thousands of railroad workers, scores of residences,

> *Old Settlers Park, or Upper Square as it was originally called, remains a hub of activities. While it was originally the site of political rallies, weddings, concerts, baseball, and the final speech by Sauk and Fox war chief Black Hawk, time and progress have not erased much.*

> *Enjoying a long history, as well as current popularity, is Fort Madison's Tri-State Rodeo, which dates back to 1948 when city officials tried to find something - an attraction or event of some sort - to attract Labor Day weekend visitors. The event now boasts evening performance attendance figures of 10,000 or more, and brings visitors to Fort Madison from all over the Midwest.*

# Fort Madison

*While the landscape, architecture, businesses, and traditions reflect Fort Madison's commitment to preserving its past and heritage, its quality-of-life investments in walking trails, bike routes, business incentives, and most recently, its plans to open a newly-designed public library show the community's eye is on the future - on providing a better life for the next generation.*

commercial buildings, duplexes and small cottages were constructed. Many of these structures remain today, offering the visitor a trip back into the Victorian and Gothic architectural era. Restored storefronts, as well as 89 other structures, make up Fort Madison's driving tour of Victorian homes.

A detailed brochure not only gives the architectural and historic significance of the structure itself, but also a brief overview of its original builders and occupants. Many of the community's restored, cherished, and historically preserved properties surround city parks, which are also reflective of the past - complete with bandstands, gazebos, park benches, and flower gardens, but still in constant use, with ball diamonds and playgrounds.

Each May and December, school and community groups traditionally sponsor tours of selected showcase homes, allowing the lucky participants to see the interior of the mansion-like homes, their restored tall ceilings, elaborate staircases, and sparkling rich wood floors, while raising money for their worthy causes.

Visitors walking or driving along the Victorian Home Tour cannot escape the beauty of two east-end parks: Old Settlers Park and Central Park. Both were public squares laid out in Fort Madison's original 1838 town plat. Old Settlers Park, or Upper Square, as it was originally called, remains a hub of activities. While it was originally the site of political rallies, weddings, concerts, baseball, and the final speech by Sauk and Fox war chief Black Hawk, time and progress have not erased much.

Because of its authentic bandstand, its shelterhouse, well-kept grounds, and vibrant flower garden cornerstone areas, Old Settlers Park is still the site of

## VISITOR ATTRACTIONS

*Each summer, usually in June, hot air balloons fly above and glow near Fort Madison's riverfront during the annual Balloons Across the Mississippi. Always wanted to ride in a hot air balloon? Here's your chance.*

# Fort Madison

baseball games, weddings, free summer concerts, community potluck suppers, and a popular scene for memorable prom, graduation, and family photo sessions. Central Park, also located on Fort Madison's east end, takes over where Old Settlers Park leaves off, with its white gazebo, spraying fountain, picnic areas, and playground area. Every Thursday afternoon, from June through much of September, a bell rings, signifying the beginning of that week's Farmers Market, and one side of the park is lined with freshly-picked produce and tables of baked goods for sale to those wanting the season's best of the best.

Other traditions grace Fort Madison's Central Park, in addition to the couples exchanging wedding vows or the people reading books while nestled under one of the enormous shade trees. Summer visitors will find music filling the air in Central Park every Sunday evening in June, July, and August. The Fort Madison City Band continues a musical tradition that has endured since 1937. The concerts always begin at 7:30 p.m., always have a specific theme ranging from show tunes and the patriotic to tunes from the Big Band era, and are always enjoyed by an audience seated on blankets or in lawn chairs. Children listen while playing, when not begging their parents to buy them ice cream being sold during the concert by a local church or civic group.

History buffs will want to stroll a couple of blocks east, away from Central Park, to what is known as "The Betsy Ross House" by some, and "The Albright House" by others. Still, others, if asked, will tell visitors some haunting, unexplainable tales connected to the house at 716 Ave. F.

The 26-room Albright House was

## Traditions

*"Iowa's Friendliest Casino" is said to be the Catfish Bend Riverboat Casino. The 1,300-passenger vessel offers unlimited gambling, with fine dining and entertainment to be found on the third floor. From May through much of October, the riverboat is docked in Fort Madison's Riverview Park, spending its winter months docked in Burlington, just 20 miles away.*

*This historic chimney structure is a Monument For The Daugthers of the American Revolution located near Riverview Park.*

106

# Fort Madison Iowa

built in 1858 by brothers William and Jacob Albright. The two operated a dry goods store nearby. Originally, the home was two residences, with separate addresses. William and his wife occupied one half, or one residence, while Jacob and his wife Rachel, who was Betsy Ross' granddaughter, occupied the other residence. Accounts from this time quote Rachel Albright recalling childhood memories of sewing flags with her grandmother.

The "hauntings" connected to the Albright House have endured decades, and allegedly come from another famous character - James Ringling Jr., an heir to the Ringling Brothers Circus fortune. James Ringling Jr. married into the family, which occupied the Albright House after its original owners sold it in the 1920s.

Actress Toni Darney, who appeared in several television soap operas in the 1960s and was nominated for a Tony award for her work on Broadway in the 1970s, inherited the house in 1978.

Ringley, who married Darney's sister, contested the will that bestowed the residence on Darney. Some say it was Ringling who kept the stories of hauntings, unexplained shadows, movements seen through windows, and abrupt sounds alive as part of a plan to turn the house into a tourist attraction. However, the home has been an attraction almost a century now mostly because of its connection to Betsy Ross and the prominent local Albrights, and most recently - because it is listed on the National Register of Historic Places.

Rob and Carol Davis, a Chicago-area couple who saw the house and fell in love with it, purchased it in 2000. They visit when they can,

*The water slide and diving board are perhaps the biggest attractions to the Fort Madison Municipal Swimming Pool, located next to Fort Madison High School, but it is also the site of swimming lessons, private pool parties, and other fun events.*

*One of many examples of preserving the past while serving the purpose of today is the Fort Madison Art Center. The old train depot, restored and preserved, is now the home of monthly exhibits, art classes, demonstrations, and ceramic pottery workshops.*

# Fort Madison

> Fort Madison's Tri-State Rodeo ranks as one of the best PRCA Rodeos in the country. The outdoor arena welcomes rodeo fans to four performances featuring top professional cowboys and national musical entertainers.

hoping to retire in Fort Madison and occupy the residence and continue to restore the house to its original luster. Graceful arches and woodwork said to be similar to that in the White House are found throughout the structure.

Although Ringling did not want Darney to own the Albright House, he occupied a mansion on the far east end of town. In fact, in 2005, the estate of James Ringling was auctioned off, attracting collectors and history buffs from all over the Midwest. Soon after the auction, more than 500 attended a public tour of the mansion which once housed circus animals and an astounding amount of memorabilia.

Antique lovers and collectors of fountain pens aficionado will feel as though they have arrived home when entering Fort Madison. Across from the Mississippi and beautiful Riverview Park, visitors will see the landmark business that put Fort Madison on the business community map - The Sheaffer Pen Company.

Sheaffer Pen Corporation had its origins in the jewelry store of Walter A. Sheaffer, the man who invented the first fountain pen in 1913.

When the Chicago fire in 1871 cost his father his investment in an insurance company, Walter, then just 11 years old, went to work as a printer's assistant for $1 a week. He held several jobs and, using his savings, later became a partner in his father's jewelry business. After reading a 1908 advertisement for a pen that filled with ink much like an eye-dropper, Sheaffer decided there had to be a better way. After some trial and error, he developed a self-filling pen, and five years later,

> Built in 1909, this mission revival style depot is the home of the North Lee County Historical Museum. Because of its unique architecture, it is listed on the National Register of Historic Places. The railroad complex is a classic for those interested in railroad history, firefighting lore, Sheaffer fountain pens, and the state's territorial and pioneer days.

# Fort Madison IOWA

*While touring many neighborhoods and homes in the hills of Fort Madison, residents and visitors stop and enjoy the various views of the Mississippi River and riverfront properties.*

he held the patent on his inventory and prepared to open his own small factory.

Sheaffer was regarded as a master marketer, as well as creative inventor He made his first big splash in the Saturday Evening Post and, through the years, continued to make the Sheaffer name synonymous with top-of-the-line luxury fountain pens in the 1950s with radio and early television commercials and by being the national sponsor of the Jackie Gleason television show.

The Sheaffer product line expanded in the 1920s to include Skrip, a writing fluid available in 12 colors in both washable and permanent form, invented by a Fort Madison chemist, Robert Casey. A propel-expel-repel mechanical pencil, desk sets, inks, and more were added throughout the years.

But the debut and increasing demand of cheaper, disposable pens in the 1960s provided the first real competition to the products. The Sheaffer family sold the company in 1966 to Textron Inc. Several transactions later, the company ended up with its current owners, the Paris-based BIC S.A., in 1997. The Fort Madison plant continues to manufacture pens, however, BIC officials have announced plans to close the landmark business in 2006.

Sheaffer pens and memorabilia, as well as the

*History buffs will want to stroll a couple of blocks east away from Central Park to what is known as "The Betsy Ross House" by some, and "The Albright House" by others. Still others, if asked, will tell visitors some haunting, unexplainable tales connected to the house at 716 Ave. F. One of its original occupants, Rachel Albright, was the granddaughter of famous American seamstress Betsy Ross. Accounts from this time quote Rachel Albright recalling childhood memories of sewing flags with her grandmother.*

# Fort Madison

like products of other trusted names, can be admired and purchased at 'Pendemonium', a retail store located in downtown Fort Madison not far from the Sheaffer Pen plant itself.

### Attractions

Enjoying a long history, as well as current popularity, is Fort Madison's Tri-State Rodeo, which dates back to 1948 when city officials tried to find something - an attraction or event of some sort - to attract Labor Day weekend visitors.

After a series of negotiations, the first Tri-State Rodeo was held in September of 1948 and featured famous cowboy entertainer Gene Autry, professional cowboys competing for prizes, and an extensive Saturday morning parade.

*The North Lee County Courthouse at Seventh Street and Avenue F was built in 1841. It is listed on the National Register of Historic Places, and is the oldest courthouse still in use in Iowa.*

## RODEO NOTEABLES

The rodeo became an annual event from the start, growing every year in terms of its professional rodeo and its pre-rodeo events, which include a kickoff breakfast the Saturday of each Labor Day weekend, a "downtown hoe-down" dance, and a regional talent competition the following Sunday evening, the Lil' Spurs Rodeo for youngsters on Sunday of that weekend, the Special Olympics Rodeo, suppers, and special events or contests each evening the following week, an elaborate two-hour parade on Saturday of Rodeo weekend, and four evening professional rodeo performances - two of them featuring rising country music stars.

The likes of Reba McIntyre, Michael Landon, Fess Parker, Jimmy Dean, Toby Keith, Brian

*As if the Mississippi River does not provide enough beauty for those strolling the Fort Madison riverfront, a host of decorative walks and gardens can be enjoyed in Riverview Park.*

*Fort Madison*

> *Victorian homes are not the only architectural example found along the scenic parks of Fort Madison. "The castle," now owned by Ron and Connie Barnes, as well as others, are often included on home tours throughout the year that raise funds for worthy local causes.*

White, 'Little Texas,' Charlie Daniels, Neal McCoy, and more have graced the main stage and entertained crowds at the Tri- State Rodeo.

And not long after the Tri-State Rodeo each September, visitors can enjoy the annual Mexican Fiesta. Even before the Mexican revolution in 1910, there was a significant community of Mexican immigrants living in Fort Madison. Many left their war-torn and impoverished country to have jobs with the Santa Fe Railroad. Today, this sector of Fort Madison continues to celebrate their heritage and Mexico's independence from Spain during a three-day festival in the 3400 block of Avenue Q with the crowning of a Mexican and American queen, music, dancing, colorful ceremonies, and a continuous Mexican feast.

Each Fourth of July holiday brings its own red, white, and blue tradition with the annual Charlie Korschgen Fourth of July Kiddies Parade, a tradition that dates back to 1913 when Santa Fe Railroad employee Charlie Korschgen grabbed his snare drum, picked up an American flag, and went through the streets, attracting attention and gathering up children along the way.

In 1956, American Magazine claimed this parade was "the oldest Fourth of July patriotic kiddie parade in the USA." The parade continues, but has grown to include a large portion of adults and children alike.

And those who want to try their luck, even roll the dice, should be sure to board the Catfish Bend Riverboat Casino. Labeled "Iowa's friendliest casino," slot machines, blackjack - all games of chance - including poker, entertain residents and visitors alike. And that's when there isn't a special concert or program taking place on the spacious gaming vessel.

D. Looking to the future

While the landscape, architecture,

> *Fort Madison is also home to the state's only maximum security prison, dating back to 1845 and the site of the last federal hanging in 1963.*

# Fort Madison

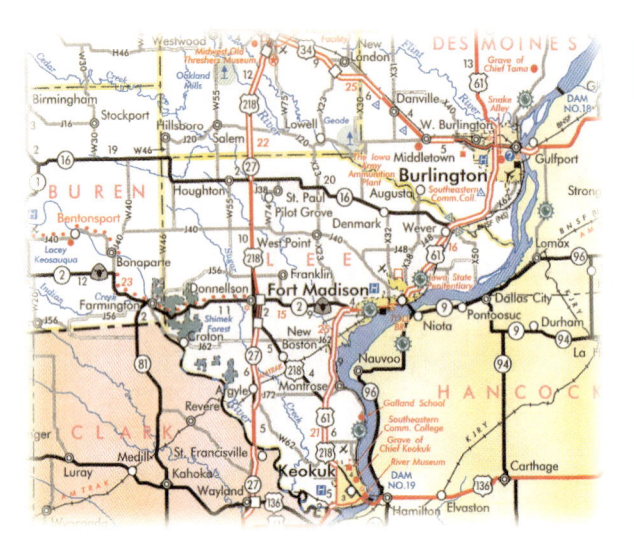

## LEARN MORE

Fort Madison is located along the Mississippi River on Highway 61, between Keokuk, which is 20 miles south, and Burlington, which is 20 miles northeast. And it is just a bridge away from Illinois, and just 10.3 miles north of Nauvoo, Ill.

For more information about Fort Madison, contact the Fort Madison Area Convention & Visitors Bureau at 1-800-210-TOUR or www.visitfortmadison.com

## STORY CONTRIBUTOR

Robin Delaney has been the managing editor of the Fort Madison Daily Democrat since 1995.

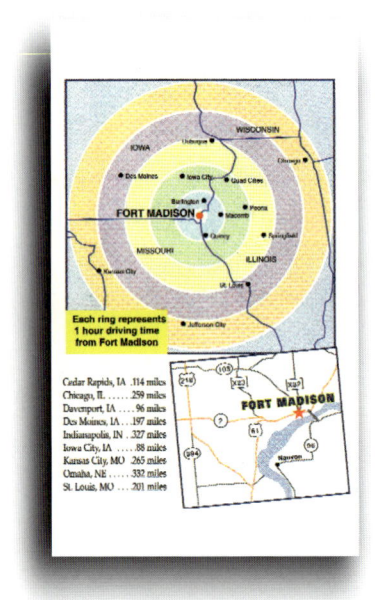

---

businesses, and traditions reflect Fort Madison's commitment to preserving its past and heritage, its quality-of-life investments in walking trails, bike routes, business incentives, and recreational activities show the community's eye is on the future: on the next generation.

Skaters, whether on skateboards or roller blades, will be in their glory at Fort Madison's west-end Ivanhoe Park Skate Park, While as rich in history as its Central Park and Old Settlers Park sisters, Ivanhoe Park is the primary headquarters for fun, athletics, and competition. Youngsters participating in the YMCA's baseball leagues rule the park most evenings at the baseball diamond, attracting their family, friends, and baseball lovers to the bleachers. Fishermen and boaters gravitate to the marina and Mississippi riverfront for recreational pleasure or sometimes, competition.

In short, Fort Madison residents work hard, and play harder. They enjoy the comforts and security of small-town living, while working to expand and build on the present assets to create a brighter, even more prosperous future. And they do this by cherishing the past, while embracing the future.

*"The old Morrison place," located at 532 Ave. F in Fort Madison, is one of 89 properties on the "Driving Tour of Victorian Homes." Dennis A. Morrison was a partner in Morrison Plow Works, and had several real estate holdings. In about 1879, Morrison had this two-and-a-half story brick Italianate residence built.*

Cedar Rapids, IA .114 miles
Chicago, IL .....259 miles
Davenport, IA ....96 miles
Des Moines, IA ..197 miles
Indianapolis, IN .327 miles
Iowa City, IA .....88 miles
Kansas City, MO .265 miles
Omaha, NE ......332 miles
St. Louis, MO ...201 miles

112

*Pride In Our Hometowns.*

# P·O·R·T·R·A·I·T·S
## OF
# *Jefferson*

## CITY ON THE RISE

*The story of Jefferson is the story of Iowa's county seat towns. Starting with river and overland settlement in the 1850s, and galvanized by the arrival of the railroad in the 1860s, the Jefferson community grew with the taming of the Greene County prairie by hundreds of hard-working farm families.*

*As technology reduced the need for large amounts of hand labor on the farm, Jefferson leaders encouraged manufacturers and other businesses to spur the community's growth. Today the Jefferson community enjoys a balanced economy and lifestyle, positioned for the 21st Century and proud of its past. It's a great place to visit, to work, and to live.*

JEFFERSON

*Pride In Our Hometowns.*

# P·O·R·T·R·A·I·T·S
## OF *Jefferson*

## CITY ON THE RISE

*Circus visits were always major occasions in Iowa towns. This one took place in the late 1890s, heralded by the traditional parade. View looks eastward down the north side of the square.*

## THE HISTORY

The story of Jefferson, Iowa, is inseparable from the story of Greene County. Staked out as the county seat in 1854, the town serves as the center of the Greene County community. The city and the county are linked from their earliest history.

The first settler family to locate in Greene County was that of Truman and May Davis, who moved up the Raccoon River valley in a covered wagon from Adel, 40 miles to the southeast, in 1849. Truman and their two older sons built a cabin 10 miles downstream from Jefferson, measuring 16 feet by 12 feet, where Truman and May children spent that first winter. They brought with them one yoke of oxen, one cow, one horse, 12 chickens, eight sheep, two pigs, one dog, a few housekeeping items, and six children.

The Davises were followed up the river by a number of other farm families, most of them from the Ohio River area and the Upper South. The land they bought from the federal government for $1.25 an acre sells today for about 3,000 times that much.

In the fall of 1854 a three-member Greene County commission selected a 2 1/2 square mile plot of upland prairie in the very center of the county as the county seat location. A $200 loan from

*Local women served as fashion models at this 1900 city-wide sale.*

*Left: The Union Bus Line in Jefferson featured an enclosed passenger bus and open-air hauling as well (with a driver's umbrella).*

*Right: How newspapers were published in the old days: the interior of the Jefferson Bee print shop in the early 1900s.*

Des Moines financier Hoyt Sherman was used to buy the land from the federal government. The name "Jefferson" was chosen as the town's name, but a town in Dubuque County had already registered that name, so the Post Office Department rejected the new community's proposal. However, when the Dubuque community died out, Greene County's Jefferson became the official holder of the name.

Growth started immediately. B.F. Robinson opened a dry goods store in 1854, and George Walton brought merchandise and moved his wife and children to the new community in the summer of 1855. In the spring of 1856 some 15 families arrived, several of them setting up craft shops. The county that year let a contract for $1,825 to build a courthouse for the new county seat.

The first Sunday school in the county met at the courthouse starting in 1857, the same year that a weekly mail route was established from Adel. The next year, in 1858, "Uncle Billy" Anderson drove a herd of fat hogs on foot well over 200 miles to Keokuk on the Mississippi River, the first Greene County pork headed to the eastern U.S. markets. The first printing press and newspaper publisher arrived in 1859.

When the Civil War began in 1861, Greene County, with a total population of 1,400, sent about 150 men to fight for the Union, about half of the entire able-bodied male population in the county. Azor R.

*Bronze larger-than-life statue of Abraham Lincoln stands on the courthouse square facing Lincolnway, the original route of the Lincoln Highway. It was donated to the community in 1918 by Judge and Mrs. E. B. Wilson, Jefferson residents.*

*Train wrecks occurred occasionally in early days. This one in 1912 on the Milwaukee line near Jefferson killed a railroad fireman.*

115

# Jefferson IOWA

Mills, a Yankee and the county's first schoolteacher, organized his entire student body of 32 young men into a military company, drilled them, and led them off to fight in several Civil War battles.

In 1866, little more than a year after the South surrendered, the Cedar Rapids and Missouri River Railway Company (later the Chicago and NorthWestern, now the Union Pacific), reached Jefferson on July 30, making shipment of goods and people much easier. By 1880 Greene County's population had mushroomed to 12,727, or 25 per cent greater than it is today.

That year 1,444 residents were counted by the U.S. Census in Jefferson. By 1886 that number was up to 1,750, and a Jefferson business directory listed the following: two banks, two newspapers, eight lawyers, five physicians, two dentists, eight teachers, five restaurants, two meat markets, seven groceries, three hardware stores, four general stores, two feed stores, two clothing stores, two shoe and boot stores, two blacksmiths, three drugstores, two furniture stores, two jewelers, two barbers, two hotels, two opera houses, a creamery, a saloon, a post office, a bookstore, a secondhand store, a billiard parlor, an abstracts and loan office, a photographer, several painters, and a sewing machine and organ shop.

By 1900, Greene County boasted 17,820 residents, the county's all-time population peak, a remarkable achievement in just a 50-year span. When some 3,500 residents gathered in Jefferson for a meeting of the Old Settlers' Association in 1904, they adopted the following resolution: "RESOLVED, That the good Lord possibly might have made a better county than Greene, but He probably never did."

Over the next hundred years the town of Jefferson, building on its early foundations as well as the technological innovations of the 20th and 21st Century, grew to become the vibrant, attractive community it is today. The town is respected statewide for the quality education it provides its young people, its healthy mix of progressive industries and other

*Spring Lake County Park draws campers from a wide area, for swimming, boating, fishing, and just relaxing.*

*Monument on the courthouse square honors the late Darrell Lindsey, Jefferson pilot who received the Medal of Honor posthumously for giving his life to save his crew over France in World War Two.*

*Jefferson-Scranton High School is recognized statewide, and by state education officials, as a leader in secondary education.*

*Marker in southeast Greene County locates the first "courthouse": a log cabin where county business was conducted in the 1850s.*

business firms, its strong professional community, and the myriad social, religious, charitable and non-profit organizations that enrich the lifestyle of its residents.

## A GREAT PLACE TO VISIT

Jefferson is also a great place to visit, with its growing collection of tourist attractions. Foremost among those is the Mahanay Memorial Carillon Tower, located on the southwest corner of the courthouse campus. Dedicated in October 1966, the 168 foot tower was a $350,000 gift to the people of the city and county by the late Floyd and Dora Mahanay, lifetime Jefferson residents. The carillon, consisting of 14 bells from the Petit-Fritzen foundry in The Netherlands, sounds the Westminster chime every quarter hour. The Bell Tower Foundation plans more bells and an additional keyboard. A popular observation tower at the 120 foot level, reached by a glassed elevator, allows visitors a panoramic view of the countryside for many miles.

Jefferson is the northern starting point of the Raccoon River Valley Trail, a hard-surfaced bicycle path that runs south to Herndon and then eastward to the Des Moines suburbs, about 75 miles in all. Opened in 1997, the trailhead is the beautiful restored former Milwaukee Railroad depot on the historic Lincoln Highway in Jefferson.

*Left: The restored Milwaukee Depot is the northern starting point of the Raccoon River Valley Trail, a beautiful 75-mile bicycle trail that ends up in suburban Des Moines.*

*Right: The observation deck of the Mahanay Memorial Carillon Tower affords a panoramic view of the surrounding countryside from a height of 120 feet.*

# Jefferson IOWA

Multi-county improvements along the trail are underway for the benefit of biking enthusiasts, and Jefferson will soon offer camping facilities and a bike hostel adjacent to the depot. A growing number of cyclists from all over the Midwest are discovering the trail and the community, and they return regularly.

The depot, in addition to its historical displays of train memorabilia, also serves as a gallery for the talented community of serious artists in the Jefferson area, organized as the Greene County Arts Council. Art shows are held there on a regular basis, displaying oils, watercolors, pencil and pen and ink work, fabric work, sculpture, carvings, computer art, photography, many crafts, and other media. Greene County artists have won many awards in juried exhibitions across the state and the Midwest.

Art in the broader sense plays an important role in the life of the community. Sculpture was commissioned for the front of the most recent addition to the Jefferson Public Library. A number of buildings downtown are graced by wall-to-wall exterior murals. The community enjoys an active community theater, a youth summer theater group, several quilters' groups, a popular garden club, and other arts-oriented organizations.

Visitors to the Mahanay Tower, the depot and the bike trail usually enjoy a stroll through the three-story Greene County courthouse at the center of town. Constructed of Bedford stone in 1917, the handsome Greek Revival building is listed on the National Register of Historic Places. A reproduction of the county seal, a "Horn of Plenty" cornucopia in mosaic tile, dominates the center of the rotunda floor. Lunette paintings grace the four walls of the dome.

On the south side of the courtyard, facing Lincolnway, stands a large bronze statue of Abraham

*The Jefferson Public Library is a blend of old and new: an original Carnegie Library building built a century ago, and a modern addition complete with electronic services.*

*The Greene County Community Center, built and operated entirely without tax dollars, attracts young and old for exercise. It also contains several meeting rooms.*

*Baller's Auto Supply in 1937 advertised "The Lowest Tire Prices in History!"*

Lincoln, a gift to the community in 1918 from Judge and Mrs E. B. Wilson. The Great Emancipator is depicted standing.

Speaking of Lincoln and Lincolnway: Jefferson sits astride the original Lincoln Highway, the first coast-to-coast thoroughfare for automobiles and trucks. Immediately following World War One, the new Lincoln Highway Association and the U.S. Army promoted a cross-country military convoy that mostly followed the route designated as the Lincoln Highway, duplicating the Chicago and NorthWestern route through Iowa.

The Army convoy, including combat tanks, camped overnight at the county fairgrounds in Jefferson. One of the tank commanders was young Army officer Dwight David Eisenhower, who 33 years later returned to Jefferson on a whistle-stop C&NW railroad tour during his successful campaign for President. Three days after the 1919 convoy left Jefferson, Greene County voters by a three-to-one margin approved a referendum that made the county the first in the state to pave the Lincoln Highway from county line to county line.

The spacious and well-designed Greene County Historical Society Museum, on Lincolnway a block east of the square, is dubbed by State Historical Society officials as one of the best historical museums in rural Iowa. The museum displays "rooms" of early-day stores and professional offices, complete with original equipment and retail goods, as well as walls and cases full of old-time Greene County historical artifacts.

There's even a life-size mock-up of an early coal mine, several of which operated in the southeast part of the county until well into the 20th Century. In February of the terrible winter of 1935-36, William Van Horn, 36, hitched four German Shepherds to a

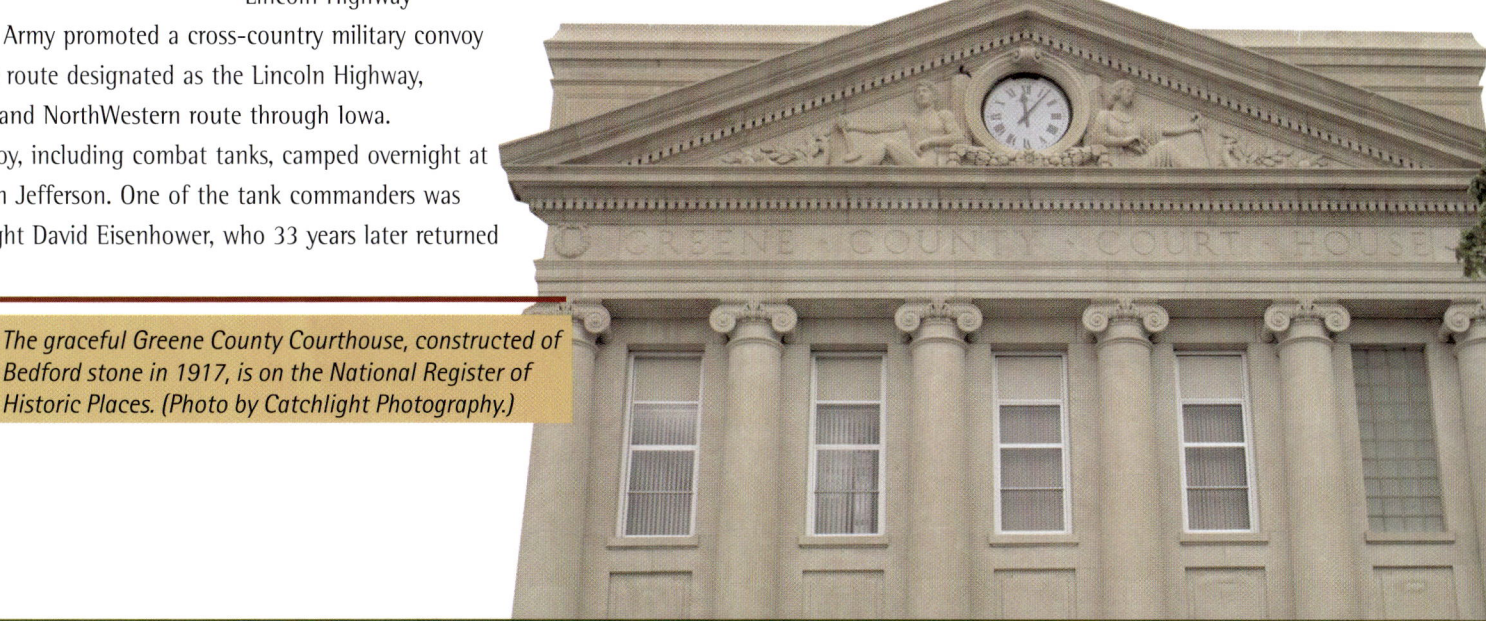

*The graceful Greene County Courthouse, constructed of Bedford stone in 1917, is on the National Register of Historic Places. (Photo by Catchlight Photography.)*

119

# Jefferson IOWA

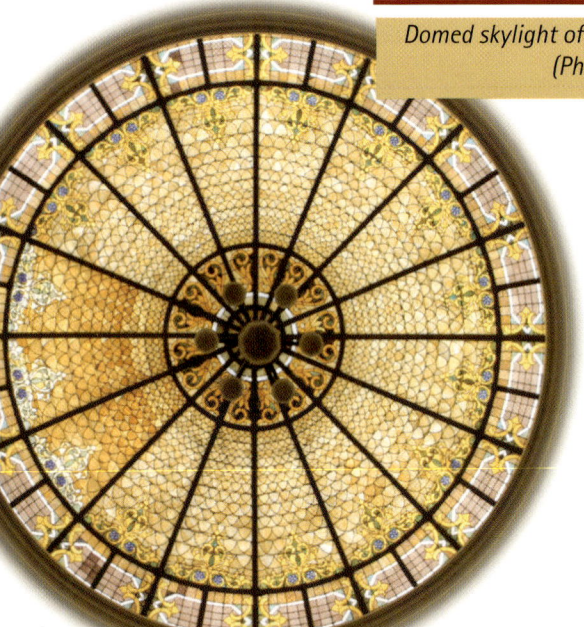

*Domed skylight of the Greene County Courthouse. (Photo by Catchlight Photography.)*

homemade sled and hauled 150 pounds of food down the frozen Raccoon River to relieve 17 miners and 58 truck drivers marooned at the Greene County Coal Company mine.

The unique Telephone Museum, located in the Communications Building of the Jefferson Telephone Company, displays antique telephone equipment from the early days of the communications industry. It's a collection that exists nowhere else in the state.

Jefferson was the childhood home of the late George Gallup Jr., founder of modern polling methods. He was born here, graduated from school (where he served as player-coach for the high school football team and edited the school newspaper), and then headed for the University of Iowa. The Gallup home, a unique eight-sided house in the south part of town, designed by George's father, is now owned by a foundation that bears his name. The home is in the early stages of a renovation/restoration project that will turn it into a tourist, conference and office site.

Visitors to Jefferson find comfortable accommodations for dining and lodging, with two motels, plenty of restaurants, and camping facilities nearby. Outdoor recreation abounds in Greene County. Spring Lake, in addition to its campsites, proffers picnicking, fishing, hiking and swimming, and a boat rental facility provides canoes, paddleboats and rowboats. Squirrel Hollow is a favorite picnic spot with its wonderful wooded trails and a shelter house and stone stairway, both built during the Depression of the 1930s. Several other county parks, most of them located along the Raccoon River, are popular both with locals and with out-of-town visitors, including the winter sled run at Seven Hills Park to the southwest.

Chautauqua Park is the site of the Jefferson Municipal Swimming Pool, a large outdoor pool that hosts the West Central Swim Conference meet every year.

*The Lincoln Square building, on the south side of the square, houses professional offices and other businesses. It was originally built as the Head House, a 19th Century downtown hotel.*

*The Greene County Arts Council heads up a mini-renaissance of the arts that currently graces the Jefferson community. This painting is by Colleen Clopton, one of many serious local artists.*

Hunters find plenty of action at Goose Lake north of Jefferson, Dunbar Slough in the west part of the county, and dozens of wooded and wetlands areas throughout the county. Fishing is productive at Spring Lake, in dozens of private farm ponds throughout the county, and along the length of the Raccoon River.

For indoor recreation, check out the Greene County Community Center just west of the square in Jefferson. Built entirely with private donations and operated with memberships and fees, no tax dollars were or are involved with the Center. The building, striking in appearance with its translucent stone sides, contains basketball courts, a second-floor walking track, a racquetball court, a fully equipped exercise gym, and several meeting rooms, as well as a day care facility.

Jefferson celebrates every year with its Bell Tower Festival, held the second weekend of June for the past quarter of a century. The gala event, centering on the downtown square, features entertainment, booths, rides, music of all types, dances, a bistro, food and more food, contests and games: everything that makes a summer festival in Iowa a joy.

*"Rooms" in the Greene County Historical Museum depict early-day business layouts.*

## PROFESSIONS AND BUSINESSES

The Jefferson professional community serves area residents' needs with competence and care. Greene County Medical Center, the county's largest employer, provides acute care, skilled care, nursing home care and outpatient services to area residents, as well as obstetrics and gynecology for mothers-to-be and their newborns. McFarland Clinic-Jefferson, physically connected to the west end of the medical center, offers highly competent family medicine, internal medicine and surgical care. A number of visiting physicians bring their specialties to the clinic on a regular basis, and emergency care is available round-the-clock.

*A number of handsome murals are painted on buildings in downtown Jefferson. This one, dating from 1976, depicts the Jefferson skyline from a point four miles east of town.*

Several Jefferson attorneys have gone on to distinguished careers as judges in state district courts, the state supreme court, and federal district court, and several of them have held key positions in the Iowa Bar Association. Three progressive banks are located in the community, with high loan-to-deposit ratios that demonstrate their commitment to local development and prosperity.

The family-owned Jefferson Telephone Company has long been a leader in the state in technological innovation, and continues as one of the community's strongest development partners. The company recently acquired Jefferson Cablevision, through which it offers a wide range of programming, and high-speed Internet service and cell phones are also integral components of the firm's range of services. The Bee and Herald newspapers, Greene County's longest business in continuous service (dating from 1866), publish twice a week, providing local news and a wide range of advertising options. Two radio stations, KGRA and KDLS, provide local news, sports and a music format along with over-the-air advertising.

The Jefferson retail community answers the needs and wants of area shoppers, with competitive

*The boyhood home of George Gallup Jr., the father of modern opinion polling, is located on South Chestnut Street in Jefferson. George's father was a firm believer in octagonal housing design, as evinced by the Gallup family home.*

*Teddy Roosevelt is among the many national candidates who have campaigned in Jefferson through the years. Photo is from a whistle-stop at the Chicago & NorthWestern depot when Roosevelt was seeking the vice presidency in 1900.*

prices and close-to-home convenience that lets consumers avoid the cost of increasing gasoline prices. Working together through the active Jefferson Area Chamber of Commerce, the business community delivers more-bang-for-the-buck promotions on a regular basis.

A sizable number of local industries provide employment for hundreds of area residents, and their products are sold nationwide, some of them around the world. Products include world-class gymnastics equipment, patented soyflakes, washing machine transmissions, rivets and fasteners, weight-lifting stanchions, and a wide variety of other items.

The close ties between Jefferson and agriculture are nowhere more evident than with the huge West Central Cooperative complex at the north edge of the city. In addition to millions of bushels of storage capacity, a West Central facility manufactures SoyChlor dairy feed additive. The co-op provides expert agronomy services to farmers over a wide area.

### QUALITY OF LIFE

Local residents are justly proud of the Jefferson-Scranton Community School District, which includes what one state education official calls "the best comprehensive high school in the state of Iowa." The school offers about 50 different college credit courses, and serves as a regional high school for Greene County, providing upper-level classes for dozens of students from the county's other high schools. Nine of the 94 J-S teachers are nationally certified, one of the highest percentages of all

*The Jefferson Municipal Swimming Pool is a popular spot for young and old on hot summer days.*

123

# Jefferson IOWA

## LEARN MORE

Jefferson is located an hour northwest of Des Moines and 45 minutes west of Ames, at the crossroads of U.S. Highway 30 and Iowa Highway 4. Its airport handles small plane traffic.

For information, contact the Jefferson Chamber of Commerce at 515-386-2155, or on-line at www.jeffersoniowa.com

## STORY CONTRIBUTOR

Rick Morain is the longtime editor-publisher of the Jefferson Bee and Herald Newspapers, and also serves as executive director of the Greene County Development Corporation. A fourth-generation Greene Countian, he lives in Jefferson with his wife Kathy.

---

Iowa school districts.

Test scores in the district at all grade levels typically rank in the top 80 per cent nationally and above the average in Iowa. The district recently received a glowing report from an evaluation team from the Iowa Department of Education, for the strength of both its academics and its activity programs.

Faith is an important aspect of the community's life. Thirteen churches offer residents their respective worship opportunities, and they also contribute significant organizational and volunteer help to worthwhile civic projects: Helping Hands home improvement for the needy, Adopt-A-Family at Christmastime, and the Webb House youth center, to name just a few examples.

The Jefferson Public Library recently celebrated its Centennial, dating its origin from the Carnegie-funded building a block west of the downtown square. The library's book collection is impressive, but the facility offers much, much more to area residents, including public computers.

### POSITIONED FOR THE FUTURE

Jefferson community leaders are positioning the community for progressive, 21st Century growth. Greene County Development Corporation executive director Rick Morain puts it this way: "With strong, generous support from city and county government, the business community, and many organizations and individuals, we see our future as very bright indeed. Our location in central Iowa, just a short drive from the Des Moines metro area and Iowa State University, is an added plus. We welcome everyone who's looking for a great place to visit, to work, or to live."

*The bronze statue of Abraham Lincoln appears to stride at a height equal to the bell tower on the downtown square.*

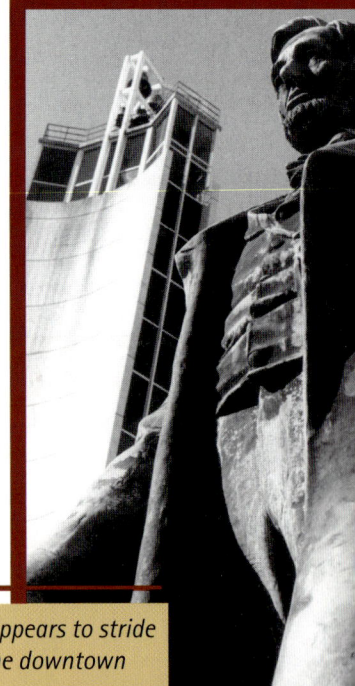

124

*Pride In Our Hometowns.*

# P·O·R·T·R·A·I·T·S
## OF
# *Keokuk*

## THE GATE CITY

*Known for its river and Native American history, Keokuk serves as a commercial center for parts of three states today: Southeast Iowa, West Central Illinois and Northeast Missouri.*

*Once a place where Native Americans hunted and fished, Keokuk is located where the Des Moines River flows into the Mississippi River. Included in the Louisiana Purchase of 1802, the area was set aside as a tract for the half breed descendants of the Indians and early fur traders as a result of a special treaty in 1824.*

*The town is named after Chief Keokuk, elected leader of the Sac/Fox Indians who made their home along the half-breed tract through Southeast Iowa.*
*With the decline of fur trading, more emphasis was placed on the transportation of freight and passengers around the Mississippi rapids using a series of canals. The wealth from the river traffic was reinvested in other businesses that serviced a growing rural population.*

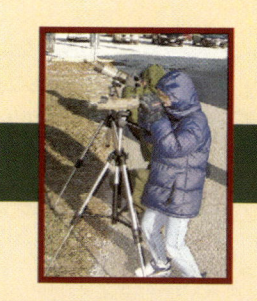

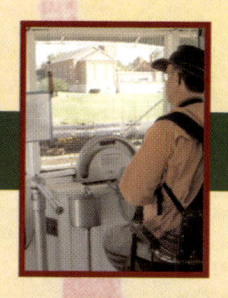

KEOKUK

*Pride In Our Hometowns.*

# P·O·R·T·R·A·I·T·S
## OF *Keokuk*

### THE GATE CITY

*The Keokuk Junction Railway Co. provides rail service for Keokuk's industries such as Roquette America, Inc.*

Americans started to settle the area en masse in the 1830s, and Isaac Galland platted the city of Keokuk in June 1837. Galland built Iowa's first school in 1830, located nine miles north of Keokuk. By 1847, there was a community large enough for a city charter to be granted by the Iowa Legislature. The mayor and council were not elected until January 1848.

Keokuk became a magnet for all types of medical care over the next several decades. In 1850, the College of Physicians and Surgeons (later a part of Drake University in Des Moines) was established at the corner of Third and Palean streets.

Keokuk played a prominent role in the Civil War, serving as a swearing-in point for the Iowa volunteers and as a major medical center. At one point, as many as seven Civil War hospitals were located in the

### A SNAPSHOT

*The Birge Fountain is one of the features at the flower garden in Keokuk's Rand Park, which was established in 1883. The fountain is named after Charles Birge, a former mayor of the city.*

# Keokuk, IOWA

*This stock certificate in the name of Keokuk Hamilton Water Power Co. dated Oct. 4, 1900, is one of the exhibits at the Samuel F. Miller House and Museum in Keokuk.*

community. Soldiers wounded on Southern battlefields were transported up the Mississippi River on hospital boats. Many of those who didn't survive were buried in the Keokuk National Cemetery, one of the original 12 designated by Congress and the first national cemetery west of the Mississippi River.

On March 7-8, 1862, Keokuk's own Gen. Samuel Curtis led the Union troops in a two-day battle in Pea Ridge, Ark., that prevented Missouri from being controlled by the Confederacy. The battle is recreated every April at Keokuk's Rand Park, which overlooks the Mississippi River.

The city got a boost in the 1870s when a railroad bridge was built across the Mississippi to connect Keokuk to several major rail systems. Progress continued when the Badger Electric Company brought electricity starting on March 2, 1885. A starch factory opened in Keokuk in 1887.

River commerce took a turn for the better when the canal that split the Des Moines Rapids on the Mississippi River at Keokuk was replaced in 1913 by Lock and Dam 19 and a hydroelectric plant, which was an engineering marvel at the time. The lock was replaced in 1957 by the present 1,200-foot structure, which still is one of the longest on the river.

In 1985, the

*A statue of Chief Keokuk in Keokuk's Rand Park overlooks the Mississippi River. The statue honors the community's namesake and leader of the Sac/Fox Indians.*

*Tablets originally used in a Jewish synagogue at Eighth and Blondeau streets in Keokuk are among the exhibits at the Samuel F. Miller House and Museum. Many of Keokuk's early merchants, including the Younker brothers, were Jewish.*

127

# Keokuk
## IOWA

*An 1895 "Keokuk Waltzes" song book by Frank Nagel of Keokuk is one of the many exhibits at the Samuel F. Miller House and Museum in Keokuk. The museum is named after a former U.S. Supreme Court justice who built the house.*

In 1993, Keokuk and the Tri-State Area overcame a momentous flood that closed the Keokuk-Hamilton, Ill., bridge for awhile and forced area residents to cross the dam by foot or rail car. At one point, the river reached 27.17 feet, or more than three feet above the old mark of 23.75 feet in 1973.

Keokuk has a proud auto racing and professional baseball history. It is known as "The Home of Champions" and "The Racing Capital of the World" with such famous drivers as Ramo Stott, Ernie Derr, Dick Hutcherson, Don White, Gordon Blankenship, Lem Blankenship, Darrell Bradley, Mike Derr, Russ Derr, Ron Hutcherson and Jerry McCredie. In fact, Keokuk has more racing champions per capita than any city in the U.S.

narrow two-lane bridge linking Keokuk with West Central Illinois was replaced by a four-lane concrete structure. The old swing span vehicular bridge has since been converted to an observation deck and is still used by trains. In addition, the old toll booth now serves as an information booth with restrooms and landscaping.

The Keokuk Westerns began playing pro baseball in the National Association of Professional Baseball Players (later known as the National League) in 1875. Although the team played only one season, Keokuk's rich pro baseball heritage began.

Minor league baseball teams made Keokuk their home until the early 1960s. Such major league notables as Roger Maris, who broke Babe Ruth's single-season home run record in

*Re-enactors dressed in period costumes are familiar sights at the annual Battle of Pea Ridge Civil War Re-enactment in Keokuk. About 800 to 900 re-enactors usually attend the three-day event.*

# Keokuk IOWA

1961, Jim "Mudcat" Grant, Tim McCarver and Gus Bell honed their baseball talent at Keokuk's original Joyce Park at one time or another.

More than 400 baseball players were on Keokuk teams during 1947-62 when Keokuk was affiliated with four major league franchises: the Pirates, Indians, Cardinals and Dodgers. Baseball America ranked the 1955 team, which won the Three-I League with a 92-34 record, No. 30 among the top minor league teams of all time.

Other famous Keokukians include Supreme Court Justice Samuel Miller, who was appointed to the nation's highest court by President Abraham Lincoln; Mark Twain (Samuel Clemens), who helped his brother Orion publish a city directory before leaving to become a steamboat's cub pilot on the lower Mississippi River; Annie Wittenmyer, the first national chaplain of the National Women's Relief Corps and first president of the Women's Christian Temperance Union; Lipman Younker, who operated a dry goods store in Keokuk, the forerunner to the Younker's department store; and J.C. Hubinger, who operated a starch factory in Keokuk and helped bring electricity to town.

Presidents also have made several appearances in Keokuk, the most recent being former President Jimmy

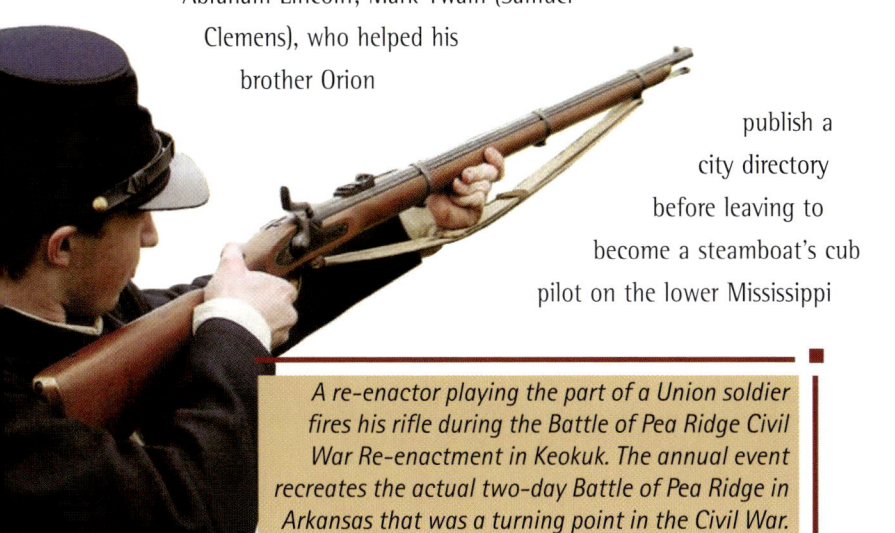

*An entertainer mixes with the crowd at Keokuk's Rollin' on the River in August, a blues festival that draws musicians and fans from a wide area.*

*A re-enactor playing the part of a Union soldier fires his rifle during the Battle of Pea Ridge Civil War Re-enactment in Keokuk. The annual event recreates the actual two-day Battle of Pea Ridge in Arkansas that was a turning point in the Civil War.*

# Keokuk, IOWA

Carter who went through Lock 19 during his trip down the Mississippi River. President Teddy Roosevelt visited Keokuk three times, including once in 1903 when he spoke at Rand Park and pushed the button to reopen Hubinger's newly rebuilt factory.

Today, Keokuk boasts a strong K-12 educational system of public and private schools, plus a branch of Southeastern Community College. Five elementary schools, one middle school and one high school serve approximately 2,200 students in the Keokuk Community School District. The public school system offers a wide array of extracurricular activities as well as the basics of reading, writing, math and science. The public school system's students and parents also are able to access grades and assignments through PowerSchool software used in conjunction with the World Wide Web.

St. Vincent's Elementary, Cardinal Stritch Junior and Senior High Schools, and Keokuk Christian Academy offer alternatives for those preferring a private school education.

The opening of Midwest Academy, a private school located in the former county home north of town, has added to the community's educational mix.

The Keokuk campus of Southeastern Community College offers associate of arts degrees. Continuing and extended education courses offer opportunities for personal enrichment and for improving employment skills. In addition, many public universities and private colleges are within a 90-minute drive, including the University of Iowa in Iowa City, Western Illinois University in Macomb, Ill., Iowa Wesleyan College in Mount Pleasant and Culver-Stockton College in Canton, Mo.

Although some of Keokuk's older industries have been adversely impacted by foreign competition and outsourcing, Roquette America, Inc., Metzeler Automotive Profile

*The Keokuk Junction Railway Co. provides rail service for Keokuk's industries. The city's old railroad depot is partially shown in the background.*

*A statue of Gen. Samuel Curtis is located in Keokuk's Victory Park along the Mississippi River. Curtis led the Union troops in the two-day Battle of Pea Ridge, Ark., a turning point in the Civil War.*

# Keokuk IOWA

*This hard helmet diving suit and related equipment once used by a Quincy, Ill., diver is on display at the George M. Verity River Museum in Keokuk. The air compressor was manually operated. The outfit also includes a weighted belt and lead shoes.*

Systems, Keokuk Steel Castings and Griffin Wheel still anchor the town's industrial base. Roquette America, Inc. has built its own 50-megawatt power plant and added a major product line.

In addition, local economic development officials are working on establishing a port authority, which could have positive international ramifications and eventually provide hundreds of jobs.

Keokuk has four industrial sites available for new and expanding companies. Located on the U.S. 61 bypass, Kindustry Park has full water, gas and sewer service and is the home of six companies: Alliance Pattern Inc., Associated Toolmakers, Carry Transit, CHMI, CCX and HEADCO/Bearing Headquarters. Three other sites, including North Park and the Montrose site, are developing rapidly.

Besides the Mississippi and Des Moines rivers, U.S. 61 is accessible from any point in Keokuk and leads to nearby IA 394, IA 218, IA 136 and many more expressways. In addition, I-80 is less than 90 minutes north and serves as one of the more important interstates in the country.

Two major railroads serve Keokuk: Burlington Northern Santa Fe Railway (BNSF) and Keokuk Junction Railway Co (KJRY).

The Keokuk Municipal Airport/Lindner Field has 5,500- and 3,800-foot runways.

Other features include

*A new Veterans Memorial has been built at the entrance of Oakland Cemetery in Keokuk. The marble structure has the names of about 1,400 servicemen and servicewomen as well as contributors. The memorial was built with private funds in a project that took about three years to complete.*

*The new and old bridges spanning the Mississippi River at Keokuk serve as a backdrop for these bald eagle viewers during Bald Eagle Appreciation Days in Keokuk.*

# Keokuk, IOWA

an instrument landing system, Unicom radio, non-directional beacon and localizer DME. More commercial airline options are located less than an hour away in Burlington and Quincy, Ill.

Three large barge terminals in Keokuk help many companies that ship products on the Mississippi and Des Moines rivers. As a result, the barge terminals assist products such as grain, coal and petroleum reach their destinations throughout the world.

Keokuk's retail sector has been bolstered by a change of ownership at the River City Mall, investment in the downtown and the opening of a new Wal-Mart Supercenter that replaced a Wal-Mart on the north edge of town. In addition, a new Hampton Inn hotel is planned for Keokuk on land formerly owned by the city and a new mini-mall has been built near the Supercenter.

With more than 450 businesses employing more than 1,700 people, the city's commercial district draws shoppers from Lee County in Iowa, Hancock County, Ill., and Clark County, Mo. Keokuk's commercial mix ranges from financial institutions to hair salons to retail stores to restaurants to health clubs.

Tourist attractions abound, with the above named observation deck and information booth as well as the George M. Verity River Museum at Victory Park and the Samuel F. Miller House and Museum on North Fifth Street. Keokuk has 14

*The annual Rollin' on the River blues festival in Keokuk draws some of the best blues musicians in the Midwest. The event is held in August in Victory Park along the Mississippi River.*

*Dancers enjoy the blues in front of the stage at the annual Rollin' on the River blues festival in Keokuk. The event attracts big name blues musicians from throughout the Midwest each August.*

*The George M. Verity River Museum in Keokuk's Victory Park pays homage to the community's river heritage. When it was in service, the Verity normally moved about 10,000 tons of cargo per trip, while most ocean going freighters of the day moved about 5,000 tons or less.*

# Keokuk IOWA

*The Keokuk National Cemetery has several graves of Union and Confederate soldiers from the Civil War, including this one for Union soldier John Wood, dating back to Oct. 7, 1862.*

city parks: Bluff Park, Gateway Park, Hubinger Landing, Joyce Park, Kilbourne Park, Kiser Park, Rand Park, Rees Park, Riverview Park, Roadside Park, Tolmie Park, Triangle Park, Tumelty Park and Victory Park. The Keokuk Public Library has been remodeled extensively and is undergoing renovation in the basement to provide space for the Keokuk Art Center and Lee County Historical Society as well as library staff and the community.

The latest attraction is a Veterans Memorial with nearly 1,400 names of veterans and contributors at 18th and Carroll streets. The memorial, which was dedicated July 4, features six nine-foot pillars, five grand arches and 16 black plates of granite. Eventually, pillars kept from the demolition of the 1927 Keokuk High School will form an entry arch to the veterans memorial.

Keokuk's natural beauty is matched only by its architectural beauty as shown by its fine examples of Victorian architecture. Many of the community's architectural masterpieces overlook the Mississippi River along Grand Avenue. The mix of Keokuk's architectural styles also includes Tudor, Italianate, Queen Anne, Revival and Greek Revival.

People looking for communal or senior living options can choose between several centrally-located apartment complexes. Safe and affordable, rental alternatives include duplexes, multilevel buildings and converted 19th-century mansions. Condominiums also are available, giving citizens a chance to own a home with many of the conveniences of apartment living.

*The 1,200-foot lock at Keokuk serves as a major transportation component on the Mississippi River. The hydroelectric power plant operated by Ameren UE and dam are shown in the background. Completed in 1913, the dam was one of the biggest public works projects of its era.*

# Keokuk IOWA

Keokuk also has several cultural attractions, including the Great River Players, a theatre group, and Marilyn Hart Children's Theatre. Most of the theater and music productions are held at the historic Grand Theatre, a restored 1920s opera house used by the Keokuk High School band and choirs, Keokuk Concert Association, McNamara's Band and dance recitals, too.

Recreational opportunities include baseball and softball diamonds, fields for soccer and other sports, basketball courts, jogging and walking trails. Playgrounds for children, tennis courts and a disc golf course can be found in Keokuk, too. The Hoerner YMCA has a swimming pool as well as a basketball court and racquetball courts. In addition, two private golf courses and several public courses are located in or near the city.

Keokuk's proximity to the Mississippi and Des Moines rivers provides easy access for water skiing, rafting and fishing. Boat clubs, canoeing and kayaking also are popular.

There are many opportunities to observe and hunt ducks and geese since the Mississippi River serves as a major flyway for migrating water fowl. The uninhabited area around the city has a plentiful population of deer, squirrel,

*Keokuk has the only National Cemetery in Iowa. The first National Cemetery west of the Mississippi River, many soldiers from the North and South in the Civil War are buried in the cemetery as well as soldiers from wars and conflicts since then.*

*The former toll booth at the old Keokuk/Hamilton, Ill., bridge has been converted to a tourist information site. The bricks in the foreground were taken from the reconstruction of Keokuk's Main Street. Landscaping and period lighting add to the pleasing atmosphere.*

*A Union artillery unit fires a cannon during the Battle of Pea Ridge Civil War Re-enactment in Keokuk. The original two-day battle in 1862 is recreated over a two-day period in April each year at Rand Park in Keokuk.*

# Keokuk IOWA

*This office exhibit at the Samuel F. Miller House and Museum in Keokuk includes a chair used by Maj. Montgomery Meigs, the engineer in charge of the canal and new locks at Keokuk.*

wild turkey, pheasant, quail and other assorted game. Nearly 40 churches are located in the community, including several Protestant and one Catholic. Two congregations – the First Christian Church and Faith Family Church – use former big box retail stores. The first Catholic services were held in 1833, while the first Protestant services were conducted in 1835.

Keokuk Area Hospital is one of the community's largest employers and serves as a medical center for the Tri-State Area. Recent improvements include a major renovation of the obstetrical department.

All tolled, the 120-bed hospital has a staff of 450 medical professionals including almost 40 doctors and is fully authorized by the Joint Commission on Accreditation of Healthcare Organization. Physicians specialize in several areas, including radiology, anesthesiology, pediatrics, internal medicine and more.

The hospital also provides numerous specialized services, including a full ambulance service, airlift capabilities, an on-site pharmacy and workout center.

Keokuk Area Hospital operates a Home Health Care program, too, that allows recovering patients to get health care from trained professionals in their home. Home Care specialties include physical therapy, diabetic teaching, pain management, catheter care and medication assessment.

Dentists, chiropractors, orthopedic surgeons, internists,

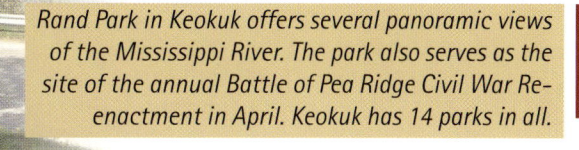

*Gateway Park greets motorists entering Keokuk from Illinois on the four-lane bridge (shown in the background) completed in 1985. A walkway cuts through the park, which also includes benches and landscaping.*

*Rand Park in Keokuk offers several panoramic views of the Mississippi River. The park also serves as the site of the annual Battle of Pea Ridge Civil War Re-enactment in April. Keokuk has 14 parks in all.*

# Keokuk IOWA

## LEARN MORE

Keokuk is located in Southeast Iowa at the tip of Lee County, bordering the Mississippi and Des Moines rivers. It is accessible by U.S. Highway 61 and Iowa Highways 218 and 136. It is four miles from the four-lane Avenue of the Saints highway from St. Louis, Mo., to St. Paul, Minn.

For more information contact the Keokuk Area Chamber of Commerce at 319-524-5055 or visit the Web site at: www.keokukchamberofcommerce.com.

## STORY CONTRIBUTORS

Steve Dunn, managing editor, D<
Gate City, Keokuk
Keokuk Area Chamber of Comm<
Web site: Keokuk-ia.com/history

---

psychiatrists and other specialized doctors have offices near the hospital and elsewhere in the community.

Annual attractions include Bald Eagle Appreciation Days in January, the Battle of Pea Ridge Civil War Re-enactment in April, Rollin' on the River in August and the City of Christmas in late November/December.

Because of its dam on the Mississippi River, Keokuk hosts one of the largest concentrations of bald eagles during the winter. In addition to viewing the majestic creatures, the public has an opportunity to enjoy several other activities during Bald Eagle Appreciation Days.

The Civil War re-enactment draws hundreds of re-enactors and their families from throughout the country. Besides the battles, the public can attend a Ladies Tea and Fashion Show and hear Civil War-era music.

Billed as the best "dam" festival, Rollin' on the River attracts some of the finest blues musicians in the country. The festival was featured in a 2004 issue of Gig magazine.

Operated by volunteers, the City of Christmas features more than 100 Christmas displays and 300,000 lights in Rand Park from Thanksgiving through December each year.

The newest attraction is the annual Native American pow wow in July. Several descendants of Native Americans who once lived in the area return to Rand Park where Indian customs, dances and music are displayed.

**Steeped in history, Keokuk looks forward to a new century while maintaining its role as the gateway to the Tri-State Area.**

*The Armco Steel Corporation donated the George M. Verity River Museum to the City of Keokuk in 1961. The boat was built in Dubuque by the U.S. government in an attempt to spur river transportation. The steel company bought the boat in 1940 and put it into service on the Ohio River.*

*Pride In Our Hometowns.*

# P·O·R·T·R·A·I·T·S
## OF
## *Newton*

NEWTON

### RED PRIDE

*It's an intangible thing, hard to grasp or initially even understand. But spend time in Newton and you learn what it means to be hit with "Red Pride."*

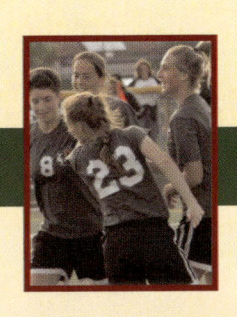

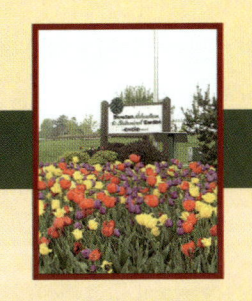

## Pride In Our Hometowns.
# PORTRAITS OF Newton

### RED PRIDE

*The north side of the Newton square in the early part of the century.*

## A Snapshot

"Red Pride" shows itself in little things - like Renew Newton's and Project AWAKE's efforts at community beautification and the local sculpture group's efforts at bringing permanent art displays to common areas throughout the community.

"Red Pride" shows itself in big things - like a local Fortune 500 company's effort at transforming an unused warehouse into a community college campus that now boasts an affiliation with two state universities and a four-year private college.

And "Red Pride" shows itself in huge things - like resident support and financial contributions for a new library, upgraded public school facilities, hospital renovations and expansion, new swimming pool, new airport facilities and community center.

Should the measure of a community's strength and success be the willingness of its citizens to work toward its common goals, then Newton has few peers.

We call it "Red Pride." Come take a look at Newton, we've saved a place for you.

Like nearly all early Midwestern communities, Newton - which derived its name from a noted Revolutionary War soldier, Sergeant Newton - grew on the number of farmers settling the area and the merchants catering to their needs. While agriculture today continues to be a vital component of the local economy, the early

# Newton IOWA

## F.L. Maytag

industrialization of Newton and its growth to prominence as the "Washing Machine Center of the World" has pushed Newton beyond its agrarian beginnings to be a hub for a host of manufacturing, specialty advertising and telecommunication business headquarters. Although global in its outreach and look, it promotes the conveniences, benefits and ease of small-city living that has given Newton residents quality of life for a lifetime.

An act of the Legislature made possible the formation of Jasper County in 1846. A commission named by the Legislature in the 1845-46 session to select a site for the courthouse chose the ground where the first of three courthouses was later erected. A pole set up on the open prairie marked the place which became the public square and the center of town of Newton.

The rich prairie land with a small amount of timber lent itself at once

## The History

to the settlers' need for fuel, building materials and farms. In the 1860s, the Mississippi and Missouri Railroad, predecessor of the Rock Island (and later the Iowa Interstate Railroad) came through the county bringing tools and products from the East.

One of the most flourishing businesses in the early days was the milling of lumber and later the manufacturing of farm implements. In the pioneer days, numerous privately-owned colleges were developed, such as the Wittemburg Manual Labor College which was established just north of Newton in 1855. Students entering the college, in exchange for room and board, were required to work at least two hours a day on the plat reserved for farming. An economic depression and the Civil War hindered the school's ability to make it financially and the property was foreclosed upon and the school closed in 1860.

By the 1880s, all the land

*The Newton Daily News has been publishing a newspaper in the community for the past 104 years. The building now housing the paper was built in 1920-21 and sits one block east of the downtown square.*

*A dog is dressed in its finest multi-colored pattern in advance of a pet fashion show held in connection with the annual Fourth of July parade.*

# Newton IOWA

worth farming was in use. Over the course of the next decade, the rural population decreased, since larger acreages could be farmed successfully by one man with machinery and manufacturing had created a demand for more labor.

Frederick Louis (F.L.) Maytag sowed the seed of his company's laundering fame in Newton.

As a 16-year-old farm hand, Maytag had seen many men injured while they fed grain into large threshing machines. In 1893, with $2,400 in capital, a workable idea and an abundant fund of confidence, Maytag joined forces with George W. Parsons and two brothers-in-law to form a farm equipment company to manufacture an accessory which would eliminate the dangerous job.

The Parsons Band Cutter and Self Feeder Company thrived. By 1902, the company had become the world's largest manufacturer of threshing machine feeders.

But because the business was seasonal, the company began manufacturing clothes washers, a product that could be manufactured during the winter months. Maytag introduced its first washer, a wooden tub model called the "Pastime," in 1907. Maytag's next model, the "Hired Girl," followed in 1909, the same year he acquired full ownership of the company and gave it his name. One year later, a swinging reversible wringer was added, a first in the industry. And the next year Maytag introduced an electric-powered model.

Maytag was not the only washing machine company in Newton at the time. In 1911, five Newton factories turned out 60,000 washing machines

> The Newton Kart Klub hosts weekly go-cart racing on a dirt track just south of town. The facility hosts national competition each summer with drivers coming to the track from throughout the Midwest and beyond.

> A customer inspects an Automatic Washer Company washing machine hooked up to "Smiling Thru," the private air office of H.L. Ogg, president of the company. The Wright Whirlwind J6 300 hp motor let Ogg cruise at 135 mph while conducting company business. Local historians say Ogg would blow a horn attached to the plane and drop candy and trinkets from the plane to attract customers before landing at a community's airport.

> "Family Outing," a sculpture commissioned for display by the Newton Rotary Club, the Newton Board of Realtors and Renew Newton, sits at the entrance to the community near the head of the city-long hike and bike trail.

# Newton
## IOWA

*A hike and bike trail winds its way through a wooded area in Newton. The hard-surface trail crosses the southern half of the city with plans eventually to have the trail circle the community.*

annually. In addition to Maytag, other Newton manufacturers included The Newton Washing Machine Company, Automatic Electric Washer Company, One Minute Manufacturing Company and the Disc Plow Company. Woodrow Washing Machine Company started in 1914.

But Maytag's business acumen, insistence on quality products and continuous innovations led his company to continued success while the local competitors eventually fell by the wayside. In 1915, Maytag filled the need of many a rural family without access to electric power. The MultiMotor, the first gasoline engine attached to a washer, powered a half-horse-power engine that not only cleaned clothes but was capable of operating other farm equipment, as well. In addition, a host of attachments - including a butter churn, ice-cream freezer and meat-grinding equipment - were available for use with the machine.

Within six months, sales and production of washing machines doubled and for the first time the washing machine division of Maytag outperformed farm implement production.

As World War I raged overseas, Maytag did what many said couldn't be done - cast a lightweight and sturdy, non-rusting aluminum-tub washer. And in 1922, Maytag turned the industry on its head by flipping the agitator from the lid to the bottom of the tub. Maytag's "Gyrator blades" forced water through the clothes rather than pulling clothes through the water.

By 1924, Maytag was making one out of every five American washing machines. Between 1922 and 1926, washer production in Newton increased 300 percent. By 1927, Maytag had produced its one millionth washer.

This phenomenal industrial boom impacted Newton's growth. Workers poured into the city as production could not keep up with demand. Rent and real estate prices skyrocketed and living costs mounted. During

*Left: A refurbished Maytag Company building.*

*Right: A motocross rider acknowledges the photographer during a jump while riding in Newton.*

# Newton IOWA

the warm months, new workers lived with their families in a tent town on the Jasper County Fairgrounds, now Maytag Park. From 1925 to 1929, $3 million was spent in building homes, most small structures for the incoming workers. At the time, an Iowa columnist wrote: "Sprawling spaciously over the fields and hills on both sides of U.S. 32 (now First Avenue/U.S. Highway 6) Newton probably has more new suburbs and additions and real estate development than any town its size in North America."

During World War II, the Maytag Company was not allowed to produce any washing machines and was engaged entirely in the production of war materials. The company produced special components for airplanes, tanks and other military equipment, an effort largely undertaken by women workers. Throughout the war, Maytag employees purchased war bonds and used them in 1943 to buy a B-26 bomber dubbed the "Maytag Marauder."

When Maytag started making washers again in 1945, the building boom was on and demand was so great that production hit the highest mark in Maytag history. In 1947, the company produced its five millionth wringer washer (the last of which was produced in 1983).

In 1949, Maytag introduced its first automatic washer. Demand was so strong that a second manufacturing plant, solely dedicated to the production of automatic washers, was opened. Clothes dryers were added in 1952, when Maytag's eight millionth washer was produced.

Maytag continued to operate as a family-owned business until 1962 under the direction of two of F.L. Maytag's sons, Lewis Bergman Maytag and Elmer Henry Maytag, and his grandson, Fred Maytag II. For the past 43 years it has been a publicly owned company and expanded to become a manufacturer of a full line of home appliances.

F.L. Maytag's philanthropic efforts on behalf of the community and his public service stints as Newton city councilman, mayor and Iowa Senator reaped benefits for the community's residents. He was chiefly responsible for the installation of a city light and power plant in the late 1890s, saw to the paving

> *The Cardinal is the team mascot for Newton Senior High School. The high school football team is closely followed by the community with games at H.A. Lynn Field on Friday nights played before a standing-room-only audience. The game is so popular locally that reserved seating along Newton's sidelines is passed on from generation to generation.*

# Newton IOWA

*Newton band students prepare for a concert.*

of more than 18 miles of roadways within the city as mayor in 1919 and was instrumental in the organization of the Newton Water Company. He helped raise funds to build the Skiff Memorial Hospital, built a citadel for the Salvation Army and gave the YMCA a building and endowment fund. He also helped finance the construction of the Maytag Hotel in downtown Newton, one of the first buildings in the state to be air conditioned. He was also instrumental in the transformation of the old county fairgrounds into Maytag Park, including the construction of a swimming pool for use by Newton residents. The pool was dedicated on Sept. 8, 1935. A sportscaster for WHO radio, Ronald "Dutch" Reagan, was on hand for the Maytag Park pool dedication ceremonies. Reagan went on to become the governor of California and President of the United States.

Maytag was not the only manufacturer in Newton. Companies involved in the manufacture of items ranging from earth excavators to specialty advertising products were also leading manufacturing establishments in the community at that time. A partial list includes:

- **The Parsons Company** - manufacturer of trench excaving and dirt moving machinery.
- **DunLap Manufacturing Company** - manufacturer of advertising specialties, name plates and decals.
- **Maytag Dairy Farms** - manufacturer of what still today is considered by many the best blue cheese in the world.
- **Newton Manufacturing Company** - still today one of the prominent specialty advertising companies in the United States.
- **Cline Tool & Service Company** - continues to design tools, dies and jig work.
- **Skow Manufacturing Company** - manufacturer of wood and metal caskets and disc sharpening machines.
- **Thombert Company** - continues to manufacture plastic fabricated items.
- **The Vernon Company** - now more than 100 years old, the specialty advertising company is another of the most prominent companies in its field

*Sir Rust-O-Lot sits in front of the Newton Public Library.*

143

# Newton, IOWA

*The Newton Municipal Band performs an evening concert at the Maytag Park Bowl on a summer evening. The bowl hosts a number of various musical events and is the site of the high school graduation ceremonies each year.*

and is still family owned and operated.

- **WinPower Manufacturing Company** - manufacturer of electric generators, rotary hoes, post hole diggers, farm wagons and machinery.
- **Salmon's Products** - paint products.
- **Davis Advertising Company** - decal transfers.

Newton provides a quality of life for a lifetime. Truly, there is something for everyone.

Newton boasts outstanding public and Christian education systems. Voter approved bonds, special tax assessments and targeted school district funding has allowed the community to expand and modernize all its school facilities.

Newton is also home to the Newton Polytechnic Campus, a branch of Des Moines Area Community College. Buena Vista College also houses classes in the facility and the University of Iowa provides an evening/weekend master's in business administration program on site. Skiff Medical Center, Newton's state-of-the-art, full-service medical center, has expanded considerably in recent years and now serves as a regional hub for medical care.

A strong community playhouse, arts council and numerous groups devoted to promoting the arts provide residents with a diverse array of cultural programs. Civic groups are active in promoting the community and conduct numerous community betterment projects. A strong sister-city relationship with a Ukrainian community has resulted in numerous business and cultural exchanges that has enhanced Newton's reputation in the international community.

Community events abound. The city's annual Fourth of July parade draws thousands along its route each year to view the bands, floats, clowns, fancy cars and horses that make their way down the city's main street for nearly two hours.

And Newton is famous for its courthouse Christmas lighting ceremony. Each year the historic, Bedford limestone, Neo-Classic structure is transformed into the world's largest Christmas tree. The lights are flipped on during extravagant ceremonies the Friday after Thanksgiving following a downtown parade.

## PRESENT DAY

Monthly downtown art walks, a yearly live blues music festival, a juried sculpture festival, Friday night football games, annual alumni reunion,

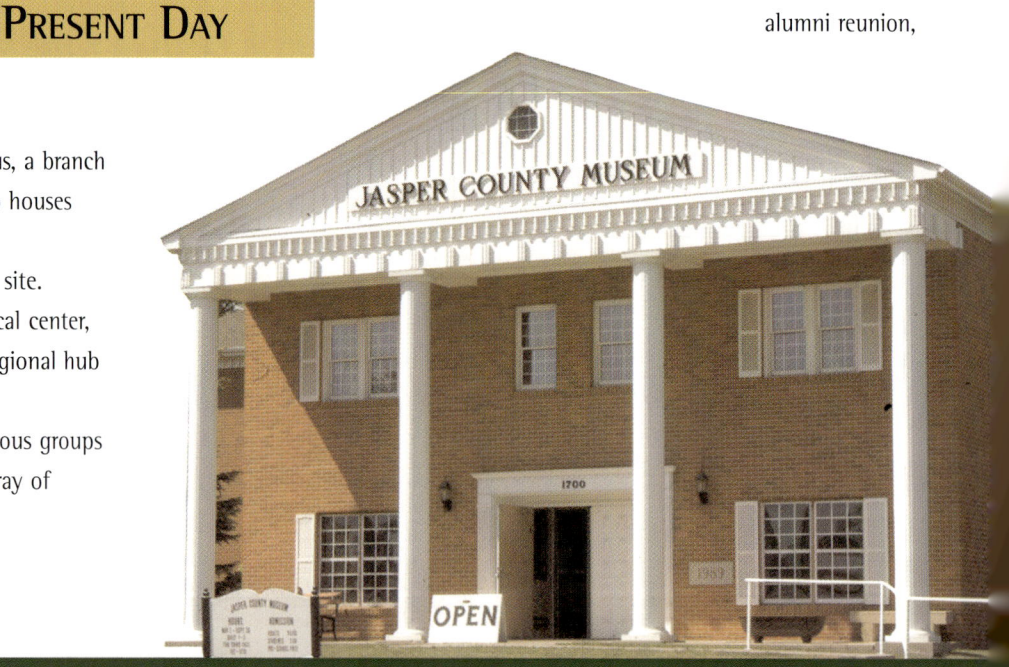

# Newton IOWA

*The Maytag Park swimming pool is enjoyed by swimmers all summer long.*

Passion Play performance and summer farmer's markets are just some of the happenings that keep residents active throughout the year.

The community's top-notch and full-gamut recreational facilities help keep the body strong. The stately 18-hole Westwood Municipal Golf Course challenges even the most proficient golfers while the 18-hole disc golf course at Maytag Park draws players from throughout central Iowa and recently hosted a junior nationals competition. Bicyclists and walkers take advantage of the new fully-paved hike and bike trail that winds for miles through the city. The Newton Arboretum and Botanical Garden, located in Agnes Patterson Park and the site of the Daniel J. Krumm Horticultural Learning Center, also offers more than a mile of hiking trails through its lovely landscaped setting featuring various woody shrubs, conifer and deciduous trees, ornamental grasses, perennial and annual flower beds. A water garden with native prairie flowers and grasses and a butterfly garden are located along the walkways.

The Newton YMCA provides a full scope of both exercise and arts programs for all ages and operates ACES Teen Center, a place for teens to do some wall-climbing, pick up a roller-hockey game, dance a weekend evening away or just hang out. Skate Castle roller rink is popular with young and old.

Swimming enthusiasts take advantage of the recently revamped Maytag Park pool. It's zero depth entry allows even the youngest to splash away the warm afternoons of summer while its two water slides, basketball hoops, umbrella waterfalls and diving boards give even the oldest children opportunities for play.

History buffs can get their fill at Newton's two museums. The Jasper County museum boasts more than 8,000 artifacts including a bas-

*La Corsette Maison Inn is a five-star gourmet dining establishment and bed and breakfast situated along Newton's main thoroughfare just east of the downtown area. The opulent, mission-style mansion was built in 1909 by early Iowa State Senator August Bergman. It is listed on the National Register of Historic Places.*

*Marchers at the annual Relay for Life event set off on the 24-hour walk.*

145

# Newton IOWA

relief sculpture depicting the history of Jasper County. At more than 40-feet long, it was created by Newton artist Herman L. Deaton. Another highlight is the display of washing machines from Newton's era as the Washing Machine Center of the World. Machines built in Newton by the Woodrow, One Minute and Automatic companies are on display. The Maytag display starts in 1907 with representative models up to the present.

The International Wrestling Institute and Museum is dedicated to educating the public about the grand history of what is known as mankind's oldest sport. Wrestling dates back 5,000 years and plays a key role in The Epic of Gilgamesh, the oldest piece of extant literature in the world. It is also mentioned in the Bible and in the great epics of ancient Greece. Items on display include artwork of Abe Lincoln as a wrestler in 1831, Olympic history from 1896 to present, collegiate wrestling history from 1928 to present, displays dedicated to Dan Gable and Cael Sanderson, the Glen Brand Wrestling Hall of Fame and the George Tragos/Lou Thesz Professional Wrestling Hall of Fame. Each year, the Museum holds induction ceremonies into its halls of fame, as well as a celebrity golf outing and banquet.

The drive-in theater tradition still lives in Newton at the Valle Drive-In, the only drive-in theater remaining in central Iowa. Residents arrive early for a chance at the prime parking spots (front for some, back for others) to view the first run, double-feature shows.

Racing will soon take center stage for visitors to Newton as construction of the Iowa

*A balloonist fires his burner in preparation for a hot air balloon ride across the community.*

*Luminaries line the track at H.A. Lynn Field as part of the ceremonies surrounding the annual Relay for Life event to raise money for the American Cancer Society.*

*A bronze sculpture honoring veterans of World War II was erected on the 50th anniversary of the war's end. Local sculptor Nic Klepinger was commissioned to complete the larger than life depiction of a soldier assisting his fallen comrade. A local committee has recently established the Iowa Sculpture Festival @ Maytag Park which this year drew more than 60 sculptors in a variety of media to display and sell their artworks. The committee purchases one piece each year and places it for display in various common areas of the community in an effort to promote the visual arts.*

146

# Newton IOWA

*The annual lighting of the Jasper County Courthouse during the holidays dates back to the 1930s in Newton. Each year thousands of lights are draped from the courthouse dome to make what Newton residents call the world's largest Christmas tree. Events surrounding the annual lighting ceremony - held each year on the Friday after Thanksgiving - include a parade, carolers and a visit from Santa. Local historians say that in the 1940s and 1950s, airliners headed for landing in Des Moines would often fly low over Newton in order to give passengers an aerial view of the display. Focal point of the downtown square, the Neo-classic courthouse building, with stained glass dome, hand-painted murals, fresco design and ceramic tiles laid in mosaic patterns has been restored to its near period condition when erected in 1911. It is listed on the National Register of Historic Places.*

*A garden provides a relaxing setting at Skiff Medical Center.*

Speedway is now under way. The U.S. MotorSport Corp., is in the process of developing the $70 million project on a 225 acre tract of land adjacent to the Newton Municipal Airport. The 7/8 mile paved motor speedway is being designed by NASCAR racer Rusty Wallace, the first such signature facility designed by an active NASCAR race driver. It will have permanent grandstand seating for 25,000 seats (with capability of future expansion), plus provisions for temporary seating. It includes 22 luxury suites located above the grandstand, 60 motor home parking and viewing spaces, vendor and display areas and 52 garages in the infield. Total accommodation for 80,000 is possible. The facility will include a Rusty Wallace restaurant and museum. Planned events include auto racing, car shows, driving schools, concerts and other entertainment activities.

Just outside Newton's corporate limits, and not more than a 15-minute drive, include a host of other recreational opportunities.

The Neal Smith National Wildlife Refuge and Prairie Learning Center is the largest prairie reconstruction project in the United States. Set among the rolling hills of prairie grasses and flowers are more than 5,000 acres of protected prairie and oak savanna habitats. The grounds are inhabited by bison and elk. The Learning Center offers a variety of interpretive displays.

*Bison graze in front of the Neal Smith National Wildlife Refuge and Prairie Learning Center.*

# Newton IOWA

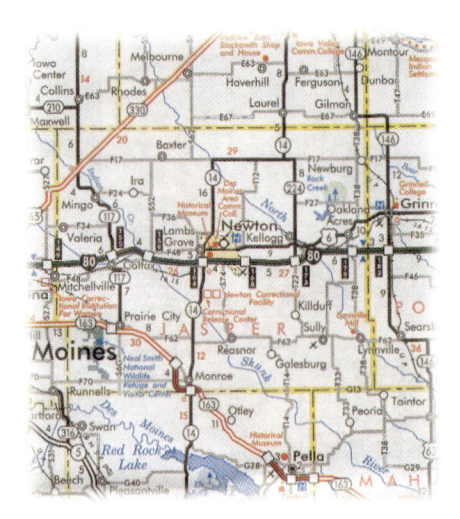

## Learn More

Newton is located along the Interstate 80 corridor, just 30 minutes east of Des Moines.

For information, contact the Newton Convention and Visitors Bureau at:
800-798-0299 or online at:
www.visitnewton.com

## Story Contributor

Peter Hussmann has been Editor of the Newton Daily News for the past 15 years and has worked at the newspaper since 1986.

---

The Newton Kart Klub offers go-cart racing on Friday nights with as many as 100 racers competing an any given weekend. Rock Creek State Park offers camping, fishing and boating opportunities while Ashton Park provides residents a look at the stars with its observatory.

Newton also has a thriving business community. In addition to Newton being home to the headquarters of Maytag, Iowa Telecom, one of the largest telecommunications companies in the state, calls Newton home. Specialty advertising, with long roots in Newton, continues strong through the operations of The Vernon Company and Newton Manufacturing. Keystone Laboratories is growing into one of the state's largest chemical analysis operations while Cline Tool continues its long history of manufacturing various casts and dies for a variety of industries. Thombert Manufacturing, also a long-time component of the Newton business community, manufactures items for the plastics industry. Maytag Dairy Farms continues to produce its world's famous blue cheese, along with a host of other cheese delicacies, from its production facility in Newton. Plans are under way for the construction of a new multi-million gallon biodiesel production facility to be located adjacent to the community's intermodal railroad facility, and two working wineries have recently located near Newton.

Newton's location adjacent to Interstate 80 positions it well for future growth. Just 30 minutes east of Des Moines, residents take advantage of the ease of small-city living while being able to easily access the amenities of Iowa's largest community.

But to really understand Newton today is to understand the spirit of its people and their willingness to put forth the effort to make the community what it needs, wants and expects to be. It's a "never-say-die," "can-do," "bring-it-on" attitude that sometimes even leaves those involved in awe of what can be accomplished through the common efforts of a community united.

Former Newton Mayor, life-long resident and long-time downtown retailer Dave Aldridge may have put it best. Newton "is a town full of citizens who care about each other, who volunteer for any and all needy causes, who share of their talents and their resources in order to retain our excellent city facilities and to aid those in distress."
That's "Red Pride."

## Skiff Medical Center

148

*Pride In Our Hometowns.*

# P·O·R·T·R·A·I·T·S
## OF
## *Osceola*

### A CITY ON THE MOVE

*At the end of the 80s Farm Crisis, many local farmers turned to industrial jobs in Osceola to help make ends meet and supplement their agricultural operations. Jimmy Dean was Osceola's top employer.*

*With the changing of the decade, those jobs disappeared much like many southern Iowa family farmers in Clarke County. The plant, then under Sara Lee ownership, closed leaving many people in a financial bind and contemplating their next move. Unemployment rates skyrocketed in Clarke County. In 1994, Osceola and Clarke County had the highest unemployment rate in Iowa.*

OSCEOLA

*Pride In Our Hometowns.*

# P·O·R·T·R·A·I·T·S
## OF *Osceola*

### A CITY ON THE MOVE

*Downtown Osceola is rich in architectural design as well as history. The downtown has been a retail anchor as well as home to many people, who live in apartments located on the second floor of the buildings.*

However, many Sara Lee employees took advantage of education opportunities presented to them. They became health care professionals, accountants and computer specialists.

City and community leaders also refused to sit still. They did not let adversity turn Osceola into a dying town.

Instead, they lobbied businesses, demonstrating the city's strengths: the strong work ethic, and genuine friendliness, not to mention an excellent location next to Highways 34 and 69 and Interstate 35 as well as a Burlington Northern railroad and Amtrak passenger train that travel through the community. It was those factors that played a role in Osceola's growth from its infancy as a community in the 1850s. And it was the people, logistics and strengths of the city that resurrected Osceola to what it is today.

In a short period of time in the mid-1990s, Hormel Foods built a plant for its subsidiary Osceola Foods.

### A SNAPSHOT

*The joyful sounds of children echo from the Osceola square during the community's annual Easter Egg Hunt.*

150

# Osceola, IOWA

This and the addition of a casino and resort, now Terrible's Lakeside Casino Resort in the later part of the decade brought a total of 1,500 new jobs to Osceola and Clarke County.

When someone looks at a community, they can see physical evidence of a town's prominence such as a thriving downtown, new housing and a large industrial base. However, Osceola, much like many parts of southern Iowa, is only as strong as the people who play a role in its growth. For the most part, those people may be faceless and even nameless, but their efforts and the fruits of their labor are witnessed daily at American State Bank, Clarke County State Bank, Great Western Bank, the Paul Mueller Company, Plum Building Systems, The Village Early Childhood Center, Clarke County Hospital, Clarke Community School District, Robinson' general store, Boyt Harness Company and even the Osceola Volunteer Fire Department.

Osceola's residents have become state lawmakers, secretary of state, an Iowa Supreme Court Chief Justice, published authors, Hollywood screenwriters, successful farmers, talented entrepreneurs, famous doctors and judges. Osceola currently has three district court judges sitting on the bench.

## A Look Back

Osceola was named to honor the great Seminole Indian leader who died in 1838 at the age of 34. Osceola rose to prominence among the Seminoles and led warriors who denounced treaties calling for the removal of the Seminoles from Florida to the West. A memorial statue of Osceola is located at Highway 34 and South

*The community of Osceola is named after a famous Seminole warrior. A statue of Osceola is located on highway 34 as you enter the city.*

*Like many communities, Osceola is rich in culture. Community leaders partner with a growing Hispanic population to hold the Latino Independence Festival in September.*

151

# Osceola IOWA

*Thursday Night in the Park is a popular event with the townspeople. Residents converge on the Osceola square every Thursday night during the summer months. They are treated to a meal and entertainment.*

Ridge Road.

From the very beginning, the wheels of transportation played a vital role in Osceola's growth and prosperity. The earliest wheels were the stage coach lines followed by the railroads and the military troop wagons traveling the grand plateau from Fort Des Moines to Fort Leavenworth, Kansas.

Today, Osceola is strategically situated along Interstate 35 and Highway 34 and 69. It also has access to transcontinental rail service that runs through the community.

Osceola was selected as the Clarke County seat on Aug. 16, 1851. That election was held in the cabin of John Coyers. The town was mapped out on a broad tract of fine prairie, which was purchased by the county for $100. It was surveyed into 85 lots with the average price of $22 each. Wagons hitched to five yoke of oxen pulled plows to break up the prairie sod.

Osceola's first rental housing was a double pen covered with hay built by John Shearer. He kept boarders until he completed a two-story log building. The boarding house was located on the southwest corner of the present town square.

The first store was owned and operated on the northwest corner of the square by George Howe. The business sold general merchandise such as fabric, clothing, blankets, and other items to meet the needs of the early settlers.

Businesses soon joined Howe's general merchandise and dry good operation around the five-acre central park square. Osceola's stately brick and masonry downtown commercial buildings were constructed between 1870 and 1900.

*The Banta House is one of a handful of homes in Osceola listed on the National Register of Historic Places. The house is located on Highway 34.*

# Osceola, IOWA

*Osceola's peaceful qualities are enjoyed by many local residents who can be found walking throughout the city.*

The oldest business in the community is the Sentinel-Tribune newspaper, which began in 1859.

There are more than 10 churches today in Osceola. However, in the early 1850s, church services were held in a little school house. The premier school system of today began as a small two-story frame building, located on the west side of the square where the present United States Post Office is situated.

The first county courthouse was a wooden structure built in 1854 at a contract price of $1,000. The courthouse was located on the northwest corner of the square where the fire department now sits. The second courthouse was a stately brick and masonry building constructed in 1892 in the town square. It featured a four-sided clock tower that sounded on the hour and half-hour. Serious structure defects developed in the main supporting walls of the building. It was speculated that this instability was due to the structure being built on the site of an old buffalo wallow. The courthouse was demolished and replaced by the present courthouse in 1956.

The first rail service was extended in 1868 to Osceola by the Chicago, Burlington and Quincy Railroad. North-south rail service was created by a local company, the Des Moines, Osceola and Southern Railroad in 1881. Q Pond and Grade Lake were created during this era as water sources for the steam locomotives. East Lake Park and West Lake were developed as sources of drinking water.

Passenger trains began making stops in Osceola in March 1949. The Vista Dome transcontinental train passed through the community twice a day. The same depot now serves more than 13,000 people each year for Amtrak. The depot is one of Amtrak's busiest in the state of Iowa.

The strategic location of Osceola was strengthened by the wheels of transportation when the north and south sections of Interstate 35 were completed in 1968.

*The new Clarke County Fairground celebrated its second year at its present location. More construction is planned in the coming years as fund-raising efforts continue into 2006.*

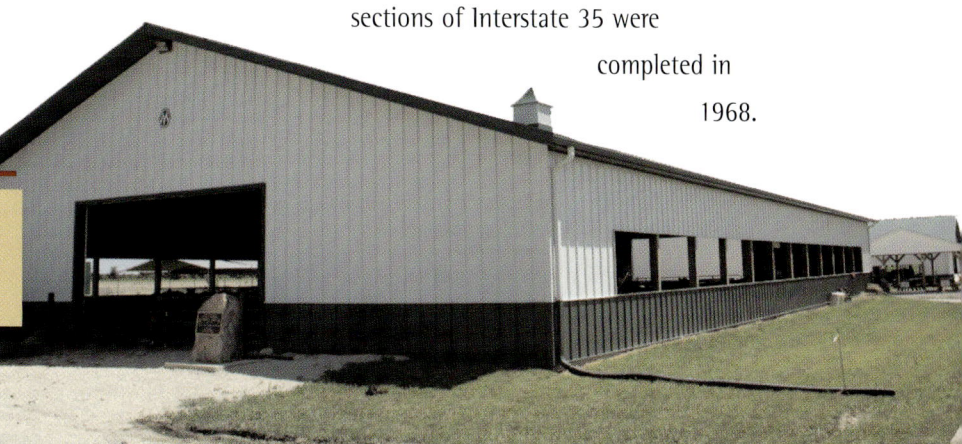

# Osceola IOWA

As the wheels turned faster, rapid industrial development came to Osceola.

When planning a day trip or weekend getaway, most people wouldn't give Osceola much thought. You won't find a major college sporting event, a zoo or an amusement park in the Clarke County seat town. However, what the community does offer are unique events centered around the different seasons and holidays.

Osceola's biggest annual event is the Fourth of July celebration. The four-day event features a carnival, nearly an hour-long grand daddy of all southern Iowa Fourth of July parades, talent show, daily musical entertainment and canoe races. Brilliantly designed and computer choreographed fireworks bring a close to the annual activities.

Some visitors travel hundreds and even thousands of miles to attend the Fourth of July celebration, which also serves as a time for class and family reunions.

The Maple Hill Cemetery Tour, in June, is sponsored by the Clarke County Historical Society. Society members research lives of deceased residents and the Cemetery Tour takes visitors on a walk through time to look into the lives of

*The Clarke County Fair remains a popular event for area youth and adults. The Clarke County Fair remains a popular event for area youth and adults.*

*The Osceola Aquatic Center is a popular place during the summer months. The aquatic center opens usually near Memorial Day and closes for the season near Labor Day.*

# Osceola IOWA

people and how they shaped the community. Members of the historical society portray the former residents in costume and tell the story of their life. The dialogue is worded as people spoke during the era of their lives. A candlelit tour is held at night.

The Clarke County Old Iron Club Farm and City Fun Weekend is in June at the Clarke County Fairground.

The event features antique tractors, garden tractors, farm machinery, homemade tractors and much more. The Farm and City Fun Weekend features a quilt display, swap meet, a garden tractor pull and a parade of the antique and restored tractors.

The annual Clarke County Fair is held in July. The event is now at the new fairground, built in 2004. The fair features highly-attended livestock shows, activities for youth and evening entertainment such as a demolition derby, mud bog races and a family fun night.

*This sculpture adds to the ambiance of the recently renovated Clarke County Hospital.*

## A Destination Stop

During the summer, scores of people gather in Osceola's downtown square for Thursday Night in the Park. Various organizations and businesses sponsor the weekly event, offering people a variety of eating options from grilled hamburgers and ribeye sandwiches to an ice cream social. Each Thursday features activities for children and musical entertainment for adults.

*Osceola boasts a strong fine arts program in the schools and in the community. There is a youth theater program as well as department in the high school that produces a musical and play each school year. The Clarke Area Arts Council also produces annual drama productions.*

# Osceola, IOWA

*Terrible's Lakeside Casino Resort is among the more popular casinos in Iowa. The gaming operation also holds regular concerts, which has featured such recording artists as Sara Evans, Brad Paisley and Diamond Rio.*

Osceola also recognizes and celebrates the Latino Independence Festival in September. The event features Hispanic food, dancing and activities for children.

The Clarke County Conservation Board sponsors an annual Halloween Wild Walk at East Lake Park. Hundreds of people attend the wild walk which winds through a candlelit path in the timber of the park. Volunteers dress up in costume and hide behind trees along the walk to offer an occasional scare.

The Clarke Area Arts Council and The Village Early Childhood Center board co-sponsor the Festival of Wreaths in November. The event is held at Terrible's Lakeside Convention Center. Beautiful wreaths created by local designers are on display during a dinner and annual talent show.

The Osceola Chamber of Commerce and Osceola MainStreet co-sponsor the annual Holiday Brilliance event in December. The festivities include a visit from Santa Claus, lighting the holiday lights around the square and a lighted evening parade.

*Grade Lake is one of many fishing hot spots in Osceola. Near a residential area, Grade Lake is a popular attraction among the neighboring homeowners and area residents to cast a line.*

# Osceola IOWA

*2005 marked the second season youth summer ball teams played at the new Osceola Municipal Recreation Complex. There are six fields at the complex, which also has a trail leading from the diamonds to the Osceola Aquatic Center.*

## CITY ON THE MOVE

Through the year Terrible's Lakeside Casino Resort offers musical entertainment at its facility, located on West Lake. Musical stars such as Brad Paisley, Charlie Daniels, LoneStar, Sara Evans, Eddie Money and K.C. and the Sunshine Band have all performed at Lakeside since 2004.

Osceola is not a city that rests on its laurels - or sits still for that matter. MainStreet Renovation of business storefronts has revitalized the downtown square since 2000. The revitalized storefronts have been a welcomed change in Osceola.

The summer of 2005 sees several large construction projects under way in the city limits. That is common for Osceola, which has witnessed significant growth since the mid 1990s. The 2000 Census shows Clarke County recording the largest growth - more than 1,800 percent from 1990 to 2000 - in Hispanic population in Iowa. The new families moving to Osceola work at Osceola Foods, own businesses around the square and contribute to culture and Clarke Community School system.

Culture is something community leaders stress as a fundamental and important building block for Osceola's growth and prosperity. Many residents participate on a regular basis in cultural activities. They take part in community theater and musicals. Organizations such as the Clarke Area Arts Council promotes architectural studies for

*The Old Iron Club's Parade of Power gives people an opportunity to witness a piece of history as a plethora of antique tractors roll through the community.*

*The Fourth of July is a time many former residents return to Osceola to get caught up with friends and family members. The annual Fourth of July parade is one of the largest in southern Iowa.*

157

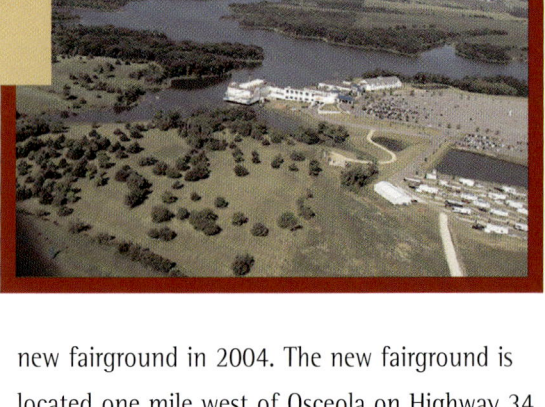

# Osceola, IOWA

students to learn about the city's history and how the community took shape in the early 1900s.

State leaders stress the importance of quality of life opportunities for a community. Osceola does not lack in opportunities. There is a plethora of activities available to residents, guests and newcomers looking to move to a community on the rise.

Civic leaders continue discussions about building a new fine arts and recreation building on the city's north side. Plans call for a facility to bring people who enjoy the arts under one roof to collaborate on artistic projects, take drawing and painting lessons as well as enjoy a swim in an indoor pool or get in shape at a proposed racquetball court.

The proposed facility would adjoin the new municipal recreation sports complex. The new facility boasts six youth ball fields, two soccer fields and a fitness trail. The trail connects the ball fields to the Osceola Aquatic Center, which was built in the 1990s. The aquatic center features an area to swim laps, a water slide and an area for youth to enjoy complete with umbrellas and sprinklers.

The Clarke County Fair Board completed the first phase of a construction project for a new fairground in 2004. The new fairground is located one mile west of Osceola on Highway 34. It features new barns and rodeo arena. With local contributions totaling more than $100,000 and grants being awarded, more construction is planned for the coming years.

A new winery is under construction and is expected to be completed in 2005. The state's

*Terrible's Lakeside Casino Resort is among the more popular casinos in Iowa.*
*The gaming operation also holds regular concerts, which has featured such recording artists as Sara Evans, Brad Paisley and Diamond Rio.*

*The city received nearly $500,000 in grants and contributions to restore the train depot, located near the downtown area.*

*The Clarke High School Marching Band is among the best in the area as it scores well each year in competitions.*

# Osceola IOWA

*The Harkin Barn was recently brought to life in a rendering by artist P. Buckley Moss.*

first winery cooperative is located in Osceola across Interstate 35 from Terrible's Lakeside Casino Resort. The Two Rivers Wine and Grape Cooperative will begin making wine and juice in 2005 and open as a tourist destination in late 2005 or early 2006.

Iowa grape industry is growing each year as renewed interest is spawning new vineyards throughout the state. Clarke County is part of that growth. The winery is expected to offer wine tastings and a gift shop as well as feature a variety of native Iowa wines.

The winery isn't the only operation testing new limits in Osceola. The Osceola Municipal Airport Commission continues to be a driving force in the community. The local airport is a constant work in progress as the commission continues to make improvements to Osceola's municipal airstrip, which has a 4,000-foot by 75-foot concrete runway, self-serve fueling with 100 ll and jet A fuels available, certified maintenance and pilot training and hanger space for 21 airplanes.

Tourism is a major economic force in the community. Some of the best wild turkey and white-tail deer hunting in the nation is found in Clarke County. Pheasants, quail, ducks, geese and other migratory birds are attracted to the area. Clarke County, much like many areas in southern Iowa, is a sportsman's paradise. Fishing at West Lake is considered one of the best bass and walleye destinations in Iowa. West Lake plays host to several Bass Masters Fishing tournaments each year.

*The Osceola Country Club is home to a challenging nine-hole golf course.*

# Osceola IOWA

### LEARN MORE

Osceola is located at the intersection of Highway 34 and Interstate 35.
Osceola is the Clarke County seat. The community is 35 miles south of West Des Moines and 146 miles north of Kansas City.

For more information, call the Osceola City Hall at (641) 342-2377.

### STORY CONTRIBUTORS

Sally and Frank Morlan, Sentinel-Tribune co-publishers

Chris Dorsey, Sentinel-Tribune news editor

Matt Pfiffner
Mickey Thomas
Mary Ellen Kimball

---

Osceola offers excellent education opportunities. Clarke Community School has approximately 1,400 students in kindergarten through 12th grade. Preschool and daycare are available at The Village, a non-profit community-based facility which opened in June 2002. Preschool is also available at Over The Rainbow preschool offered at Immanuel Lutheran Church. Higher and vocational education is available at Southwestern Community College, which has a center in Osceola.

Area farmers produce corn, soybeans and alfalfa. Cow and calf herds are raised on the beautiful rolling hills which surround Osceola. Thousands of hogs are also raised in Clarke County.

Also manufactured in Osceola are stainless steel tanks for dairy and wine industries, hunting accessories and luggage, roof trusses and pre-fabricated wall panels, screw machine products, trailers, drilling equipment and pallets. Osceola Foods produces many different product lines of ham and bacon for Hormel Foods.

None of this could be possible without the people of Osceola and Clarke County. They are volunteers, civic leaders, parents, business people, farmers, students, teachers, dedicated, hardworking employees - all of which are a spoke in a wheel that makes the community roll, progress and move toward a prosperous future.

*The Avenue of Flags at the Maple Hill Cemetery is a glorious sight during the Memorial Day holiday.*

*Pride In Our Hometowns.*

# P·O·R·T·R·A·I·T·S
## OF
# *Red Oak*

### A Shade Better

*This 6,000 population community takes its name and its theme from the beautiful "red oak" trees so prevalent in the area. Red Oak is located at the intersection of Highways 34 and 48 and is the county seat of Montgomery County. It's known for its historic old homes and proud, patriotic military heritage.*

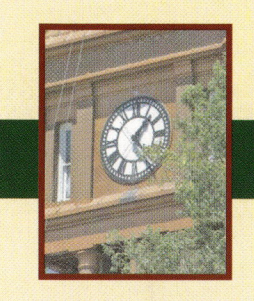

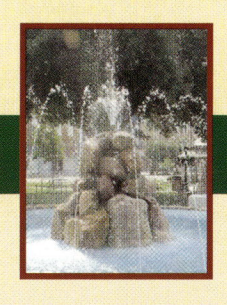

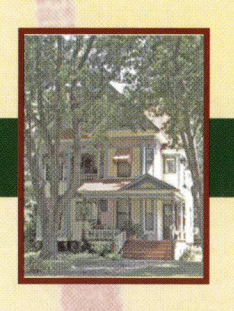

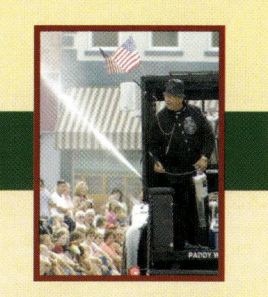

RED OAK

*Pride In Our Hometowns.*

# P·O·R·T·R·A·I·T·S
## OF
## Red Oak

## A Shade Better

*The clock tower of the Montgomery County Courthouse rises some 200 feet above the community.*

The sign on the window at the Chamber of Commerce office says, "Red Oak, A Shade Better," and that's exactly how residents of this southwest Iowa town view their home—a better place to live than most others. At a time when many small towns are shrinking into glorified housing developments that provide little more than a place to sleep for workers of the nearest city, this community continues to thrive. Located at the intersection of Highways 48 and 34 and shaded by the glorious "red oak" trees from which its name derives, the community is home to 6,000 residents.

### A Snapshot

Red Oak boasts many services unheard of in a town its size and offers a good variety and stable base of jobs. The community prides itself on its Victorian and military heritage and regularly celebrates the quality of life that keeps residents calling Red Oak—home.

Founded in 1876 as Red Oak Junction, the town grew up as many of that

Red Oak IOWA

era did, around the railroad. It became a Mecca of industrial and commercial trade with a cannery, flour mill, brick factory, meat packer, glove factory, buggy manufacturer and brewery among its earliest industries. The railroad offered easy access to Red Oak Junction for people, trade goods and building materials.

Red Oak pioneers Thomas Murphy and Edmund Osborne created the art calendar industry in 1890 when they produced a calendar which featured a woodcut illustration of the Montgomery County Courthouse (under construction at that time). Although Murphy and Osborne went their separate ways, the Thos. D. Murphy Company was born and continued as a staple of Red Oak industry for more than 100 years. Over the years it employed hundreds as sales agents, production and printing workers and office staff. Whole families and two and three generations earned their livelihoods at "Murphys," as it was known colloquially. The company developed a national and international reputation for utilizing fine art on its calendars. It also expanded into other advertising specialties and today the calendars still are prized by collectors. The

## "MURPHYS"

*Each Memorial Day, the Montgomery County Veterans Memorial Court of Honor recognizes and celebrates the lives of local veterans. More than 1,000 flags have been dedicated into the Court of Honor and all fly throughout Evergreen Cemetery on Memorial Day. Each year, more flags are dedicated into the court.*

*In addition to being a trademark of the Red Oak skyline, the bright orange water tower plays an integral part in the city's water system.*

# Red Oak IOWA

*The Montgomery County Fairgrounds shines brightly each July for the annual county fair.*

*Extreme Bull Riding comes to the Montgomery County Fair in Red Oak each July.*

massive red brick factory, with its trademark heavy wooden doors, is in the midst of an historic restoration and preservation project.

Red Oak Junction was a social hub as well as a commercial one. Early newspaper accounts describe huge crowds gathering in Red Oak for such historic events as Fourth of July spectaculars, Chautauqua programs, the laying of the cornerstone for the town's celebrated courthouse and races at the town's sporting track. Some of the best trotters and harness racers of the day started their careers in Red Oak. One in particular, Sweet Little Alix, was named to the Iowa Harness Hall of Fame in 2004. Alix Avenue in Red Oak is named after the celebrated filly. Chautauqua Pavilion, restored as the centerpiece to Chautauqua Park, is one of the few, if not the only, remaining "chautauquas" in Iowa. In Red Oak's early history it served as the location for revivals, musical programs and entertainment of all kinds. Today it offers a comfortable place for family reunions, church picnics and many other outdoor gatherings. Clear white lights adorn the pavilion at holiday time and a large star rests at the center peak of the roof. It is a spectacular and beautiful Christmas vision.

In 1901, Red Oak Junction became just, simply, Red Oak. The town continued to grow and prosper as the nation moved forward. During the war years, Red Oak and Montgomery County men marched into their country's service.

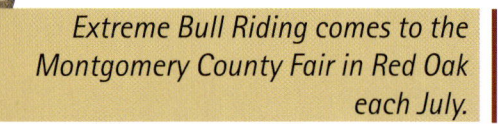

*The Montgomery County Family YMCA is located in Red Oak. It houses an indoor pool, weight room, walking/running track, gymnasium, plus indoor tennis and racketball courts.*

# Red Oak, IOWA

Company M, well-known in military histories for its heroism, was headquartered in Red Oak. During World War I, the company of 250 suffered 160 casualties—52 killed in action.

The men of Company M marched off again in World War II, once more to serve their country. You still find residents today who remember that fateful day in March 1943, when more than 100 telegrams arrived, alerting families to the fate of their loved ones, either missing or killed in action. In April, official reports confirmed that 27 members of Company M had been taken prisoner at Faid Pass.

Preserving and recognizing this proud military history is the objective for the Montgomery County Veterans Memorial Court of Honor, headquartered in Red Oak. Each Memorial Day, the court flies American flags in Evergreen Cemetery. The flags are dedicated in memory of deceased veterans. Today, more than 1,000 flags have been so dedicated. The Red Oak Depot, where many families gathered to either see off or welcome home their military loved ones, has been restored and transformed into a first-class World War II Museum. In December 2002, it was dedicated—on the 100th anniversary of the original dedication of the depot itself.

The community's military heritage and patriotic pride is evident throughout Red Oak. You'll find memorials to veterans of World War I, World War II, Korea and Vietnam in

## PATRIOTISM

*One of the more recent additions to the downtown square (Fountain Square Park) is the victorian style gazebo.*

*Red Oak celebrates every summer with Red Oak Junction Days, usually the last weekend of June. The Saturday morning parade is always a high point. Shrine parade units are a frequent and always welcome visitor.*

# Red Oak, IOWA

Red Oak's Fountain Square Park, located in the center of the downtown business district. The Memorial Fountain, originally built as a World War I memorial, was restored recently. It was rededicated in October, 2004. The Iowa National Guard continues its proud history with the location of the 1168th Transportation Company in Red Oak. The unit served in Operation Desert Storm in 1990-91 and, most recently, mobilized and served a year in Iraq as part of Operation Iraqi Freedom.

As the county seat of Montgomery County, Red Oak remains the hub of county commerce and activity. The town offers two

## Economy

grocery stores, five hardware/home/farm supply establishments, several small shops offering unique decorator and gift items, three pharmacies, four banks and a wealth of service professionals such a legal, insurance, beauty and real estate.

At the heart of the community's economic base rests agriculture. Corn, soybeans, cattle and hogs make up the farming economy. United Farmers Mercantile Cooperative operates grain elevators in Red Oak (as well as Stanton and Villisca) and recently expanded its grain storage and shipping facilities. Two sale barns provide outlets for livestock and when the Omaha, NE, livestock sale operations needed a new home, it chose Red Oak.

Nearly 2,000 jobs come from the Red Oak industrial base which includes such names as Parker Hannifin, RoMech, Traco, fres-co, Red Oak Die Casting, Minsa,

*Carriage rides through the holiday-lit downtown area are a highlight of the Red Oak Victorian Christmas celebration.*

# Red Oak IOWA

Communications Data Services and, the latest feather in the Red Oak industrial cap, Johnson Controls. Other major employers include the medical community surrounding Montgomery County Memorial Hospital, Red Oak Community Schools and Oakview Construction, which works throughout the United States and is headquartered in Red Oak.

Montgomery County Memorial Hospital, dating back to the 1920s, is firmly rooted in Red Oak's history. It has grown from the private Murphy Memorial Hospital in its infancy to a regional hospital complex, providing medical services for residents not only of Red Oak and Montgomery County, but many surrounding areas. MCMH built a new facility in 1989, added a Physicians Center in 1994 and recently completed an expansion to make MCMH a medical campus envied by many larger communities. MCMH offers more than 60 outpatient clinics, bringing specialists from larger urban hospitals and routinely provides state-of-the art diagnostic and rehabilitative services—all within the comfort of one's hometown.

From an educational standpoint, Red Oak takes a backseat to none. Community residents voted in a $10 million school bond issue in 1999. That provided the bulk of the money in a $12 million project to upgrade the district's facilities.

*Red Oak is noted for its fine Victorian homes, many of which are part of the Heritage Hill Tour.*

*Red Oak is dotted with many fine homes, renovated and restored to preserve their various architectural designs.*

# Red Oak IOWA

In late 2001 the district opened a new elementary school which houses grades kindergarten through third. The plan included renovations at the district's oldest and most historic building, the Red Oak Middle School (formerly the high school), renovations at the high school, an addition at Washington Intermediate (grades four and five) and provided support for a partnership program that resulted in a technology center adjoining the high school. College opportunities come through Southwestern Community College which operates a campus in Red Oak as well as a cooperative agreement with Buena Vista University. The tech center also provides opportunities for local industries to keep their workforce training up-to-date. Through a cooperative agreement with SWCC, Red Oak High School offers a hands-on building trades class. Support from the Red Oak Industrial Foundation allows the class to build a home each school year.

> Red Oak's victorian heritage is a big part of the community's identity. Recent efforts to maintain the beauty of that heritage include renovations to the downtown square. Victorian style street lights surround the square. Volunteers plant, water and maintain flowers on the square in the summer and the lights are adorned with Christmas decorations during the holiday season.

## RECREATION

Recreation plays a strong part in the quality of life Red Oak enjoys. The City of Red Oak operates six parks with everything from the standard children's playground equipment to horseshoe pits to a fitness and walking trail. The city swimming pool gives residents a place to cool off in the summer heat. In the last five years, many improvements have been made to the city's parks, including several new play structures with safety surfaces, more park benches, volleyball courts and a skate park. There's also plenty of space for family picnics and church gatherings. You'll also find tennis courts, baseball/softball diamonds and a soccer field.

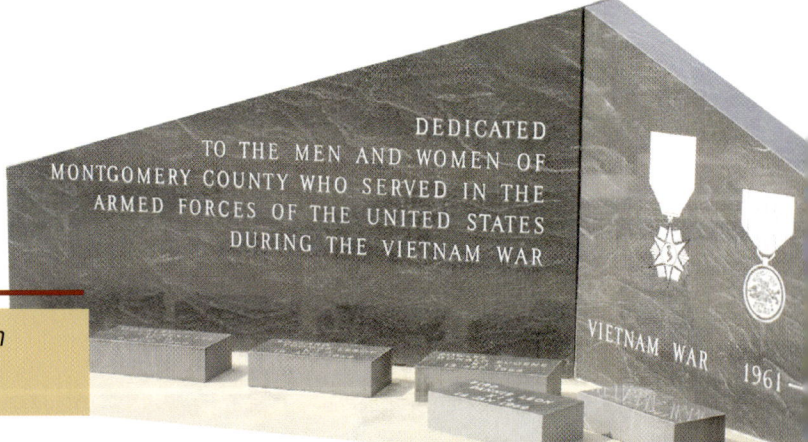

> The Vietnam War Memorial is located in Fountain Square Park.

DEDICATED TO THE MEN AND WOMEN OF MONTGOMERY COUNTY WHO SERVED IN THE ARMED FORCES OF THE UNITED STATES DURING THE VIETNAM WAR

VIETNAM WAR 1961

# Red Oak IOWA

*The Broadway Committee, a division of the Red Oak Coalition, is in the midst of a Broadway beautification project. Thanks to several Trees Forever grants, the volunteer committee, has established several "greenspace" areas along the city's main drag, Broadway.*

In 2000, the Montgomery County Family YMCA, 101 E. Cherry St., opened the doors on its facility. The massive building includes an indoor swimming pool, hot tub, weight room, walking track and gymnasium. An addition in 2001 gave area residents indoor tennis and racquetball courts. Through its core staff and countless volunteers, the YMCA operates nearly 100 youth sports and adult fitness programs. There's also an after school program. (Learn more at www.mcymca.com.)

The Red Oak Country Club offers fine dining, tennis, swimming and an 18-hole golf course.

What to do in a small town? Another reason Red Oak is "a shade better." The field is as broad as your interests and imagination. Your clearinghouse for information is the local Chamber of Commerce office, 307 E Reed St, 712-623-4821, www.redoakiowa.com.

If you like historical architecture, Red Oak will be a treat.

The Heritage Hill Tour is a self-guided driving or walking tour of several of the community's historical homes (no interior access since they are private homes). You can enjoy such architectural styles as Queen Anne, Georgian, English Tudor, Colonial Revival and Italianate. The homes on the tour were built between 1870 and 1916. Brochures are available at the chamber office.

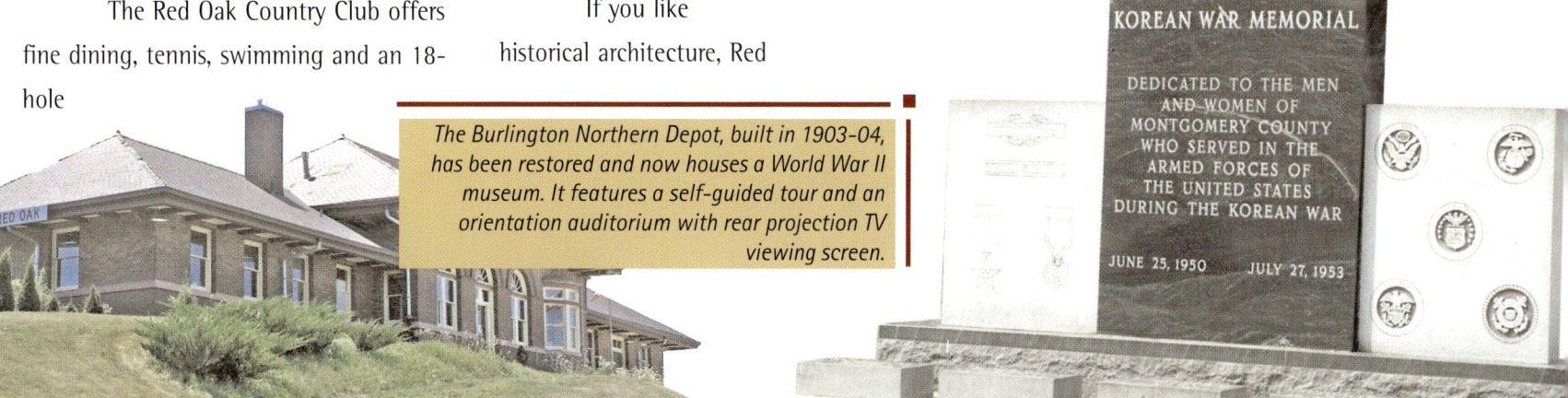

*The Korean War Memorial is located in Fountain Square Park.*

*The Burlington Northern Depot, built in 1903-04, has been restored and now houses a World War II museum. It features a self-guided tour and an orientation auditorium with rear projection TV viewing screen.*

# Red Oak IOWA

*The Montgomery County Courthouse, built in 1890, is listed on the National Historic Register. It rises nearly 200 feet into the air and continues to serve as the focus point for local government.*

Buildings in Red Oak that are listed on the National Historic Register include the Montgomery County Courthouse, Montgomery County Jail, Chautauqua Pavilion, Red Oak Library, the Osborne House and the Colonel Hebard House.

The Montgomery County History Center is a combined museum, educational and research facility. The Montgomery County Historical Society is in the midst of a fund-drive to build a new, larger museum building and once you visit the current museum, you'll see why. It's bursting at the seams with displays, historical records and artifacts. But the History Center is much more than just a museum. On the grounds you'll find the restored Nims Barn, its accompanying corn crib and the Stipe Log Cabin. A one-room schoolhouse, Pittsburg School, is located a few blocks south at the Montgomery County Fairgrounds. The History Center, 2700 N Fourth St., is open from 1-5 p.m. Tuesday through Sunday. For special tours or additional

## LANDMARKS

information call 712-623-2289.

The Burlington Northern Depot, 305 S. Second St., houses a unique World War II museum. There is a self-guided tour, research material and a variety of exhibits and artifacts, always changing as families donate new items to be preserved. Hours of operation are 9 a.m.-noon Monday, Wednesday and Friday and 9 a.m.-2 p.m. Tuesday and Thursday. For special appointments or tours, call 712-623-6340. The depot was donated to the Save Our Depot committee by Burlington Northern. Private donations and grants paid for the extensive renovation. A core of volunteers maintain the museum.

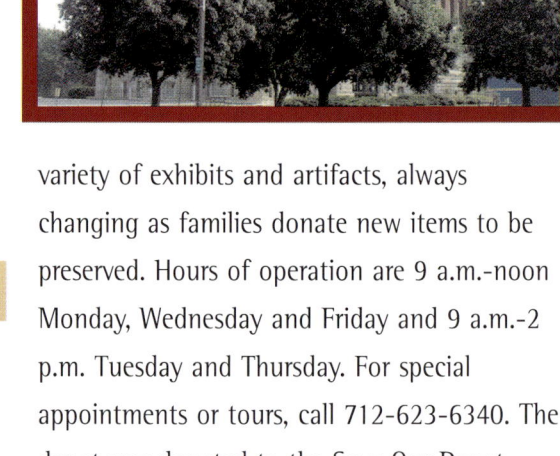

*The memorial fountain located in Fountain Square Park originally was dedicated in honor and memory of the Rainbow Division which served during World War I. The years took their toll on the fountain, however. A fund drive led to the restoration of the fountain which was rededicated in September 2004.*

170

# Red Oak IOWA

Fountain Square Park is a central location for many Red Oak activities. During the growing and harvest season, it hosts an active Red Oak Farmers Market (Thursdays from 5-7 p.m. and Saturdays from 9 a.m.-noon). Every Thursday evening during August the Red Oak Chamber of Commerce sponsors entertainment in the park. The third weekend of August the park is transformed into a parking lot—for hundreds of classic cars and trucks. The Classy Chassis Car Club sponsors the car show each year and it routinely draws some of the best classics in four states. If you prefer a different mode of transportation, don't miss the Red Oak Flight Breakfast, a project of the Red Oak Chamber of Commerce Ambassadors. It's usually the first weekend of June. Red Oak's airport, R.K. Belt Field, hosts up to 300 light aircraft.

## BIG EVENTS

Parking is available at the nearby CDS plant with shuttle service to the airport so visitors can participate in the activities and check out all the planes.

In late June (usually the last weekend), Red Oak celebrates its heritage in style with Red Oak Junction Days. The festival, begun as a celebration of the railroad heritage, is in its third decade and includes activities for all ages. The mid-morning parade gets the ball rolling and kids games, bingo and a variety of events fill the afternoon and evening.

In July, the Montgomery County Fairgrounds, 2400 N. Fourth St., takes center stage with the Montgomery County Fair. In the true tradition of county fairs, you'll find livestock shows, a carnival, bull-riding, antique tractor pull and a demolition derby. Plan to

*William Stipe was one of Montgomery County's earliest settlers. This cabin, built by him, has been moved, restored and is located on the grounds of The History Center. Tours are available by appointment. Inquire at The History Center.*

*The demolition derby is a mainstay of the Montgomery County Fair each July.*

171

# Red Oak Iowa

## Learn More

Red Oak is located at the intersection of Highways 34 and 48.

For more information, contact the Red Oak Chamber of Commerce, 712-623-4821; www.redoakiowa.com.

## Story Contributor

Jan Castle Renander is the publisher of The Red Oak Express.

---

spend several days. You'll find plenty to do.

Other annual events include Mayfest, organized around Cinco de Mayo and sponsored by the Touchstone Arts Council. Red Oak Victorian Christmas is the Friday after Thanksgiving and marks the official start of the Christmas season in Red Oak. Santa arrives in a horse-drawn sleigh and Victorian carolers stroll the downtown area.

The Red Oak community keeps going forward thanks to the efforts of many civic organizations and volunteers. A Broadway beautification plan has spruced up the community's "main drag" with trees, shrubs, flowers and new sidewalks. Civic groups such as the Red Oak Rotary, Kiwanis, Lions, Optimist, BPW, Elks and Eagles lodges provide social and civic involvement. The Red Oak community is served by churches of several denominations. Several local organizations are interested in keeping the downtown business district alive and you'll find that many have undergone facelifts thanks to those efforts. Red Oak also has been selected as the building site for the Wilson Arts Center, a regional center for the performing arts. Spearheading this effort is the Performing Arts & Educational Association of Southwest Iowa. The PAEA serves nine counties in the southwest Iowa area.

"A Shade Better"—that's what the window at the chamber office says. And Red Oak, definitely, fits that bill. The community is alive with activity throughout the year and residents know why they stay—because it just doesn't get any better than this.

*The World War II Memorial is located in Fountain Square Park.*

*Pride In Our Hometowns.*

# P·O·R·T·R·A·I·T·S
## OF
# *Sheldon*

## BORN OF THE RAILROAD

*Although by many standards, Sheldon is a small town, it's a place where life is never at a standstill. Thousands of semitrucks pass through town each week on U.S. Highways 18 and 60, some stopping to pick up farm products or manufactured goods at one of the city's booming industries.*

*Dozens of trains rumble through town on the Chicago and Northwestern Railroad. The city is a shopping hub and a medical center for a six-county region, a destination for students at Northwest Iowa Community College.*

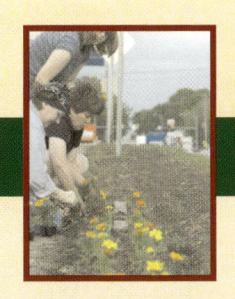

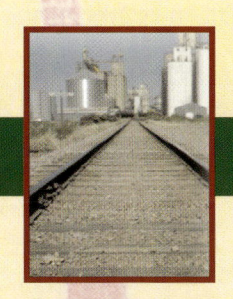

SHELDON

*Pride In Our Hometowns.*

# P·O·R·T·R·A·I·T·S
## OF *Sheldon*

### BORN OF THE RAILROAD

*Sheldon is the largest town in O'Brien county with a population of roughly 5,000. It has an agricultural and manufacturing based economy.*

It's hard to believe that less than 150 years ago this was a lonely spot on the Northern Tallgrass Prairie, ignored by settlers frightened of the frequent skirmishes in the area between the Sioux and Sac and Fox Indians. In fact, until the 1880s, much of the region was sitting on a zone established by the U.S. government to separate the two warring tribes. Only the arrival of the railroad and the promotional work of land developers led to the rapid settlement of the region in the last 125 years.

### A SNAPSHOT

Although the railroad stretched across most of Iowa by the 1860s, work was interrupted by the Civil War and so the handful of settlers in northwest Iowa had to wait for train service until the early 1870s. As workers laid track in the area in 1871, surveyors began platting a town near the Floyd River. It was named for Israel Sheldon, an east coast railroad investor.

*The vision statement by the 2011 Visionary Committee is "Sheldon will become a progressive and dynamic community by causing growth of population, jobs, incomes, opportunities and quality of life throughout the region."*

The first building in town was a saloon, and after a suitable depot was built

174

# Sheldon IOWA

along the track, a second tavern was constructed. But the hardworking northern Europeans who settled the area had commerce in mind and soon a lumberyard, hardware store, and newspaper office were in operation. Houses began to spring up and the town quickly grew.

The first community festival, an Independence Day celebration, was held on July 3, 1872. (History doesn't tell us why the Fourth of July was celebrated a day early.) The event was held on a patch of grass called "City Park" and public green space has been important here ever since.

Sheldon developed a reputation as an industrial center early in its history, with the construction of a giant mill that ground grain into feed and flour. The Prairie Queen brand became famous around the United States and gave Sheldon one of its most popular monikers: Prairie Queen City. Reminders of Sheldon's roots remain today in the names of such organizations as Prairie Queen Kiwanis, Prairie Arts Council, Sheldon Prairie Museum and Prairie Queen Bakery.

The community's largest employers include: Rosenboom Machine & Tool, which manufactures hydraulic cylinders; Van Wyk Inc., which operates a fleet of refrigerated trucks; Maintainer Corporation of Iowa, the maker of service truck bodies; Ag Processing

*The city of Sheldon supplies water from a natural well with an elevated storage capacity of 500,000 gallons.*

*The downtown area of Sheldon offers many services such as lawyers, a bakery, and clothing stores.*

## INDUSTRIAL HUB

175

# Sheldon IOWA

Inc., a soybean processing plant; Northwest Iowa Health Center, a hospital and doctors clinic; White Wolf Web, a printing company; Iowa Information, publisher of newspapers and magazines; Tanks Ltd., a plastics fabricator; and Rome Ltd., makers of meatpacking equipment.

*The Highway 60 expressway project has provided challenges and opportunities for the city of Sheldon.*

One of the city's largest employers is Village Northwest Unlimited, a non-profit center where 180 individuals with disabilities, including mental retardation, brain injury, cerebral palsy and autism, receive an array of services and training. Founded in 1974, the Village was constructed with local donations and includes five homes where eight to 12 clients are taught basic living skills in a loving, home-like atmosphere and a large campus.

The Village also offers semi-supervised, rent-subsidized apartment living in the community. Clients at these facilities receive supervision and support from staff members, but also enjoy the challenges and independency of living on their own. The community homes provide drop-in supervision for individuals capable living in a typical neighborhood. A separate program provides opportunities for up to three to four individuals to live in a house in the community with up to 18 hours of staff support daily.

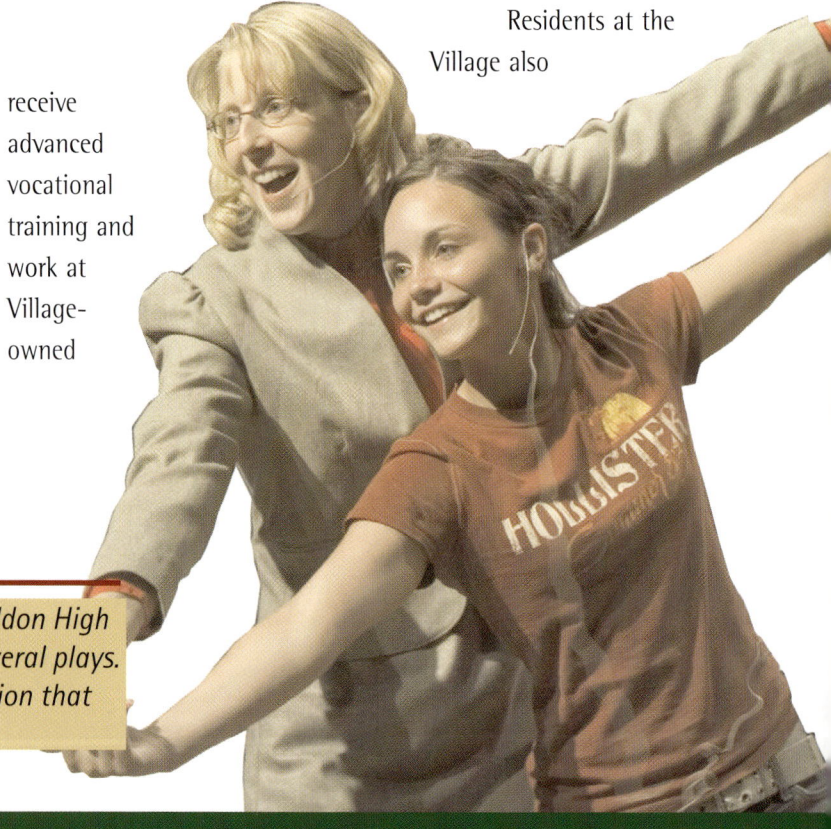

Residents at the Village also receive advanced vocational training and work at Village-owned

*During the summer months, the Sheldon High School Summer Theatre presents several plays. The troupe is one of a few in the nation that performs in the summer.*

## Sheldon IOWA

enterprises or at one of many participating privately owned businesses. It's a common site to see Village clients working throughout the city, cooking burgers at fast food restaurants, performing custodial duties at a local grocery store, helping with grounds keeping, or helping deliver appliances.

Some clients work at the local recycling center where they sort beverage containers or in the mailroom at the local newspaper, helping to count and bundle newspapers. It's a win-win-win situation for the community: the Village is one of Sheldon's biggest employers, with a staff of more than 300. The Village residents fill a hole in the workforce. And citizens get to interact with ambitious, inspiring people who are overcoming challenges to become a more active part of the community.

In addition, the Village has been a catalyst for community improvement. Administrators of the Village greenhouse program – which provides residents with jobs while growing flowers and vegetables for local customers – helped create the "Miles of Marigolds" project in the community. Each spring, scores of volunteers fan out across Sheldon planting the flowers and then caring for them throughout the summer.

The Village was founded under the guidance of Bob Hoogeveen, a former high school principal who conceived of the idea to start the residential facility, initiated many of the programs, and became a vocal advocate for the disabled until his retirement.

*The Sheldon Prairie Museum holds many items from Sheldon's past. It also houses the Sheldon Hall of Fame which includes Olympic wrestlers Tom and Terry Brands.*

*Celebration Days brings spectators to Sheldon from all over northwest Iowa during the Labor Day weekend.*

# Sheldon IOWA

But Hoogeveen will tell you the support of the community – both in Sheldon and across the region – has been instrumental in making the non-profit a success. People just seem to know how to get things done in Sheldon, whether it be raising money for a facility for the disabled, hosting 10,000 bicyclists during RAGBRAI, building a new playground, or rallying behind a sick neighbor or friend.

Pulling together for the good of the community is a trait that has served the community well. Like most small towns, Sheldon has faced unprecedented challenges that could have slowed it's growth, or even ruins it.

## DOWNTOWN

One example is the major fire in 1888 that destroyed most of the original wooden buildings in downtown Sheldon. The fire helped shore up financial support for the local volunteer fire department – still a source of pride in the community – and led to the construction of a series of handsome brick buildings that still make up a core of the businesses in the main street area.

Today, the downtown continues to offer a wide variety of services still housed in the historic brick buildings including a variety of gift shops, clothing stores, flower shops, restaurants, a bakery, banks, and professional offices.

Downtown continues to evolve, with the recent construction of a new three-screen movie theater to replace one destroyed by fire, the

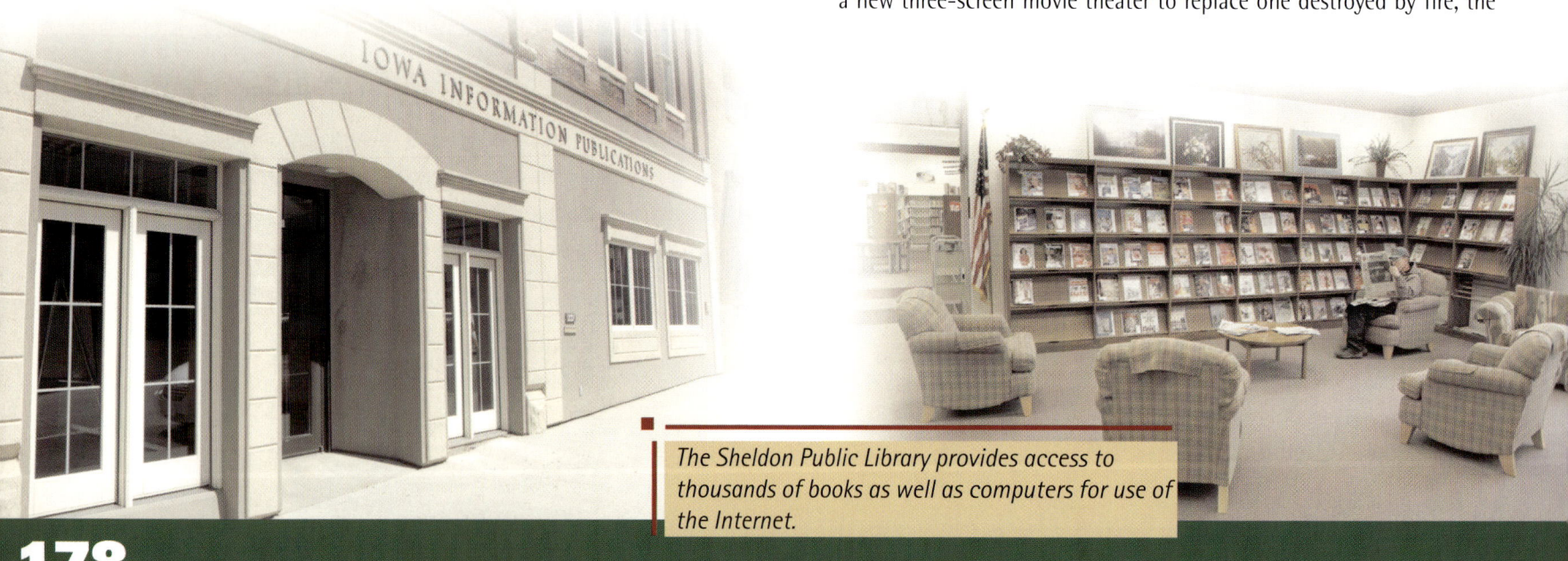

*Iowa Information Publications is the parent company of the local Sheldon newspaper, The Sheldon Mail-Sun. They also publish Okoboji Magazine, DISCOVER! Magazine, and the N'West Iowa REVIEW. The REVIEW is the nation's most award winning non-daily newspaper.*

*The Sheldon Public Library provides access to thousands of books as well as computers for use of the Internet.*

# Sheldon IOWA

development of an office plaza and furniture store, along with other buildings.

Perhaps Sheldon's most-intriguing chapter in history involves the story of Burnice Geiger. Daughter of the president of the Sheldon National Bank, Burnice could always be counted on to help a needy family or befriend a deserving cause. It seemed as if half the folks in Sheldon could have testified to her generosity. They did not, in fact, when Burnice admitted in 1961 that during the more than 40 years that she had served as the bookkeeper in her father's bank she had embezzled $2,126,859.10 of their funds—more than John Dillinger, Pretty Boy Floyd, or Ma Barker stole during their entire career.

Some of the money was used to build her beautiful house on Ninth Street. But she also contributed thousands of dollars to her church to install a slick organ and beautiful stained glass windows. Geiger served her time and then returned to the area, working in near anonymity as a receptionist in a dentist's office in Sanborn.

At the time, the embezzlement was the biggest in U.S. history and prompted federal officials to introduce a whole new set of banking guidelines that are still in effect to protect your money today. The crime, and the subsequent closing of the bank, was a shock; some people still don't like to talk about it 50 years later. But the vibrant downtown and its array of industry are testament to the community's ability to pull itself up by the bootstraps.

Folks in Sheldon have long pointed to the business community as a source of pride, an example of the strength of the people here. But a strong business community and a sense of

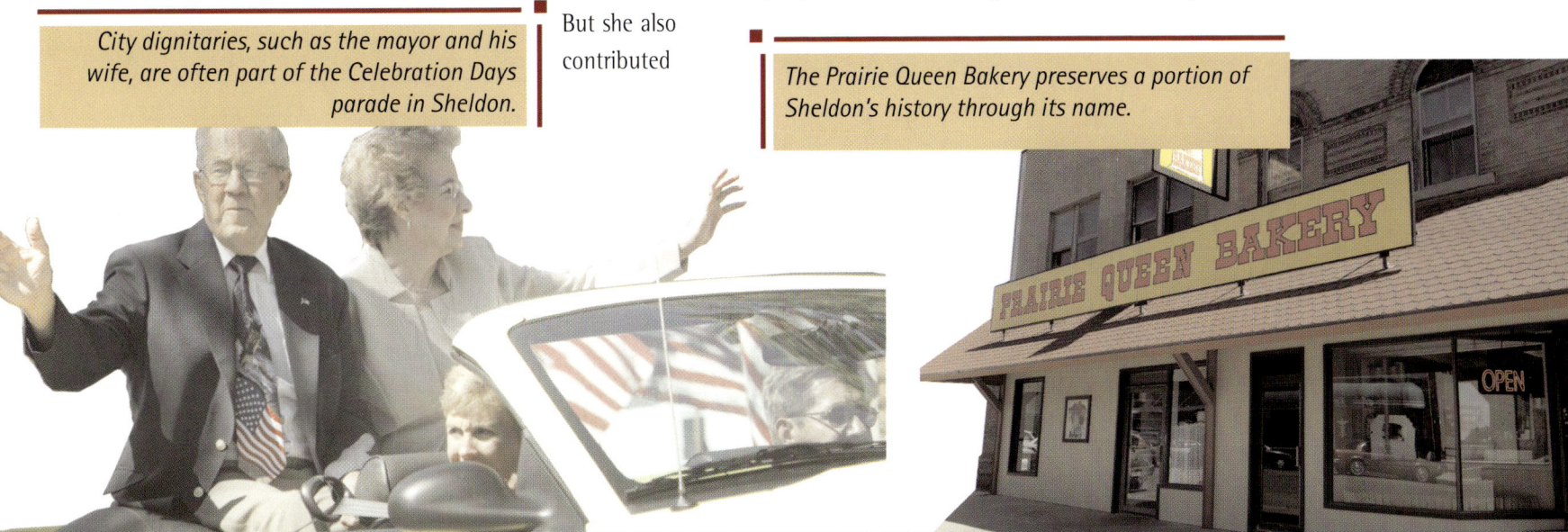

## BIG EMBEZZLEMENT

*City dignitaries, such as the mayor and his wife, are often part of the Celebration Days parade in Sheldon.*

*The Prairie Queen Bakery preserves a portion of Sheldon's history through its name.*

# Sheldon, Iowa

entrepreneurial spirit are just two of the factors that make the community a good place to live. Ask people to point to other sources of pride and you'll be surprised at the variety of their answers:

- Sheldon's fine school system includes a modern high school building, a new middle school, which opened in the fall of 2004, and East Elementary. A community daycare, Children's World, offers child care and preschool classes as well as after-school programs. Noah's Ark Preschool provides faith based preschool classes for the community. Sheldon also is home to Northwest Iowa Community College. The school, located just east of Sheldon, offers both two-year liberal arts and vocational education classes and is home to unusual courses including programs offering training for powerline workers and heavy equipment operators. Two parochial schools – St. Patrick's Catholic School and Sheldon Christian School – offer faith-based classes for kindergarten through eighth grade.

- Sheldon area churches include all major denominations including a Roman Catholic parish, four Calvinist-based Reformed churches, and Baptist, Lutheran, Assembly of God, and Methodist congregations.

- The communication needs of the community are served by KIWA, an AM-FM radio station whose signal reaches a three-state area. Iowa Information Inc., publishes two award-winning newspapers. The Sheldon Mail-Sun, the city's oldest business, covers local happenings. The N'West Iowa REVIEW covers a five-county area and has been named the best mid-sized weekly in the United States for 10 consecutive years. Since 1982, The REVIEW has been named Iowa's Newspaper of the Year 16 times by the Iowa Newspaper Association.

- Northwest Iowa Health Center is a full-service

*The railroad has always been important to Sheldon's economy. Although it no longer carries passengers through town, it is a major means of transportation for grain.*

*The new Sheldon Middle School was completed for the 2004-2005 school year. It is conveniently located adjacent to the Sheldon High School on the east side of town.*

# Sheldon IOWA

*Each year around the Fourth of July, Village Northwest Unlimited celebrates with fireworks and entertainment.*

hospital and senior living facility offering a variety of care options including obstetric and surgical care, occupational health, wellness, home health and hospice. The hospital was built in 1952, consolidating health-care services scattered in buildings throughout Sheldon.

Today, the modern facility includes a 70-bed skilled nursing facility with a 12-bed dementia unit. In 2005, hospital officials dedicated a newly renovated wing that includes inpatient facilities, obstetrics and several patient support areas. Northwest Iowa Health Center is affiliated with Sioux Valley Hospitals and Health Systems based in Sioux Falls, S.D.

In addition to the hospital's senior care center, nursing home services are offered by the Christian Retirement Home. Sheldon also has four dentists, three chiropractors and three eye-care clinics.

• Sheldon is home to the renowned Prairie Museum, housed in the former Carnegie Library at 10th Street and Fourth Avenue. The museum houses the local hall of fame as well as a variety of exhibits chronicling school life, the city's military history, the volunteer fire department, early day industry and prairie life.

• The Sheldon Public Library houses more than 30,000 books and 120 periodicals. There also is a supply of videos, books on tape, cassettes, art prints, pamphlets and telephone directories. The library is a member of the northwest Regional Library System and the State Library.

*Rosenboom Machine & Tool is one of the largest employers in Sheldon's industrial sector. Sheldon became known as an industrial hub early in it's history.*

181

# Sheldon
## IOWA

*Northwest Iowa Community College provides educational opportunities in areas ranging from nursing to heavy equipment.*

- Sheldon is home to at least three Olympic athletes. Twins Tom and Terry Brands, who both captured state wrestling titles at Sheldon High School, went on to wrestle at the University of Iowa and represent the United States in the Olympics. Tom Brands won the gold medal in 1996 and Terry won the bronze in 2000. And A.J. Kruger is one of the world's premiere track and field athletes, competing in the hammer throw at the most recent Olympic games and expected to make a bid for a spot again in 2008.

The people of Sheldon work hard, but they also enjoy their free time. The Chamber of Commerce hosts a variety of events during the year including a free hot dog feed, a Christmas lighting contest and other events. But people here mark their calendars for two particularly special events.

Celebration Days is a weekend event at the end of summer that includes a Labor Day parade, flight breakfast, arts festival, food stands, free entertainment, and other events. It replaces Soybean Days, an event that honored the soybean processing operation here that employs dozens of people and provides a market for area farmers.

Soybean Days was a victim of the Farm Crisis, when time constraints and money problems dampened the mood to celebrate agriculture and made it difficult to find enough volunteers to run a full-blown celebration. But it didn't take long until residents realized the importance of having a chance to kick back and enjoy spending time with their neighbors. Celebration Days has been a big draw across the three-state area.

The other event that people look forward to is the Independence Day Celebration

*Although the old Sheldon Depot no longer plays host to trains, it is used by the local Farmer's Market during part of the year.*

182

# Sheldon IOWA

hosted by Village Northwest each year as a sort of thank you for the support of the region. The night's main attraction is a lavish fireworks display, but it's preceded by a variety of family activities: a petting zoo, fire truck and carriage rides, carnival games, and plenty of food.

That's not to say there's not plenty to do in Sheldon year round. Besides the new movie theater in the business district, the community has a large variety of restaurants and nightspots. The Rec Bowl, the local bowling alley, is a modern facility that hosts leagues and open bowling and houses an excellent restaurant and lounge, popular with the younger crowds. The Fin 'n' Feather is known for its broasted chicken and two drive-ins – A&W and the Dairy Dandy – offer lighter fare and food for people on the go. Other popular restaurants include the Family Table and Kinbrae South, an excellent steakhouse. The community also offers a full complement of fast food, a good Chinese restaurant, and a variety of cafes, pizza restaurants and other establishments.

But man cannot live on bread alone, and there's also plenty of cultural activities to stir the soul.

Sheldon High School Summer Theatre, the only high school repertory in Iowa and one of just a few in the nation presents a different play for each week for most of June and July. Each summer, the program involves more than 50 students who handle all aspects of theatre production from promotion, to selling tickets, to acting, to constructing sets. A

*Every year, Sheldon citizens volunteer their time to plant marigolds along Highways 60 and 18, earning Sheldon the nickname "The Marigold City".*

*Northwest Iowa Health Center provides hospital as well as clinic services to Sheldon and the surrounding area. The hospital recently completed a large addition that includes a new obstetrics wing.*

# Sheldon
## IOWA

### LEARN MORE

Sheldon is located in the northwest corner of Iowa at the junction of U.S. Highway 18 and Iowa Highway 60.

For information contact the Sheldon city offices at (712) 324-4766.

### STORY CONTRIBUTOR

Jay Wagner is editor-at-large for The N'West Iowa REVIEW.

He is an author and freelance writer whose work has appeared in magazines and newspapers around the world, including Newsweek, The New York Times, The Boston Globe and USA Today.

---

community theatre production is presented every other year in June.

The Sheldon Civic Music Association presents four to five concerts by nationally and internationally acclaimed musicians and singers each season for the price of an annual membership.

Wansink Galleries, Sheldon's art gallery located on East Highway 18 displays the work of area and regional artists and collectors. At this location are three restored one-room country schools and the home of Dan McKay, which was used for church services and as a hotel and rooming house in Sheldon's early years.

Just as the railroad opened up the region for settlement in the late 1800s, local leaders are confident that a long-sought-after widening of U.S. Highway 60 will have a positive effect on the local economy in the next century. Highway 60, a popular route that provides a link from Omaha to the Twin Cities, will be completed in 2007. The four-lane highway will skirt past the east edge of the city and government leaders have already platted a commercial and industrial area near the road for businesses wanting to take advantage of the traffic. Already, about a dozen businesses have announced plans or expressed interest in locating near the bypass, including car dealers, restaurants and a new truck stop.

### THE FUTURE

The community offers a variety of economic incentives for businesses looking to locate in Sheldon including tax abatements, low-interest loans and money to train employees.

City leaders are confident that the next big growth spurt will occur on the east side of town. They have planned carefully for the strategic growth. But they also know that there are things that will happen during the next generation that they can't plan for. But they also know they have at their beck and call a community of proud citizens eager to face the next challenge head on, the way they have been doing it in Sheldon for more than 130 years.

*Sitting at the intersection of Highways 60 and Sheldon is at a crossroads, both figuratively and literally.*

*Pride In Our Hometowns.*

# P·O·R·T·R·A·I·T·S
## OF
## *Small Town Iowa*
### Avoca • Oakland • Treynor

### The Spirit Of Small Town Iowa

*In our constantly changing world, many of Iowa's smaller communities face extremely challenging problems in ensuring their future, with each having to address the issue of survival in its own unique way. These three communities have each approached the challenge differently and, in doing so, has found success.*

AVOCA-OAKLAND-TREYNOR

*Pride In Our Hometowns.*

# P·O·R·T·R·A·I·T·S
## OF
## Small Town Iowa
### Avoca • Oakland • Treynor

## The Spirit Of Small Town Iowa

While it is easy to focus on Iowa's larger cities as hubs of commerce, education, history and entertainment, it remains the smaller communities that provide the real flavor of what remains a predominately agricultural state.

Like their larger counterparts, Iowa's smaller cities are rich in history, provide many entertainment options for their residents as well as the families that live around these cities and strive to provide the best possible education for the children who live in and around them.

And like their larger counterparts, they struggle to create a niche that will assure their future. Because they are small, with fewer resources available, they are forced to be creative in paving the way for future generations. What they lack in resources, they are forced to make up through community pride – a community-wide spirit of volunteerism ... residents pulling together to address a common cause or need ... that is far less frequently found in larger cities.

### A Snapshot

Although small, these cities take great pride in the quality of life they offer their residents – the fact that residents know and care about one another. What they may lack in "amenities," they strive to make up for in "neighborliness."

Three such cities, Avoca, Oakland and Treynor, all located in the southwest quarter of the state, epitomize the spirit of small-town Iowa. All face similar

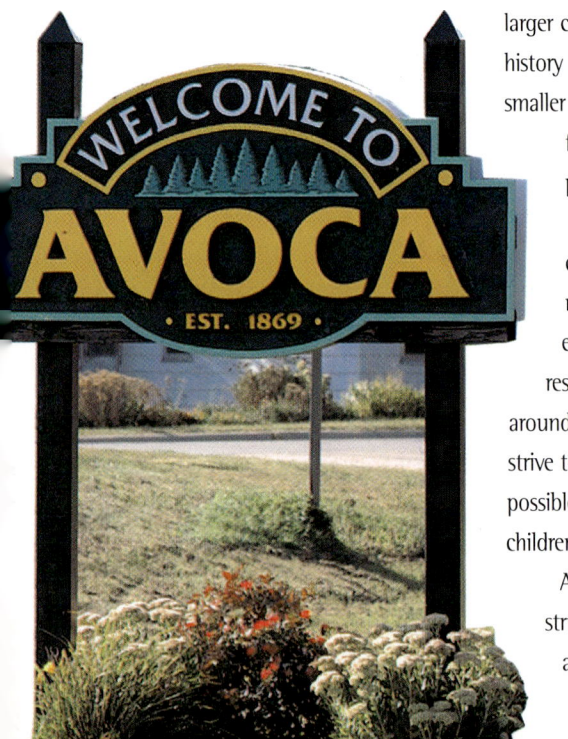

*Beautiful downtown Avoca has thriving businesses a very inviting atmosphere for both residents and visitors alike.*

# Avoca

*A shot of old-time Avoca's downtown Elm Street.*

problems in ensuring their future vitality. All have taken somewhat different approaches in meeting those challenges. And all have been successful in their own way.

## AVOCA

A connection to a major transportation system designed to move people and material swiftly across the country has been a key feature throughout Avoca's history. The original town plat was laid out in 1869 when the Rock Island Railroad reached a spot nestled in the Botna Valley of northeast Pottawattamie County.

As tracks were laid and a station of the Rock Island was established, trains began bringing individuals and families to the location. Some stayed briefly on their way to other destinations, but many initial visitors decided to remain.

First called Pacific, it later became Botna.

In late 1869, a group of individuals traveled to the area as part of an excursion organized by the railroad company. Upon viewing the scenic region, one of the women of the party, apparently inspired by what she saw as she gazed from a hill overlooking the town in the valley before her, recalled a poem by Tom Moore, in which he rhapsodized about the "Sweet vale of Avoca . . . how calm could I rest/In thy bosom of shade with friends I love best . . ."

It was agreed that "Avoca" captured the essence of the town, and would be the optimal choice for its permanent name.

Even now, Avoca maintains a link to a national transportation network - an interstate highway that spans the breadth of the country. Cars and trucks carrying people and goods on Interstate 80 are now only an off-ramp away from the entrance to the city.

"We're on both sides of the interstate now," said Avoca Mayor Marvin Piittmann. "We've expanded enough so that travelers can get a lot of what they need by stopping here."

A large Wings of America center is at the interchange, offering fuel, food and amenities to drivers. Also at the location is a new Motel 6. City officials hope that the existence of the interstate link can be utilized as an incentive for luring new businesses and industries to this community of 1,610.

But Avoca retains a

*Mckenzie Moore, 6, rides the slide during the Pottawattamie County Fair in Avoca. Ben DeVries/Daily Nonpareil*

# Avoca, Iowa

healthy downtown business district, featuring a number of retail shops and numerous service providers. Also located downtown is the East Pottawattamie County Courthouse, built in 1877. In that era, a trip of any distance was a time-consuming endeavor, and for residents of the eastern section of the county who needed to take care of legal matters, a journey to the courthouse in Council Bluffs posed an inconvenience, if not an actual hardship. So the decision was made to construct a separate building in Avoca.

The courthouse remains a part of the state's judicial system. It houses offices for the county sheriff, a magistrate judge, public health nurses and personnel from the Loess Hills Area Education Agency. The building has been remodeled, and efforts are ongoing to raise money for its maintenance and for any other restoration that may be required. The initial project, which began in late 1995 and was completed in 1998, was intended to "bring the appearance and condition of the building back to the original," said Norma Pierce, who was involved in the work.

She said she believed local residents appreciated the results of the project, since the building, which is on the National Register of Historic Places, "has been such a vital part of the community for so long."

Volunteer work is also under way to catalog and index dozens of old documents, including records of probate proceedings and land transfers, stored in the basement of the courthouse. Additional artifacts and material related to the community's past can be found at the Sweet Vale of Avoca Museum a few blocks north of the courthouse.

Information of a general nature is available at the Avoca Public Library, situated right next to the courthouse.

The facility has about 22,000 volumes and contains books popular with readers of all ages. Sherry Jacobsen, library director, said the facility offers special programs for children, and seeks to "help them enrich their experiences through reading."

*The Avoca Bakery and Cafeteria was common grounds for many residents and people in the area.*

Jacobsen said officials are evaluating the technology required to put the library's catalog online.

Technology is a notable component of one of the community's industries.

Ci Direct, founded in 1997, provides licensed agent sales and customer support for the insurance industry and financial services market. It employs almost 100 people who service major national insurance accounts.

Personnel provide expertise to design and manage communications programs for the financial services market, and the firm offers multi-channel technology to keep information and data accurate and flowing in any method the customer chooses – voice, Web or fax.

When the company expanded into Avoca in late 2001, president Mary Bro noted, the availability of local workers to perform high-tech work was

*Bryce Carroll (right), 4, and his twin brother Brandon swirl around on one of the rides at the East Pottawattamie County Fair in Avoca.*
*Ben DeVries/Daily Nonpareil*

# Avoca-Oakland

essential to opening the new facility

Bro said the addition of other insurance carriers to the client list could allow Ci Direct to expand further, creating new openings at the Avoca site, which has room for 40 more workstations.

Attracting more jobs to the community is a goal that city officials are always trying to achieve, Piittmann said.

In other areas of concern to local residents, projects were implemented in recent years to address utility, health care and recreation needs.

Under an arrangement with Regional Water Inc., the community acquired a reliable, long-term source of water.

When city officials learned that Regional Water was planning to install a new treatment facility just a few miles from the existing Avoca plant, a decision was made to form a partnership with the private company.

In late 2002, the U.S. Department of Agriculture's Rural Development Administration authorized more than $5.8 million in grants and loans for the new treatment plant and for necessary well fields.

Using Regional Water as a source, Avoca maintained its own distribution system, so the transition was basically seamless for local residents.

On the health care front, an assisted living facility, Avoca Lodge, was built, opening in early 2002 with room for 20 individuals. The facility joined an existing 46-bed nursing home, the Avoca Nursing and Rehabilitation Center.

With both facilities in operation, Piittmann said, the community can accommodate individuals who require various levels of supervision and care. Health care services for local and area residents are also available at the Avoca Physicians Clinic.

Avoca's need for upgraded recreational opportunities was met with the construction of a new aquatic center at the city park. After a two-year period of fund raising, the new pool opened in the summer of 2002.

## Avoca Growth

Recreational options in the community also include the Avoca Golf Course, which features a nine-hole layout and watered fairways.

For music enthusiasts, the attraction is the Avoca Country Music Jamboree, during which artists display their talents to crowds that gather from throughout the country.

The Pottawattamie County Fair, which has been a tradition in Avoca since the late 1890s, brings thousands to Avoca.

A year after Avoca's founding, a school was built in the community, and the first brick school building was constructed in 1871.

*Chuck Obrecht sheers one of three sheep preparing for competition in the Pottawattamie County Fair in Avoca. Ben DeVries/Daily Nonpareil*

# Oakland IOWA

*Oakland's downtown area provides both unique architecture and growing economy to the area.*

In the ensuing decades, newer buildings replaced older ones, and school systems were changed and reorganized to meet shifting educational requirements. Avoca is now part of the A-H-S-T Community School District, which encompasses Avoca, Hancock, Shelby, Tennant and the surrounding rural areas. More than 600 students attend classes at district sites. The elementary and secondary schools are in Avoca, with the middle school in Shelby.

Giving a general assessment of Avoca as a place to live, Piittmann said the community offered a "good quality of life" for its inhabitants.

"People are friendly, and they care about making the town better," he said.

## OAKLAND

During the early part of the 20th century, the Chautauqua movement brought a stimulating mixture of education and entertainment to thousands of Americans.

Under covered pavilions or beneath huge tents, teachers, politicians and performers kept audiences enthralled.

*Top: Oakland's first framed Methodist church.*
*Middle: 1965 Oakland Methodist Church*
*Bottom: 1977 picture from the Oakland Museum*

Among localities where Chautauqua activities took place was Oakland. On a broad expanse of land in the southwest section of the community, lectures, debates, presentations and instructional lessons attracted large crowds

Events that included notable presenters were especially popular, and the Chautauqua in Oakland had the distinction of having William Jennings Bryan, famed orator and presidential candidate, as a speaker in 1907.

Nearly a century after his appearance, the spirit of the Chautauqua as a place where community members can come together is evoked at a city recreational complex called, fittingly enough, Chautauqua Park.

It is situated in the same spot where those lectures and presentations occurred decades ago.

The name was selected as a way to "recognize our past while creating something important for people now and into the future," said Oakland Mayor Gayle Perkins. "We hope

# Oakland IOWA

residents will make the connection between the Chautauqua of the past and what it represented, and with the park as a vital segment of the community."

The complex includes baseball and softball fields, a soccer field, a basketball court, a sand volleyball court and an array of playground equipment. Also at the site are picnic tables and a large shelter, plus a concession stand and rest rooms. A trail for walking, jogging or biking winds through the area.

Bringing the park into existence was a community effort, Perkins said, and the endeavor demonstrated the commitment that people in Oakland had to improving this city of 1,487 in east-central Pottawattamie County.

Establishing a wetland area was a requirement for obtaining the funds, but the benefits were immediately obvious, Perkins said.

The new park is only a short distance from Oakland's downtown district that contains a number of buildings with architectural styles representing previous eras in the history of the city, which was originally called Big Grove, a reference to the thick forests that covered much of the region in the mid-1850s.

The first house built in the community, in 1856, was actually a storeroom in which groceries were stocked. Soon after, a general store was opened to serve pioneer families who were moving into the area.

## A Gathering Place

Traveling by horse or wagon was the main form of transportation until the Rock Island Railroad constructed a branch line south from Avoca to Big Grove. The rail connection allowed the delivery of more goods to the community, as well as making trips for people to and from the city more convenient.

The number of residents and businesses began to increase. By 1881, the community had two general stores, a blacksmith shop, a hotel and about a dozen homes.

In a special election, residents voted to change the name of the community to Oakland, and the city was incorporated in 1882.

An exhaustive collection of artifacts from the city's early years, as well as from other bygone times, can be viewed at the Nishna Heritage Museum, which occupies four storefronts and interiors on Main Street.

"We want individuals to understand their heritage by seeing what came before them," said Norm Helmts, museum curator. "Touring this place can be a very worthwhile history lesson, especially for younger people. It can help them appreciate what their ancestors went through."

In Oakland, honoring the community's heritage is also paired with

*Children in Avoca enjoy a new park and playground equipment in Oakland.*

# Oakland, IOWA

ongoing efforts to achieve a prosperous present and future.

"We have a good selection of businesses that offer residents a lot of what they need right here," said Christy Baker, president of the Oakland Chamber of Commerce. "We're always looking at ways to bring in more businesses so that people will have additional shopping choices."

Perkins said that "for a small town, we have a real good business base." He cited the presence of numerous stores and service firms downtown. In addition, health care services are available at a medical center and a pharmacy.

Retail business development has also occurred along Highway 59 in the south section of the city, with a variety of stores and agriculture-related firms there.

## OAKLAND GROWTH

The community's main industrial anchor is Oakland Foods, part of the OSI Group. The company's plant, situated north of the city, produces more than 200 different fully cooked and ready to cook custom products, from sausages and hot dogs to bacon and home-style meatloaf.

The 262,000-square-foot facility, occupying 90 acres, employs more than 600 people, producing items for such customers as Otto & Sons, Fair Oaks Farms and Glen Oak Foods, as well as for OSI International.

The state-of-the-art plant is the only facility in the country that utilizes a proprietary "individual quick freeze" process.

Efforts to attract more industries to the community are continuing.

To entice more residents to Oakland, the City Council approved an incentive program for developers and builders to create more housing in the community. The goal is to encourage people to move to Oakland rather than to commute from other locations to work at Oakland

*Richard Miller and Doug Coziahr, president of Trees Forever, help children at Treynor Elementary plant a tree weighing approximately 250 pounds. Funds for the trees were raised by the Optimist Club and Trees Forever, as well as other local organizations. Ben DeVries/Daily Nonpareil*

*Former Nike missile site east of Treynor. Now home to Loess Hills Area Education Agency 13.*

Foods

Meanwhile, improvements have been made at the Oakland Community Center, a building that is utilized for a number of public and private events.

"The building is used all year long, and several events are scheduled each month," said Sabrina Johnson, Oakland city clerk.

To enhance the facility, which was made handicapped accessible, wainscoting was added to the interior, and a covered carport was constructed at the main entrance.

Oakland is part of the Riverside Community School District, which enrolls about 700 students from Oakland, Carson, Macedonia and nearby rural areas. The high school and elementary school are located in Oakland, with the middle school in Carson.

The Eckels Memorial Library in Oakland receives "a lot patronage" from local residents, said Patrice Vance, library director. "For a community our size, it is a well-used facility." Containing more than 26,000 volumes, the library features summer reading programs for young people and story times for grade school children during the year.

A major annual observance in Oakland is a Fourth of July celebration that features a parade, car show, midway and fireworks.

"This celebration always attracts a big crowd, and is a good way for people of the community to come together," Baker said. From preserving their heritage to planning for the future, the willingness of residents to cooperate to achieve goals that benefit everyone is a hallmark of the community, said Jack Chaney, co-publisher of the Botna Valley Reporter.

"That's a positive approach to take because we all will be better for it," he said.

Perkins said he is proud of what Oakland has accomplished. "The quality of life is good in Oakland," he said. "It's a great place to live."

But, he said, "We have to look to the future and find ways to keep making progress. We need to adapt and adjust to changing conditions in order to thrive."

## TREYNOR

The name of a community can be descriptive, geographically referential, commemorative or inspired by notable events. Each of those guidelines has been applied, at different times, in identifying Treynor.

As pioneers arrived in Pottawattamie County to establish homesteads from the mid-1800s on, a settlement arose in the southwest part of the county near several creeks that provided a steady source of water.

In the years that followed, the

*Treynor's water tower is a constant landmark to the community and its surroundings.*

# Treynor IOWA

community acquired a succession of names, all considered appropriate for the particular period in which they were commonly used.

Known as Four Corners for a while, the name indicated a place where people could meet, discuss the weather or other pertinent topics and obtain supplies essential to their farming operations.

When called Eybergsville, the name suggested a connection to a family deemed worth mentioning in the development of the community.

Homesteading on the prairie could be a harsh way of life, and any chance for a respite, however brief, from the exhausting demands of daily survival was welcome.

Card playing became a favorite pastime for many people, and large numbers of them would gather in the settlement on a regular basis to participate in the game of "Hi-Five." The association of the recreational activity with its location became so integrated that the community soon shared its name with the title of the card game.

But the settlement's name did not always reflect such colorful links. In a telling example of pioneer era practicality, the community was sometimes simply called "Town."

In 1893, a salesman, Fritz Ehrig, while visiting the community, was impressed by the vibrant nature of the town and suggested that a post office be established.

Securing signatures on a petition for this purpose, he presented the proposal to the postmaster in Council Bluffs but received a negative response initially. Ehrig was persistent in his goal, however. To the postmaster, he made a another proposal. If the postal official approved the recommendation, the town would be named after him.

Upon this stipulation, the proposal was accepted by the postmaster - whose name was Treynor. The name remains.

During the next decade, procedures leading to incorporation were carried out so that Treynor's first municipal officials began their duties at the start of 1905. At that time, commercial enterprises in the city included a bank, two general stores, a furniture store, an implement dealer, a livery stable, two saloons, several blacksmith shops

*Firefighters from Neola (front) and Griswold compete in the Treynor Firemen Water Fight during Treynor Days.*
*Ben DeVries/Daily Nonpareil*

*Treynor* IOWA

and an assortment of small shops and service providers.

In subsequent years, the community made progress on several fronts. By 1920, a high voltage electrical system was in place, and in 1939 a new telephone dial system was installed. In 1955, a municipal water system was constructed.

The development of paved roadways had put a well-traveled state route through Treynor, and by the late 1950s a newly designated Iowa Highway 92 facilitated the rapid movement of motorists from the community and nearby areas to and from Council Bluffs and Omaha.

Treynor's proximity to the metropolitan region has been a major factor in the city's growth and progress.

"We're close enough so that people can commute and can enjoy the quality of life in our community," said Charles Killion, Treynor mayor.

To maintain that quality, he added, the city must make realistic plans to successfully meet the needs of current residents as well as those individuals who may be interested in adding to Treynor's population of 950.

"It's always best to look forward and anticipate what the town will require in the years ahead," Killion said.

Guaranteeing that the city's infrastructure is capable of handling increased demand is essential, Killion noted, and the addition of a new well has helped ensure that adequate water is available to support the

### TREYNOR GROWTH

creation of more housing developments.

A similar aim of infrastructure improvement was behind the city's decision a few years ago to upgrade the municipal sewer system.

With utilities in place, Killion said, developers can create new subdivisions in the community, expanding housing options for existing or potential residents.

A reliable supply of water also strengthens the Treynor Fire Department's ability to carry out its functions. The department has the further advantage of being housed in the new Treynor Community Center.

Construction of the center has been one of the most impressive accomplishments in Treynor recently. The culmination of an effort that involved hundreds of community supporters, the $2.3 million facility has become a popular site.

The center has two separate rooms available. The Four Corners Room, a reference to one of Treynor's previous names, is designed for large events and receptions, and has seating for up to 600 people. The American Legion Room offers a setting for smaller groups, 100 people or fewer.

*Julie Danker (left) and Shelly Guttau look at items on Guttau's table at the Flea Market outsie the Treynor Community Center during Treynor Days. Ben DeVries/Daily Nonpareil*

195

# Treynor IOWA

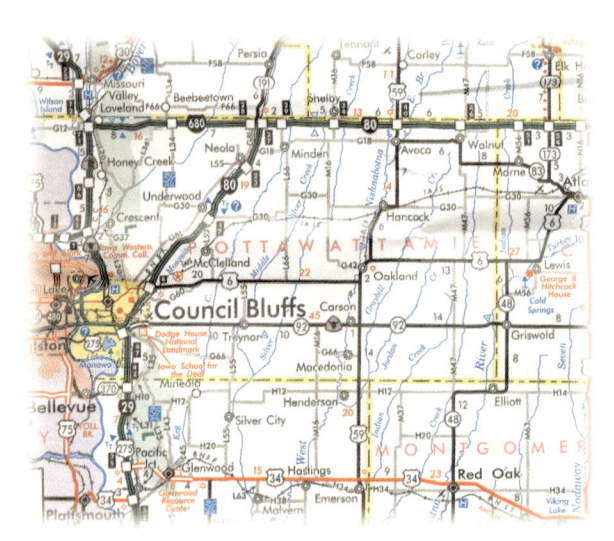

## STORY CONTRIBUTORS

*Dan Eshelman*
*Contributing Editor*

*Jon Leu*
*Managing Editor, The Daily Nonpareil*

Also clearly visible on Highway 92 inside Treynor are buildings of the Treynor Community Schools. The structures trace their lineage to one- and two-room buildings in which pupils were taught in the early part of the last century. In the 1920s, the district was consolidated with outlying rural areas, and a new building was erected.

Now, the district serves an area of about 100 square miles, and enrolls more than 600 students. Open enrollment accounts for about a fifth of the student population.

The current high school building was completed in 1984, and a new addition was constructed in 2000. Facilities include an auditorium and two gymnasiums, with seating for 800 and 1,200 people.

Several construction projects have increased the size of the elementary building. In 2004, new offices, seven classrooms, a new library, a new computer lab and a new gymnasium were added.

The pride that Treynor residents have of their heritage and of their achievements in the present is displayed during Treynor Days, an observance originally conceived as part of the effort to raise money for the community center.

"It's a good way for people to meet and have fun participating in a variety of activities," said Julie Sealock, Treynor city clerk. "It's also an opportunity for former residents to come back to the community and see friends and relatives."

Along with pride in accomplishments, the community's strength lies in the commitment of people in Treynor to cooperate for the benefit of all residents, said Michael Guttau, president of Treynor State Bank.

One example of this determination, he noted, was a project through which the Optimist Club raises money that is subsequently distributed to different youth programs and organizations. "This gives several groups an opportunity to share in the funds raised," Guttau said.

The Optimists joined other residents in another community project - the addition of new playground equipment at a park in the east section of the city. A lot of the labor needed to assemble the equipment was voluntarily provided, said Larry Kramer, Optimist member. Boy Scouts did much of work of placing gravel in the area.

Viewing the future, Killion said he had a positive attitude about Treynor's prospects, an assessment that was shared by Guttau.

"Treynor is a good place to live and to raise a family," Killion said. "It's the kind of location many people are looking for."

Guttau said the growth of recent years, reflected by his own institution and by related evidence such as expanding school enrollment and new housing, could be sustained as improvement efforts continue in the community.

Both men said challenges exist, including the need to bolster the city's retail business sector, but that success can be achieved.

"By working together, we can do what needs to be done," Killion said.

*Pride In Our Hometowns.*

# P·O·R·T·R·A·I·T·S
## of
# *Washington*

## THE CLEANEST CITY IN IOWA

*It's said the slogan began when, in the 1800s, a Health Department official visited the city and declared it so. Epidemic raged elsewhere in the West and in Iowa. But the visiting doctor found no ill residents in Washington. It was unheard of. He could only attribute the anomaly to the city's superb sanitation.*
*"This must be the cleanest city in Iowa!" exclaimed the baffled doctor.*

*Through the generations, Washington's motto has become a frame of mind. A community tacked to faith, goodwill and volunteerism, Washington is as picturesque as it is kind-hearted. With many services and attractions usually reserved for larger cities, Washington is, and always has been, a source of great civic pride. Its residents strive to create a better quality of life for each other with each passing year. That keeps Washington "clean," not only in its physical beauty, but also in its way of life.*

WASHINGTON

*Pride In Our Hometowns.*

# P·O·R·T·R·A·I·T·S
## OF
# *Washington*

## THE CLEANEST CITY IN IOWA

*Washington's downtown district, which centers on its square, shows the city's rich history in its architecture.*

Standing on the plain between the Iowa, English and Skunk rivers, Washington has been a hub of booming business as well as cutting-edge social services. A city rich in opportunity throughout the ages, Washington today clings to its history as it looks to the future and adapts to the demands of the 21st century. With a citizenry fiercely dedicated to keeping Washington one of the best small towns in America, the city welcomes visitors with open arms while it continues to provide for its own and foster growth. Its outstanding recreational opportunities, its commitment to top-quality education, and its desire to constantly better itself makes Washington an ideal place to live. Community life is active, and neighbors helping neighbors is the norm.

### A SNAPSHOT

Washington was platted and its first lots sold in 1839, when it was designated the seat of Slaughter County, which eventually became known as Washington County. (Residents didn't like the sound of Slaughter.) Washington was incorporated in 1864; by then, the town's population was a healthy 2,500.

The County Courthouse, which still stands today as a looming icon of the city's rich history, was built in 1886.

*An impromptu ensemble of musicians performs from the back of a pickup truck during Washington's annual Ridiculous Day parade.*

# Washington IOWA

*Washington, which now boasts its participation in the Tree City USA program, was founded on the prairie, where no trees grew. All the trees you see today in Washington have been planted, or were volunteers, since the city was platted in the early 1800s.*

Washington grew quickly and enjoyed the service of the Milwaukee Rail line and the Rock Island line. The town library was established in 1878, when the city council authorized a tax that raised $500 for books, which were added to those donated by prominent citizens. Space for the first library was donated. More than a hundred years later, Washington now looks to finance—again mainly through private donations—a stunning new library that will be the cultural center of the community downtown.

In 1912, Washington County Hospital was built. Still in existence today, the hospital was the first county hospital in the United States west of the Mississippi River financed publicly. Tax dollars paid for the building.

Over time, many persons of historical significance have lived in Washington. Smith W. Brookhart, a United States Senator, was known as "the man who taught the Army to shoot." He was a teacher of master marksmen, among them an Olympic gold medal winner from Washington. Brookhart literally "wrote the book" on rifle marksmanship, and with an endorsement from Gen. Pershing, Brookhart's practices and tips became the basis for marksmanship training still used in today's military.

Ola Babcock Miller, wife of the long-time editor of the Washington Democrat and gubernatorial candidate, became Iowa's first female Secretary of State and founded the Iowa Highway Patrol.

And Frank Brinton was an early

*The east side of the downtown square as it appeared in the early 1900s.*

*The Washington County Courthouse, a magnificent structure that can be seen from afar, was built in the late 1800s.*

199

# Washington IOWA

theater man, filmmaker and inventor, who built an early flying machine "that almost flew," according to reports.

In Washington, citizens maintain the memory of countless other persons famous locally, such as horsebreeders, businessmen, philanthropists, ministers, journalists and many others.

In the mid 20th century, two Washington staples were established: Its large retirement communities.

The first was United Presbyterian Home, begun in 1947. The second was Halcyon House, constructed in 1955. While Halcyon House is now associated with the Methodist Church, it began as a private corporation. Each community today still thrives.

A booming retail sales community had been a part of Washington's history for some time, reaching its peak in the mid to late 20th century. So great was Washington's pull to southeast Iowa shoppers that Iowa State University's Dr. Henry Stone, widely recognized as "Iowa's retail sales doctor," used Washington as an example "of how things should be done" in retail trade. Per capita, Washington generated more retail sales than any other town.

Recent history shows Washington's continuing strength as a people dedicated to

## THE HISTORY

each other. In 1998, a major tornado tore through town, scattering buildings before leaving the city limits to terrorize the local countryside. Volunteers from all over the community spent countless hours helping their neighbors stand back up after such a terrible event. Today, community spirit is

*Left: The downtown fountain, at the center of Central Park, is a rallying point for many of the city's cultural events, and is also Washington's most recognizable landmark.*

*Right: An old photograph of the downtown fountain.*

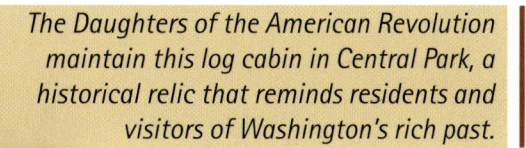

# Washington IOWA

*The Daughters of the American Revolution maintain this log cabin in Central Park, a historical relic that reminds residents and visitors of Washington's rich past.*

evoked, when, quite often, a citizen hearkens back to the post-tornado days.

Today, Washington uses its rich history and sense of self as an attraction to day-trippers and new residents, alike. Downtown, cupolas on the square are still in evidence, reminiscent of earlier years. In stunning Central Park—at the center of the downtown square—one can lounge in the shade of hardwood trees and look at the fountain that is Washington's grandest icon. A fountain has stood at the center of the square since a local resident, who wanted it to be the most glorious spectacle around, donated one in the 1930s. Today, a unique, octagonal white fountain sprays translucent streams of water during the day, and is lit in multicolored splendor at night. On Thursdays during the summertime, visitors to Central Park can also shop the Washington Farmers Market, widely known across the state as one of its best. Dozens of vendors from all over southeast Iowa flow to the park to offer inexpensive and savory vegetables and homemade baked goods, as well as arts and crafts. Several events are planned for Farmers Market Thursdays, including barbecue and salsa competitions. Live entertainment is always the norm on Thursdays in summertime, and the Washington Municipal Band takes the stage late to roll out numbers that often include traditional marches and patriotic tunes.

Performances are a

*A barbecue competition is one of many exciting events that have helped make Washington's Farmers Market renowned statewide as one of the best.*

*The sign showing the way to the Washington Aquatic Center, southeast Iowa's finest.*

201

# Washington IOWA

large part of Washington's community history and traditions. A grand community theater auditorium was built with private donations in the 1970s and survives today as one of the state's finest public showplaces. The stage is used by the community theater group and several service clubs that put on shows annually. Performances include stunning dramas, hilarious comedies, and show-stopping musicals.

But as much as Washington loves shows, it also holds its outdoor recreation opportunities dear. Its city parks system is second to none in a county whose own conservation division is a statewide leader in providing recreational and educational opportunities.

While Central Park is the city's cultural center, Sunset Park is Washington's vast playground, with rolling hills and wonderful amenities. The Washington Aquatic Center, located in Sunset Park, is southeast Iowa's finest public pool, with a huge waterslide, diving board, various water toys children can play with, and a shallow toddler's area. Built primarily on private donations, the Aquatic Center brings Iowans from all over the southeast to Washington for summertime family fun. Nearby, the park's nine-hole disc golf course is gaining popularity, and is host of The Sunset Classic, an amateur tournament held in August. The disc golf course is one of the world's largest nine-hole courses, and features Mach III chain catchers for reliable play. For young children, the park's New Dawn play area features swings, climbing equipment, and a wooden "castle" on which to frolic. This structure was built entirely with donated labor and materials and is one of the park's jewels. On the south side of the park the Daughters of the American Revolution

*Washington County Hospital was established in 1912 and even now looks to future expansion.*

*Statues adorn downtown's Central Park, where many of the city's community events take place.*

maintains an ancient log cabin that is another Washington treasure. It stands near the Flowers Forever gardens, which bloom with a dazzling, multicolored fury in spring and summer, and make for an inviting place to stroll. The flower gardens are maintained through volunteer effort.

On the west side of town, the Kewash Nature Trail begins and shoots north some 13 miles through the small town of West Chester to Keota, on the border of Keokuk County. A hiking and biking trail, it is a symbol of Washington's olden days of rail transport: the trail is an abandoned railbed, even and smooth for low-impact riding and walking. Near the Kewash, a nature loop can take a walker through Hays Timber, where woodland birds like chickadees, cardinals and titmice, and other animals congregate, and a native prairie area, where meadowlarks and red-winged blackbirds hold court.

## RECREATION

For the golfer, the Washington Golf and Country Club offers a stunning nine-hole, sloping course that can be challenging and rewarding for both the duffer and the seasoned amateur alike.

Since history plays such a large role in Washington, a city that likes to know where it has been before deciding which direction to take into the future, it's no wonder there is a museum dedicated to it. The Washington County Historical Society's Conger House Museum contains many of Washington's artifacts and sheds light on its own past. The museum is open on Sunday afternoons in the summer months.

Washington's educational

*Children line the streets in downtown Washington, waving at zany parade floats.*

*Sunset Park is the city's vast outdoor playground. Truly a place for all ages!*

# Washington IOWA

system is valued as one of the city's strengths that will drive it into the future. With a top-quality administrative and instructional staff throughout, the Washington Community Schools District has both a junior and senior elementary school, both a junior and senior high school, and an alternative high school. The Catholic Church also maintains an elementary school in Washington. The status of the school district is a source of both community debate and great pride, as Washington's residents look to provide the best education available for future generations. Washington is also home to a Kirkwood Community College satellite campus, through which students can take junior college and continuing education courses via satellite feed and on-site instruction.
Health care is still a priority to the people of Washington, who continue to support Washington County Hospital and Clinics, the public health care facility located in Washington. Since its inception in 1912, the hospital has been the leading source of health care in the community, and is looking to future growth. It sponsors a well-attended Kidzfest fair in the spring each year, drawing businesses and organizations to Wells Park, adjacent to the hospital, for fun and educational activities.

For seniors, Washington is a center for wellness, comfort and community. Its two main retirement communities continue to thrive and provide seniors with independent living or assisted care. Downtown, the Central Park Community Center offers a kind of clubhouse

## COMMUNITY

*A bust of George Washington, after whom the city is named, graces Central Park.*

*Washington's Sunset Park is home to one of the world's longest nine-hole disc golf courses.*

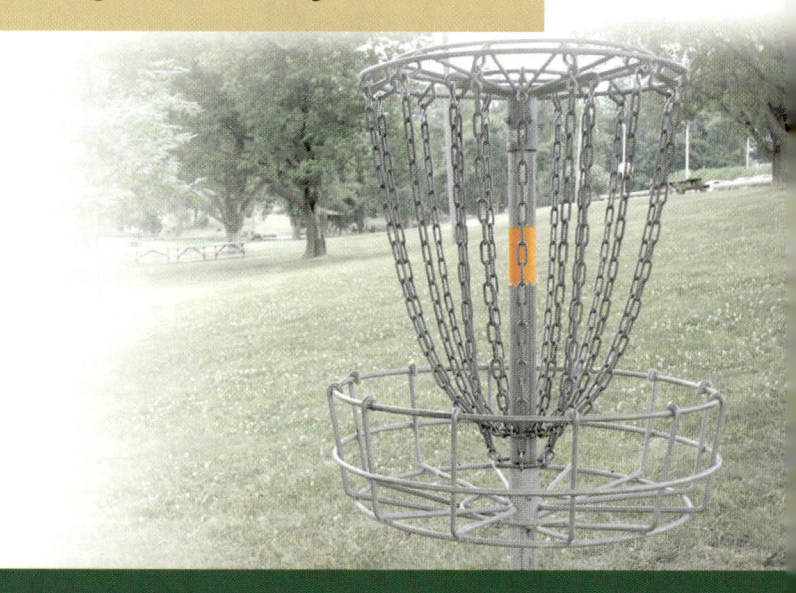

# Washington IOWA

*A stroll through the Flowers Forever gardens on the south side of Sunset Park can be a refreshing trip for both the mind and the body.*

for seniors, who come and go to chat, play games, or craft.

Washington is slowly making a transition from a major base of industry to a more service-oriented market. Located 30 minutes from much larger Iowa City, Washington is showing signs of becoming a bedroom community while remaining a city with an independent feel, voice and economy. There are four banks in Washington and real estate is a big business. New homes have been and will continue to be built in subdivisions while historic homes remain at the center of town, especially along "The Boulevard," which, itself, is a candidate for the National Register of Historic Places. A walk along this cobblestone street is visually stunning, as the grand houses complement the beautiful landscaping and tree and floral growth along it.

Washington, once a place devoid of trees, cut from the grassy prairie, is now proud to boast its status in the Tree City USA program, which it has been a part of for more than a dozen years. Trees line almost every street, sometimes in thick, venerable groves. Each year, the Trees Forever group continues Washington's arbor-loving tradition, giving away hundreds of new trees in a heavily attended event in Central Park.

Washington is a place of strong faith. It is home to numerous Christian churches of many

*The Blair House, built in 1880, is one of many Washington places on the National Historical Register. Today, it serves as office space to some of Washington's many small businesses.*

205

# Washington, IOWA

denominations. The religious community is a strong one, and area congregations work to make Washington a better place to live. They sometimes work together on missions or other special projects.

Service clubs, too, abound in Washington. Too numerous to completely list, the various service clubs of the city constantly organize community-building projects and events, through which the entire city is benefited, from senior living to the support of youth.

Many of Washington's children, when not at school or at the park, can often be found, along with adults, at the Washington Community Y. A combination YMCA and YWCA, it sits just off the square and is a central point for many community events and recreation. Washington is one of the smallest cities in the United States to have a full-service YMCA.

A tour of Washington can leave a visitor breathless. On the map, it's a county seat town of small population. But Washington is not just a map dot; it's a place that thrives in its own uniqueness, its sense of self and self-betterment. From the historic feel of downtown to the modern advances of the County Hospital; from the natural beauty of the parks to the bustle of shopping near the highway; from the way people smile and say hello when you walk by to the way they shake your hand and mean it when they tell you something important, Washington is a community with a lot of life, and a lot to give.

Washington is home to several annual

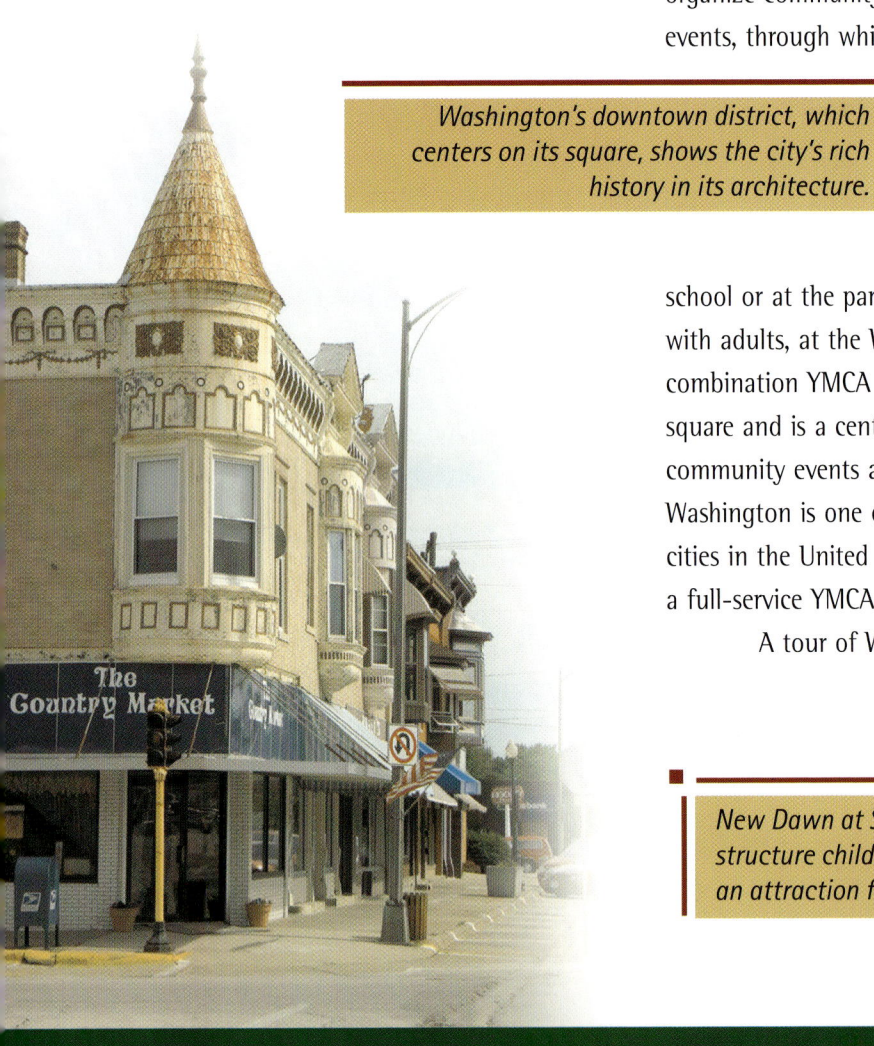

*Washington's downtown district, which centers on its square, shows the city's rich history in its architecture.*

*New Dawn at Sunset Park is a volunteer-built structure children flock to in all seasons, and is an attraction for visitors to town.*

# Washington IOWA

> The Kewash Trail runs some 13 miles from Washington to the town of Keota, on the Keokuk County Line. The trail is an abandoned railbed, and offers low-impact biking and hiking opportunities

events, including, most notably, the Washington County Fair. While many counties in the state have their own fair, Washington's is one of the finest, with great participation from both the County's 4-H clubs and Future Farmers of America, as well as a staggeringly rich entertainment schedule. From livestock events and shows to the demolition derby and truck and tractor pulls, the county fair is a weeklong event each summer that draws thousands from all over southeast Iowa and beyond. As the agricultural hub of the county, Washington shows its prowess in the barn and in the fields at the fair, displaying top-quality livestock and other exhibits, many of which go on to win in state fair competition. Nightly entertainment at a grandstand and arena allows fairgoers to relax and enjoy the cool of the evening after a hard day's work or play.

## EVENTS

Also an annual event, Washington's Ridiculous Day—the first of its kind in the nation—is a salute to lightheartedness and the city's retailers. Founded as a festival to draw people downtown to shop in local stores, the annual Saturday event has become much more, with children's activities and a flea market in Central Park. And, of course, the parade: What could be more ridiculous than a man dressed as a clown, walking two children and a goat, wearing a sign that proclaims: "Three kids and one old goat"? You'll see it next year, as Ridiculous Day prides itself on bizarre float entries.

An emerging annual event of great significance is the Washington County Relay

*The sign at Washington County Hospital and Clinics.*

# Washington IOWA

## LEARN MORE

Washington is located on Highway 92, eight miles west of US Highway 218.

To learn more about Washington, contact The Washington Evening Journal at 319-653-2191, the Washington Chamber of Commerce at 319-653-3272, or the Washington Economic Development Group at 319-653-3942. Or visit online at www.washjrnl.com, www.washingtoniowachamber.com, or www.washingtoniowa.net.

## STORY CONTRIBUTOR

C.T. Kruckeberg is managing editor of The Washington Evening Journal.

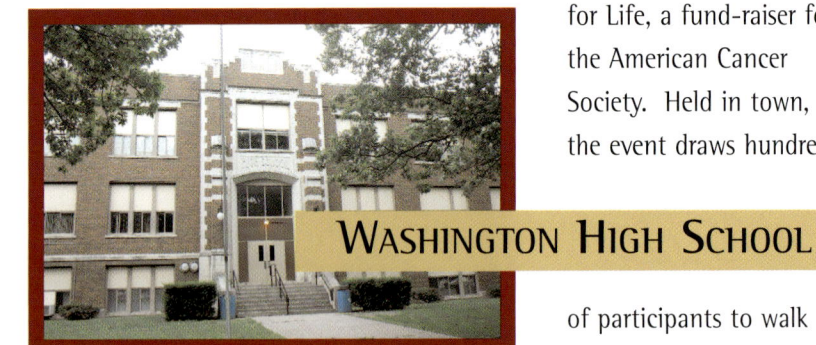

---

**WASHINGTON HIGH SCHOOL**

for Life, a fund-raiser for the American Cancer Society. Held in town, the event draws hundreds of participants to walk "laps" around a course and accumulate donations for charity. The event also promulgates hope for cancer victims and cancer survivors, as well as their families. A touching event of great power, the local Relay for Life has been growing in leaps and bounds since its inception not 10 years ago.

Washington is a city with a great past that is looking forward to a great future. In a transitional phase, growing from a retail and industrial-based economy to a bedroom community and service-oriented business sphere, its residents have not lost their passion for community improvement and betterment that has marked it one of the best small towns in America. While the world, country, state and community change with the times, Washington refuses to let itself become a carbon copy of someone else's vision. The community drives this fair city, with its goodwill and faith, and keeps it as beautiful to the eye as it is dear to its residents' hearts. Whatever forms Washington's business, social and civic realms take on in years to come, we can be assured they will be poured into a uniquely Washington mold.

*While the county seat and Washington County's largest city, Washington still clings to its roots in agriculture.*